# SCRIPTURE, METAPHYSICS, AND POETRY

# Ashgate Studies in Theology, Imagination and the Arts

*Series Editors:*

Jeremy Begbie, Duke University and University of Cambridge, USA
Trevor Hart, St Mary's College, University of St Andrews, Scotland
Roger Lundin, Wheaton College, USA

What have imagination and the arts to do with theology? For much of the modern era, the answer has been 'not much'. It is precisely this deficit that this series seeks to redress. For, whatever role they have or have not been granted in the theological disciplines, imagination and the arts are undeniably bound up with how we as human beings think, learn and communicate, engage with and respond to our physical and social environments and, in particular, our awareness and experience of that which transcends our own creatureliness. The arts are playing an increasingly significant role in the way people come to terms with the world; at the same time, artists of many disciplines are showing a willingness to engage with religious or theological themes. A spate of publications and courses in many educational institutions has already established this field as one of fast-growing concern.

This series taps into a burgeoning intellectual concern on both sides of the Atlantic and beyond. The peculiar inter-disciplinarity of theology, and the growing interest in imagination and the arts in many different fields of human concern, afford the opportunity for a series that has its roots sunk in varied and diverse intellectual soils, while focused around a coherent theological question: How are imagination and the arts involved in the shaping and reshaping of our humanity as part of the creative and redemptive purposes of God, and what roles do they perform in the theological enterprise?

Many projects within the series have particular links to the work of the Institute for Theology, Imagination and the Arts in the University of St Andrews, and to the Duke Initiatives in Theology and the Arts at Duke University.

Other titles in the series

*Christian Theology and Tragedy*
*Theologians, Tragic Literature and Tragic Theory*
Edited by Kevin Taylor and Giles Waller

*The Poet as Believer*
*A Theological Study of Paul Claudel*
Aidan Nichols, O.P.

*Between the Image and the Word*
*Theological Engagements with Imagination, Language and Literature*
Trevor Hart

# Scripture, Metaphysics, and Poetry

## Austin Farrer's *The Glass of Vision*
## With Critical Commentary

Edited by

**ROBERT MACSWAIN**
*The University of the South, USA*

**Routledge**
Taylor & Francis Group

LONDON AND NEW YORK

First published 2013 by Ashgate Publishing

Published 2016 by Routledge
2 Park Square, Milton Park, Abingdon, Oxfordshire OX14 4RN
711 Third Avenue, New York, NY 10017, USA

First issued in paperback 2016

*Routledge is an imprint of the Taylor & Francis Group, an informa business*

**British Library Cataloguing in Publication Data**
A catalogue record for this book is available from the British Library

**The Library of Congress has cataloged the printed edition as follows:**
Farrer, Austin, 1904-1968.
[Glass of vision]
Scripture, metaphysics, and poetry : Austin Farrer's The glass of vision, with critical commentary / edited by Robert MacSwain.
    pages cm. – (Ashgate Studies in Theology, Imagination and the Arts)
  Includes bibliographical references and index.
  ISBN 978-1-4094-5083-2 (hardcover)
  1. Revelation–Christianity. 2. Farrer, Austin, 1904-1968. Glass of
  vision. I. MacSwain, Robert. II. Title.
  BT127.3.F37 2013
  231.7'4–dc23

                                                                      2013011280

ISBN 13: 978-1-138-27940-7 (pbk)
ISBN 13: 978-1-4094-5083-2 (hbk)

# Contents

# Contributors

**Austin Farrer (1904–68)** was Warden of Keble College, University of Oxford, England.

**David Brown** is Professor of Theology, Aesthetics and Culture and Wardlaw Professor at the University of St Andrews, Scotland, where he is also a Professorial Fellow at the Institute for Theology, Imagination and the Arts.

**Ingolf Dalferth** is Professor of Systematic Theology, Philosophy of Religion and Symbolism at the University of Zürich, Switzerland, where he directs the Institute of Hermeneutics and Philosophy of Religion. He also holds a joint appointment as Danforth Professor of Philosophy of Religion at Claremont Graduate University, USA.

**Hans Hauge** is Senior Lecturer in the Department of Aesthetics and Communication at Aarhus University, Denmark.

**Douglas Hedley** is Reader in Hermeneutics and Metaphysics at the University of Cambridge, England, and a Fellow of Clare College.

**David Jasper** is Professor of Literature and Theology at the University of Glasgow, Scotland, and Director of Centre for Literature, Theology and the Arts. He also currently holds a joint appointment as Changyang Chair Professor at Renmin University of China.

**Gerard Loughlin** is Professor in the Department of Theology and Religion at Durham University, England.

**Robert MacSwain** is Assistant Professor of Theology and Christian Ethics at The School of Theology of the University of the South, USA.

# Permissions

**Part I**

Austin Farrer, *The Glass of Vision: Bampton Lectures for 1948*, originally published by Dacre Press in 1948, reproduced by permission of SPCK Publishing.

**Part II**

*Chapter 1*

Originally published in David Jasper, *Coleridge as Poet and Religious Thinker* (London and Basingstoke: Macmillan, 1985), pages 145–53, reproduced by permission of Palgrave Macmillan.

*Chapter 2*

Originally published in Brian Hebblethwaite and Edward Henderson (eds), *Divine Action: Studies Inspired by the Philosophical Theology of Austin Farrer* (Edinburgh: T & T Clark, 1990), 103–22, reproduced by permission of Continuum, an imprint of Bloomsbury Publishing Plc.

*Chapters 3, 4, and 5*

Originally published in Ann Loades and Michael McLain (eds), *Hermeneutics, the Bible and Literary Criticism* (London: Macmillan/New York: St Martin's Press, 1992), pages 71–128, reproduced by permission of Palgrave Macmillan.

*Chapter 6*

Originally published in Douglas Hedley and Brian Hebblethwaite (eds), *The Human Person in God's World: Studies to Commemorate the Austin Farrer Centenary* (London: SCM Press, 2006), 106–34, reproduced by permission of Hymns Ancient and Modern Ltd.

# Acknowledgements

There are several groups of people whom I must thank for helping me bring this project to completion. First (and most) of all, Trevor Hart of St Andrews, Jeremy Begbie of Duke, and Roger Lundin of Wheaton for kindly accepting this volume in their series. Likewise, Sarah Lloyd of Ashgate and her staff for their efficient and cheerful assistance.

Second, Nick Newton of the Farrer Estate, and SPCK (the current holder of the rights to Farrer's publications), for permission to publish a critical edition of *The Glass of Vision*. I was also delighted that Thomas Denny gave us permission to use a detail from his magnificent Transfiguration Window at Durham Cathedral for the cover image.

Third, the six additional authors whose stimulating work on Farrer is included in Part II of this volume: David Brown (St Andrews), Ingolf Dalferth (Zürich and Claremont), Hans Hauge (Aarhus), Douglas Hedley (Cambridge), David Jasper (Glasgow), and Gerard Loughlin (Durham). Special thanks to David Brown for translating Farrer's Latin citations and phrases, identifying most of the classical sources and a suggestion regarding Farrer's German sentence in the first lecture.

Fourth, I consulted several other scholars in regard to my notes in Part I: Paul Holloway (University of the South), Benjamin J. King (University of the South), Fergus Kerr (Blackfriars, Edinburgh), Stephanie McCarter (University of the South), Steven Nadler (Wisconsin-Madison), Edmund Santurri (St Olaf College) and Reinhard Zachau (University of the South). They all kindly responded to questions regarding their respective areas of expertise, although only I can be held responsible for the notes themselves.

Fifth, a number of past and present Sewanee students read these texts along with me in the Advent Semester of 2012 and offered much insight: Jeannie Babb, Nathan Bourne, Pete Burgess, Rachel Bush-Erdman, Brooks Cato, Rebecca Cato, Candice Frazer, Bentley Manning, Laurel Mathewson, Quinn Parman, Ashley Sullivan, and Michael Thompson. Drew Courtright assisted with the proofing and index.

Sixth and finally, I am extremely grateful to The University of the South for a research grant to cover the cost of the various permission fees to republish the material in this volume; and for the University's Media Services for scanning the documents to be reformatted.

Without all of the assistance listed above, this volume would not be in your hands.

Robert MacSwain
Sewanee, St Augustine of Hippo, 2013

# Introduction:
# 'The form of divine truth in the human mind'

Robert MacSwain

> If there was a moment in my new life at Oxford at which I experienced a conversion, or rather realised that a conversion had occurred, it was while listening to Austin Farrer's Bampton Lectures, given in St Mary's Church for the Michaelmas term 1948 and published under the title *The Glass of Vision*. The restrained delivery, the precision of utterance, the controlled imagination, together with the capacity, without apparent alteration of pace or emphasis, to raise the discourse to the most intense level of religious contemplation without loss of philosophical substance, were unlike anything I have ever experienced before or since.[1]

So wrote Basil Mitchell in 1993, in retirement after a distinguished career at Oxford as Nolloth Professor of the Philosophy of the Christian Religion.[2] Forty-five years later, Mitchell still vividly remembered the lectures he had attended as a young philosophy tutor finding his way toward Christian faith, recalling how they had crucially shaped his intellectual and spiritual life. Above all, it was the perfect fusion of 'religious contemplation' and 'philosophical substance' that seemed to impress Mitchell the most. Indeed, in his address at Farrer's memorial service – held in the Chapel of Keble College, Oxford, on 1 February 1969 – Mitchell said of these Bampton Lectures that 'surely St Mary's had seen and heard nothing like

---

[1]  Basil Mitchell, 'War and Friendship', in Kelly James Clark (ed.), *Philosophers Who Believe: The Spiritual Journeys of 11 Leading Thinkers* (Downers Grove, IL: InterVarsity Press, 1993), 38–9. The Bampton Lectures were founded in 1780 and have since been one of the primary sources of English theology, comparable to the Gifford Lectures in Scotland. For the record, Farrer's Bamptons were delivered in the Spring of 1948, not the Autumn (Michaelmas), as recalled by Mitchell: see Austin Farrer, *The Glass of Vision: Bampton Lectures for 1948* (Westminster: Dacre Press, 1948), xii / 14 in this volume; Oxford University, Bodleian Libraries, MS Eng. Lett. d. 272, folios 71–3; and Philip Curtis, *A Hawk Among Sparrows: A Biography of Austin Farrer* (London: SPCK, 1985), 133. Note that all future references to *The Glass of Vision* will be cited as 'GV' followed by both original pagination and page number in this volume.

[2]  For a brief biography and critical assessment of his career, see David Brown, 'Basil George Mitchell: 1917–2011', *Biographical Memoirs of Fellows of the British Academy* XII (2013), 303-21.

it since John Henry Newman occupied that pulpit'.[3] But who was Austin Farrer, and what were these eight lectures – rather obliquely titled *The Glass of Vision* – about?

Austin Marsden Farrer (1904–68) was an English philosopher, theologian, New Testament scholar, priest and preacher, considered by many to be 'possibly the greatest Anglican mind of the twentieth century'.[4] Raised in a scholarly and devout Baptist family in London, he joined the Church of England during his first year of university, at Balliol College, Oxford.[5] After a curacy in Dewsbury, West Yorkshire, he spent his remaining career back in Oxford, first as Chaplain and Tutor at St Edmund Hall (1931–35), then Fellow and Chaplain of Trinity College (1935–60) and finally as Warden of Keble College (1960–68).[6] One of the leading Anglo-Catholics of his generation, Farrer wrote a number of brilliant and creative books spanning several academic fields, as well as some luminous devotional works – but Charles Hefling asserts that *The Glass of Vision* is 'undoubtedly the most important source for understanding the breadth of Farrer's genius'.[7] According to Farrer himself, the primary theme of these lectures is 'the form of divine truth in the human mind'.[8] But in the preface he announces that he actually wished to explore not one but three topics, topics often considered apart but in this instance intentionally and provocatively brought together:

---

[3]  Basil Mitchell, 'Austin Marsden Farrer', in Austin Farrer, *A Celebration of Faith*, edited by Leslie Houlden (London: Hodder and Stoughton, 1970), 16.

[4]  Thus Archbishop Rowan Williams in 'Debate on *The Gift of Authority* – Archbishop of Canterbury's Remarks', delivered at the Church of England's General Synod in London on Friday, 13 February 2004: http://rowanwilliams.archbishopofcanterbury.org/articles. php/1836/general-synod-debate-on-the-gift-of-authority-archbishop-of-canterburys-remarks (accessed on 28 January 2013).

[5]  For the details of this difficult decision, see Robert MacSwain, 'Documentation and Correspondence Related to Austin Farrer's Baptism in the Church of England on 14 May 1924', *Anglican and Episcopal History* 81 (2012), 241–76. For a more general study of Farrer's Anglicanism, see Robert MacSwain, 'Above, Beside, Within: The Anglican Theology of Austin Farrer', *Journal of Anglican Studies* 4 (2006), 33–57.

[6]  For more information on Farrer's life and work, see Curtis's biography cited in note 1 above; Ann Loades, 'Farrer, Austin Marsden', in Alister E. McGrath (ed.), *The SPCK Handbook of Anglican Theologians* (London: SPCK, 1998), 120–3; and I.M. Crombie, 'Farrer, Austin Marsden (1904–1968)', in H.C.G. Matthew and Brian Harrison (eds), *Oxford Dictionary of National Biography: Volume 19* (Oxford: Oxford University Press, 2004), 121–3.

[7]  Charles C. Hefling, Jr, *Jacob's Ladder: Theology and Spirituality in the Thought of Austin Farrer* (Cambridge, MA: Cowley Publications, 1979), 130. This book is an excellent introduction to Farrer's thought, and especially helpful on *The Glass of Vision*. For an accessible anthology that provides an overview of Farrer's work in several fields and genres, along with a bibliography of primary and secondary literature, see Ann Loades and Robert MacSwain (eds), *The Truth-Seeking Heart: Austin Farrer and His Writings* (Norwich: Canterbury Press, 2006).

[8]  GV 1 / 15.

the sense of metaphysical philosophy, the sense of scriptural revelation, and the sense of poetry. Scripture and metaphysics are equally my study, and poetry is my pleasure. These three things rubbing against one another in my mind, seem to kindle one another, and so I am moved to ask how this happens.[9]

So, 'the form of divine truth in the human mind', understood through scripture, metaphysics, and poetry 'rubbing against' and thus 'kindling' one another – this is what *The Glass of Vision* is 'about'.

I will return to this fascinating combination of theme and topic in a moment. Let me first, however, address the crucial question of genre. As stated above, Farrer was a philosopher, theologian, and New Testament scholar, and wrote significant books in each of these three fields. But it is at least arguable that Farrer's greatest work may be found not in his academic publications but in his sermons, where he drops the disciplinary fences maintained by the academy and simply allows his mind to 'kindle' without restraint, with philosophy, theology, biblical interpretation, and spirituality all flowing and fusing, expressed with a strong poetic sensibility and in often exquisite prose, not to mention occasional gleams of puckish wit and whimsy. In most cases, each sermon is self-contained and focused on a single idea. But Hefling's statement that *The Glass of Vision* best captures 'the breadth of Farrer's genius' is compelling for reasons already provided by Mitchell above and further elucidated (if unintentionally) by Farrer in the book's preface: unlike Farrer's more academic books or individual sermons, these are in fact eight inter-connected 'Lecture Sermons' delivered from the pulpit of a Christian church – admittedly not during a worship service, but in a church building nevertheless – with all of the associations such a setting conveys.

Farrer states that he fears he has thus produced 'something unscholarly and impressionistic' and points out that 'lectures are, in fact, rhetoric'.[10] But it is precisely the impressionistic and rhetorical character of these lecture-sermons that gives them their unusually provocative power 65 years after they were first delivered. Or, put differently, the fact that this book was originally *preached* to a live audience is actually what makes it one of Farrer's most successful efforts. Using the distinctive genre of the lecture-sermon, Farrer was inspired to develop his argument with rhetorical skill and spiritual insight as well as intellectual subtlety. It was the perfect assignment for him, and released his genius to a sustained degree that he perhaps never again achieved.[11]

So much for genre; what then of the theme and topics? I will say very little about scripture, metaphysics, and poetry in this introduction, as they are discussed

---

[9]  GV ix / 12.

[10]  GV ix–x / 12.

[11]  For a substantial study that explores the relationship between theology and rhetoric, and considers the degree to which theology can be construed in rhetorical terms, see David S. Cunningham, *Faithful Persuasion: In Aid of a Rhetoric of Christian Theology* (Notre Dame, IN: University of Notre Dame Press, 1991).

extensively by Farrer and the essays that follow his text in Part II. I will rather focus here on the primary theme of 'the form of the divine truth in the human mind', first in its own right, and second as it relates to the series in which this current volume appears. Then, after some very brief evaluative and critical remarks, I will conclude with some comments on the format of the current volume itself.

By 'the form of the divine truth in the human mind', Farrer primarily intends the theological doctrine of supernatural revelation, but he inevitably finds himself drawn into a discussion of divine inspiration as well. William J. Abraham has argued that revelation and inspiration, while intimately connected, are nevertheless conceptually distinct and should not be confused or conflated.[12] Farrer, however, at least comes close to fusing them in his insistence that supernatural revelation comes to humanity via divinely *inspired thinking*. That is, while Farrer does not deny the validity of the term 'inspired' to the biblical text itself – that is, to its very *words* – he thinks that it applies first of all to the *minds* of those who composed these words. So, Farrer explores the question of what it could mean for human thoughts to be divinely inspired, and thus to become vehicles of divine revelation.[13]

Farrer's distinctive theory, which warrants at least a mention in standard surveys of the doctrine of revelation, is that supernatural revelation itself is conveyed, not in the more familiar categories of propositions or events, but through *images*, or more specifically through the 'interplay' of image and event.[14] As Farrer put it:

> Now the thought of Christ himself was expressed in certain dominant images. He spoke of the Kingdom of God, which is the image of God's enthroned majesty … Again, he spoke of the Son of Man, thereby proposing the image of the dominion of a true Adam … He set forth the image of Israel, the human family of God … These tremendous images, and others like them, are not the whole of Christ's teaching, but they set forth the supernatural mystery which is at the heart of that teaching … The great images interpreted the events of Christ's ministry, death and resurrection, and the events interpreted the images; the interplay between the two is revelation.[15]

David Brown points out, however, that by 'images' Farrer primarily means *verbal* or *literary* images – that is, evocative symbolic terms such as 'Kingdom of God' or 'Son

---

[12]   William J. Abraham, *The Divine Inspiration of Holy Scripture* (Oxford: Oxford University Press, 1981).

[13]   For a recent study of the doctrine of inspiration, which contains an extensive discussion of Farrer's 'non-verbal' theory, and which draws heavily on Farrer in formulating the author's own original proposal, see David R. Law, *Inspiration* (London and New York: Continuum, 2001), esp. 114–22.

[14]   See, for example, the brief discussions in John Baillie, *The Idea of Revelation in Recent Thought* (Oxford: Oxford University Press, 1956), 36–40; and Avery Dulles, *Models of Revelation* (Maryknoll, NY: Orbis Books, 1992), 201–2. Dulles associates Farrer with his own 'symbolic' approach.

[15]   GV 42–3 / 42.

of Man'. Or, put differently, by 'images' Farrer means images described in words and mediated through the biblical text: basically, metaphor, simile, and analogy.[16] While these verbal images may well conjure various mental images for those who read them or hear them described, and while they may well have first 'come to' Christ and the biblical writers as vivid mental images, it is as literary or verbal images that we readers encounter them – and thus, in Farrer's theory, encounter supernatural revelation.

Farrer's theory of revelation through images, verbal or otherwise, crucially leads him to consider the role of *imagination* as well, not just in theology but in general human thought. This is where the current volume intersects most directly with the themes of the series in which it appears. Very few people have followed Farrer's theory of supernatural revelation through inspired images as explicitly articulated in *The Glass of Vision*. A number of scholars, however, have been influenced or 'inspired' by it and have adapted it into their own perspective, and even more have been fascinated or provoked into engaging with it to some degree. Unusually for a work of mid-20th-century English theology, *The Glass of Vision* has been a remarkably generative text, drawing international commentary from philosophers, theologians and literary scholars for almost seven decades.[17] In the current ferment of interest in theology, imagination and the arts, *The Glass of Vision* is, in fact, a foundational text that has – nevertheless and ironically – been unjustly neglected due to its being long out-of-print, not easily available and never in a critical edition. This volume rectifies that situation.

Farrer's Bampton Lectures receive extensive critical analysis in the chapters that comprise Part II, and so I will not engage that task here. However, for those who have not previously read *The Glass of Vision*, this introduction should include at least some evaluative and critical observations. So, just two points readers should bear in mind. First, it is important to note that Farrer's project is not motivated entirely by academic or even theological concerns. As Farrer himself indicates, he is looking for a theory of Scripture that justifies the practice of *lectio divina*, or 'spiritual reading' – a theory of Scripture in which the practice of *lectio divina* (to which he is committed) makes sense.[18] Likewise, as noted earlier, *The Glass of Vision* consists of 'Sermon

---

[16] David Brown, 'The Role of Images in Theological Reflection', in Douglas Hedley and Brian Hebblethwaite (eds), *The Human Person in God's World: Studies to Commemorate the Austin Farrer Centenary* (London: SCM Press, 2006), 85–105, especially 86 and 88–9. This important essay certainly merits inclusion in Part II, but for several reasons I opted for Brown's earlier 'God and Symbolic Action' instead.

[17] Some of that commentary has been assembled in Part II. Another important discussion that I was not able to include due to space restraints is Wayne Proudfoot's '*The Glass of Vision*: Imagination and Discourse' from his book, *God and the Self: Three Types of Philosophy of Religion* (Lewisburg, PA: Bucknell University Press / London: Associated University Presses, 1976), 137–46. This section concludes a chapter dealing with Farrer's thought more generally, construed as one of the three 'types' of the volume's subtitle: 'The Self as Will or Agent: The Individualistic Type' (88–148).

[18] See GV 36 / 37. I am grateful to Michael Thompson for helping me formulate this insight.

Lectures' that intentionally blur the boundaries between theology and spirituality: hence their closing Trinitarian doxologies, which made such an impact on their original hearers and which may impress (or not) contemporary readers as well.[19] For example, Hans Frei (1922–88) commends an understanding of theology as 'first of all the contemplative and devotional habit of the mindform of the knowledge and love of God, and second, the use of the trained intellect in penetrating that abiding mystery. (Austin Farrer's Bampton Lectures, *The Glass of Vision*, come to mind.)'[20] Farrer's work can thus also be read as contributing to recent discussions of the relationship between theology and spirituality.[21]

Second, more critically: no matter how brilliant or ahead of his time Farrer may have been, there are undoubtedly places where *The Glass of Vision* has dated, and dated badly. While some of Farrer's cultural prejudices or temporal peculiarities can be contextualised, perhaps most challenging to his project are the ways in which our understanding of the composition and compilation of biblical texts has continued to develop since the 1940s. For example, Farrer's paradigm of inspired thinking, and thus revelation through images, is the individual prophet (Jeremiah) or apostle (Paul) or gospel writer (Mark). But in the light of our evolving sense of how the Biblical texts came to their present form, it is evident that a satisfactory doctrine of either inspiration or revelation must take account of a far more complex reality than that envisaged by Farrer, including memory, eyewitnesses, communal oral tradition, individual original writers, pseudonymous revisers, anonymous editors, unknown arrangers of the various canons and so forth. Whether or not Farrer's insights can be translated effectively into the contemporary context remains to be seen.[22]

---

[19]   See Curtis's biography for the statement that at 'the end of every sermon – more particularly for the Bampton Lectures – there is the mounting excitement of waiting to see how eloquently the final words of praise to the Triune God will be phrased' (213). As noted above, Farrer belonged to a specific generation of Anglo-Catholic scholars, a generation which also included figures such as Gregory Dix (1901–1952), Michael Ramsey (1904–1988), and Eric Mascall (1905–1993). *The Glass of Vision* thus emerged from a very particular set of ecclesial commitments and practices that are crucial to understanding Farrer's arguments but which will not receive the attention they deserve here. For some thoughts on this generation, contrasted with those who came afterward, see Rowan Williams, *Anglican Identities* (London: Darton Longman and Todd, 2003), 109–10.

[20]   Hans W. Frei, *Types of Christian Theology*, edited by George Hunsinger and William C. Placher (New Haven and London: Yale University Press, 1992), 120. Frei's essay collection *Theology and Narrative*, also edited by Hunsinger and Placher (New York: Oxford University Press, 1993), contains a number of appreciative references to Farrer as well.

[21]   For a brief overview, see Mark A. McIntosh, 'Theology and Spirituality', in David F. Ford with Rachel Muers (eds), *The Modern Theologians: An Introduction to Christian Theology since 1918*, Third Edition (Oxford: Blackwell, 2005), 392–407.

[22]   However, for a significant recent monograph that discusses both *The Glass of Vision* and Farrer's later book *A Study of St Mark* (Westminster: Dacre Press, 1951) and brings them into conversation with more recent New Testament scholarship, see Robert Titley, *A Poetic Discontent: Austin Farrer and the Gospel of Mark* (London and New York: T&T Clark

Part I of this volume consists of a critical edition of Farrer's Bampton Lectures. There are no footnotes in the original text, and so all of the footnotes and citations in Part I are provided by the editor. I have not striven to annotate every detail but rather to provide references and information that some readers may find helpful, especially those without a background in theology or philosophy. The primary text itself has been left almost untouched, with only a few minor corrections to obvious printing errors and some small formatting changes. As for the secondary material in Part II, these chapters have been chosen out of a wide range of possible essays and chapters, which has obviously entailed a process of selection and some hard decisions. Not every topic of *The Glass of Vision* receives equal treatment in Part II, but I have selected essays with an eye toward those elements most relevant to the Ashgate Series in Theology, Imagination and the Arts.[23]

I am not here going to summarise, note agreements or disagreements among, offer critical commentary upon or take sides in the debates between the various chapters in Part II, either as they relate to the interpretation of Farrer's texts or to the individual arguments of the contributors. That is work for the readers of this volume to do themselves, after reading *The Glass of Vision*. Each chapter in Part II is provided with a brief introductory note that places it in the context of its original composition and publication, as well as how it relates to the author's own work more broadly. These chapters, of course, do not necessarily reflect their authors' *current* perspectives, either on Farrer or on the general theme of their chapter. Each has been provided with a specific date of publication to locate it chronologically. In order to provide a sense of how the scholarly conversation has developed over the decades, revision been kept to a strict minimum, with no substantial changes to the main texts; this is especially important as some later chapters refer back to some earlier ones. Likewise, chapters have not been adapted to current standards of gender-inclusive language. However, with the permission of the authors, obvious corrections and occasional clarifications have been made; the style of citation is now consistent across the chapters; some footnotes have been adapted or updated to better suit a contemporary audience, especially if the original information would now be misleading; and entirely new footnotes or

---

International, 2010). For just two general studies that take account of recent developments, see Christopher Bryan, *And God Spoke: The Authority of the Bible for the Church Today* (Cambridge, MA: Cowley, 2002) and Paul. J. Achtemeier, *Inspiration and Authority: Nature and Function of Christian Scripture* (Grand Rapids, MI: Baker Academic, 2010).

[23]     Some readers may note that all of the contributors to this volume are male. Farrer has not lacked female commentators and critics on various topics, and indeed a major figure in the subsequent pages is Helen Gardner (1908–86), whose classic critique of *The Glass of Vision* is summarised by David Jasper in the first chapter of Part II and discussed in further chapters as well. While I initially considered including the work of earlier commentators such as Gardner, H.D. Lewis, and Frank Kermode, as well as some other important texts by Farrer, for various reasons it made more sense to start with Jasper's summary of these debates instead. See the Selected Bibliography for more detail.

material from the editor is provided in brackets. Two chapters have been edited for length, and excisions are noted with reference to the original publication.

To conclude, the goal of this volume is certainly not to endorse *The Glass of Vision* uncritically, but rather to bring a neglected masterpiece of 20th-century English theology back into ongoing conversations regarding revelation and imagination, and to provide some sense of the rich discussion it has already generated. I hope that readers will get at least as much benefit from engaging with these multiple texts and authorial perspectives as did the editor. Scripture, metaphysics, and poetry are rarely in close enough proximity to 'rub together', so it will be interesting to see what fires they may 'kindle' for a new generation of imaginative readers.[24]

---

[24]    I am grateful to David Brown, Christopher Bryan, Ann Loades, and Charles Taliaferro for helpful comments on earlier versions of this introduction.

# PART I
## Austin Farrer, *The Glass of Vision*:
## Bampton Lectures for 1948

Bampton Lectures for 1948

# *The Glass of Vision*

## Austin Farrer
### Doctor of Divinity and Fellow of Trinity College, Oxford

Now we see through a glass darkly

I Corinthians, xiii, 12[†]

DILECTISSIMAE CONIVGI
AVRIVM QVAE PATIENTIAM ACVMEN MENTIS
HIS ADHIBVIT CORRIGENDIS

['To my beloved wife
who applied patient listening and mental insight
to the improving of this manuscript']

---

[†]   Farrer's title and scriptural epigraph from the Authorised Version of 1611 both bear some comment. While contemporary readers may naturally assume that both Farrer and Paul are referring to cloudy but transparent glass that we 'see through' with some difficulty and distortion, the original reference was to an ancient mirror of polished but nevertheless entirely opaque metal such as silver or bronze. Hence, what is 'seen' is a reflection rather than something 'on the other side'. Thus, the New Revised Standard Version renders 1 Corinthians 13.12 as: 'For now we see in a mirror, dimly' and a note indicates that 'dimly' is literally 'in a riddle'. Earlier English translations such as the AV provide 'glass' for 'mirror' because later mirrors were indeed made not of metal but of glass with a silver backing, and were hence known as 'looking glasses' (cf. Lewis Carroll's *Through the Looking Glass, and What Alice Found There* [1871]). An interesting ambiguity is thus introduced into the meaning of Paul's statement. On one level, Farrer's book should thus apparently be titled, *The Mirror of Vision*, and the epigraph should be modernized accordingly. However, on another level, it seems that Farrer is deliberately trading on the anachronistic ambiguity of 'glass' as mirror in English usage, and yet also 'glass' as a translucent substance through which one indeed sees something, and perhaps sees it differently (cf., perhaps, the third verse of George Herbert's 'The Elixir' [published 1633]). Garrett Green, for example, suggests that Farrer's title 'recalls Paul's seeing "through a glass darkly" as well as Calvin's scriptural spectacles': *Imagining God: Theology and the Religious Imagination* (Grand Rapids, MI: Eerdmans, 1998), 111. Here we see Farrer's own poetic and imaginative faculties at work, in that both title and epigraph seem to be intentionally ambiguous and evocative. In either case, it must also be stressed that the epigraph of course is only part of the verse, and Farrer no doubt expected his readers to fill in the rest: '… but then face to face: now I know in part; but then shall I know even as also I am known' (AV). In a work dealing with divine revelation, Farrer certainly intends for the entire verse to be kept in mind.

# Preface

The lectures which follow are no more than a modest attempt to state what I do, in fact, think about the relation borne to one another by three things – the sense of metaphysical philosophy, the sense of scriptural revelation, and the sense of poetry. Scripture and metaphysics are equally my study, and poetry is my pleasure. These three things rubbing against one another in my mind seem to kindle one another, and so I am moved to ask how this happens. I would not dream of undertaking to give an adequate treatment of such a question. Perhaps, after each of the three subjects of my interest had claimed a great volume to itself, a fourth volume (but I should have broken down long before) might begin to draw them into relation with one another. If we were never to say anything unless we said everything, we should all be best advised to keep our lips sealed: but we are all vain enough to think that if we express within a limited compass what in fact interests us, it may have the luck to interest our indulgent friends. The limited compass is happily prescribed to me by the course of eight lectures allowed to a Bampton Lecturer. Here is a conveniently narrow vessel in which to mix together my three ingredients. Since any interest the experiment may have consists in a combination of things we have often considered apart, the smallness of scale may be a positive advantage – the unity will be less likely to get lost in the detail.

I fear that in touching so many and great themes with the boldness of treatment required for a lecture, I have produced something unscholarly and impressionistic. It is not only that the style may be rhetorical, for as to that, perhaps the reader will remember that lectures are, in fact, rhetoric. It is much more that there are many inconsistences in statement between one lecture and another, and it seems too much to ask of the reader that he should imagine for himself how I would have reduced them if I had written a full-scale scholastic treatise.

But I am most penitent of all for the seeming arrogance with which I have pronounced on the form of scientific and metaphysical thought, when I am very ignorant of the first, and too entramelled in the second to get it into focus. What I have said I have only said to give a broad impression relevant to the purpose I had in view: to speak of scientific thinking only in an aspect of it which contrasts with metaphysical thought; and then, no doubt, with gross exaggeration of the contrast. To generalize about the form of natural science is really absurd; every science must be allowed its own form: at the most we could arrange the sciences in a sort of scale, from the more rigidly mathematical at the one end, to the more humane and historical at the other. Let me repeat, then, that I say what I say about the characteristically scientific procedure for no other purpose but to raise a discussion about metaphysics by way of contrast. I am more concerned to say that metaphysics *is not* this than to say that any particular scientific procedure *is* just this.

In the third lecture I have used by way of illustration the Trinitarian symbolism of St John's Revelation. The reader who is acquainted with the commentaries on that book will know that a different account of these symbols, and especially of the Seven Spirits of God, has often been preferred, and so he will be likely to complain that my citation is a piece of arbitrary and unsupported dogmatism. I would not have dogmatized if I had thought that the interpretation was open to serious doubt. I have defended it at length in a study of the Apocalypse which will be published, I hope, not long after these lectures appear.[1]

My debts are to such obvious sources for the most part that there will be no real fraud in leaving them unacknowledged; but I would like to mention M. Gabriel Marcel, from whose *Être et Avoir* I have lifted the distinction between problems and mysteries repeated, I dare say with much distortion, in my fourth lecture.[2]

It is the privilege of the Bampton Lecturer to commemorate from the pulpit before every lecture the Reverend John Bampton, Canon of Salisbury; recalling, it may be, with some awe the river of good doctrine which through so long a time has flowed into learned ears from that munificent source. Now here are the exact provisions of his testament:

> ... I give and bequeath my Lands and Estates to the Chancellor, Masters and Scholars of the University of Oxford for ever, to have and to hold all and singular the said Lands or Estates upon trust, and to the intents and purposes hereinafter mentioned; that is to say, I will and appoint that the Vice-Chancellor of the University of Oxford for the time being shall take and receive all the rents, issues, and profits thereof, and (after all taxes, reparations, and necessary deductions made) that he pay all the remainder to the endowment of eight Divinity Lecture Sermons, to be established for ever in the said University, and to be performed in the manner following:

> I direct and appoint that, upon the first Tuesday in Easter Term, a Lecturer be yearly chosen by the Heads of Colleges only, and by no others, in the room adjoining to the Printing-House, between the hours of ten in the morning and two in the afternoon, to preach eight Divinity Lecture Sermons, the year following, at St Mary's in Oxford, between the commencement of the last month in the Lent Term and the end of the third week in Act Term.

> Also I direct and appoint, that the eight Divinity Lecture Sermons shall be preached upon either of the following subjects – to confirm and establish the Christian Faith, and to confute all heretics and schismatics – upon the divine

---

[1]   It was published the following year: Austin Farrer, *A Rebirth of Images: The Making of St John's Apocalypse* (Westminster: Dacre Press, 1949).

[2]   Original French edition published in 1935; Farrer's wife Katharine translated the first English version, which likewise appeared the year after *The Glass of Vision*: Gabriel Marcel, *Being and Having*, translated by Katharine Farrer (Westminster: Dacre Press, 1949).

authority of the holy Scriptures – upon the authority of the writings of the primitive Fathers, as to the faith and practice of the primitive Church – upon the Divinity of our Lord and Saviour Jesus Christ – upon the Divinity of the Holy Ghost – upon the Articles of the Christian Faith, as comprehended in the Apostles' and the Nicene Creeds.

Also I direct, that thirty copies of the eight Divinity Lecture Sermons shall always be printed, within two months after they are preached; and one copy shall be given to the Chancellor of the University, and one copy to the Head of every College, and one copy to the Mayor of the city of Oxford, and one copy to be put into the Bodleian library; and the expense of printing them shall be paid out of the revenue of the Land or Estates given for establishing the Divinity Lecture Sermons; and the Preacher shall not be paid, nor be entitled to the revenue, before they are printed.

Also I direct and appoint, that no person shall be qualified to preach the Divinity Lecture Sermons, unless he hath taken the degree of Master of Arts at least, in one of the two Universities of Oxford or Cambridge; and that the same person shall never preach the Divinity Lecture Sermons twice.

Not again, says the wise testator. But, *O si melius*![3]

Oxford
June 1948

---

[3]    'If so, it would have been better!'

# Lecture I:

# The Supernatural and the Natural

That which may be known of God is manifest among men, for God hath
manifested it unto them. For his invisible attributes since the creation of the
world are clearly seen, being perceived through the things that are made, even
his everlasting power and deity.

Romans, I.19

The subject of these lectures is the form of divine truth in the human mind: and
I begin today with the distinctive character of supernatural and revealed truth.
For the truth of which I have principally to speak is not simply truth about God,
it is revealed truth about God; and God himself has revealed it. So we believe:
and in so believing we suppose that we exalt this truth, as something above what
our faculties could reach; as something we could not know unless God himself
declared it. Our intention is not to make truth as narrow as the Church which
professes it, but as high as the God who proclaims it. There is indeed, we say, a
truth about God which human reason can discover; and man might have supposed
it to be the highest he could know, had it not been that God himself had spoken a
higher truth to him.

Since revealed truth is exalted by comparison with natural truth, we are
disconcerted to hear some Christian philosophers attack the whole basis of
distinction between the two, equating revelation and reason, so far as either is able
to speak truly of God. The instinct of our faith reacts against such an equation, and
inclines us to look into its credentials. The equation of reason and revelation is, we
find, supposed to be proved by two propositions.

The first is this: if we believe in God at all, it is absurd and impious to imagine
that we can find him out by our own reason, without his being first active in
revealing himself to us. Therefore all our discovery of him is his self-manifestation,
and all rational theology is revealed theology.

And this is the second proposition: if God does reveal himself to us, we cannot
acknowledge or master what he reveals without the use of our reason. Therefore
all his self-manifestation is also our discovery of him, and all revealed theology
is rational theology.

The first proposition, assuming reason, proves revelation: the second, assuming
revelation, proves reason. We are intended to add the two together and establish the
joint conclusion that, wherever there is knowledge of God, both factors operate:
man reasons, and God reveals. We need not of course conclude that the proportion
between the two factors is everywhere the same. In the wide and continuous field
of human experience we shall find places at which God's operation appears more
personal and more striking, and man's 'reason' has more the character of simple

recognition. Again we shall find places at which God's operation is less evident or less clear, and man's reason must be consciously strained in the effort to apprehend or to interpret it. Such differences there are admitted to be, but they are not admitted to be differences of principle. Indeed, to distinguish between natural and revealed theology is positively misleading; it would be better to substitute other distinctions: say the distinction between a theology based on God's action in the general laws of nature, and a theology based on God's action in particular historical fact – in the lives, let us say, of prophets and saints. It would be more significant on this shewing to call Christianity an historical religion than to call it a revealed religion.

Such is the argument. In proceeding to discuss it, we begin by observing that the two propositions on which it stands are flat platitudes, which can scarcely have been ever contested. Who has supposed that God can be found out without his own previous act of willing self-manifestation? Or who has supposed that revealed truth can be acknowledged without any use of our rational faculties? Is it really likely that a pair of incontrovertible truisms have strength to overthrow a doctrine long maintained by philosophers and saints? One would hesitate to think so. It is not, in fact, the substance of traditional doctrine that the two propositions assail, but simply the title by which it has been frequently and infelicitously called. 'Reason and Revelation' is a current description, but a bad description, for the antithesis we have to discuss. We ought to say '*Natural* Reason and *Supernatural* Revelation', and we ought to throw the emphasis on the adjectives rather than upon the nouns. We have not to distinguish between God's action and ours, but between two phases of God's action – his supernatural action, and his action by way of nature. It is difficult to see how anything resembling Christianity can survive the denial of this distinction. For Christianity is faith in Christ, and Christ is God acting not by way of nature, but supernaturally. If you reduce Christ to a part of God's natural action, is he Christ any longer?

Let us first consider God's self-revelation by way of nature. To a theist, everything which happens in the world reveals God acting through his creatures, or, to put it otherwise, it reveals the creatures acting as themselves the effect of the Creator's act. For this reason the creatures have traditionally been called 'second causes', and God the 'first cause' of every action. The creatures, all together, make up the realm of Nature. Human minds, being themselves creatures, are parts of Nature in the sense here understood. It is particularly necessary to observe this, because German idealism has popularised the distinction between Nature and Spirit, a distinction which exempts the human spirit from the realm of nature. Let every man use words in the way best suited to make his meaning plain. For our present purpose we define Nature in such a sense that the activities of human spirit, of intellect, that is to say, and will, are parts of nature. For intelligence and voluntary choice are certainly the natural endowments of man. Without them human nature would not be human nature, but some other thing.

By Nature, then, we mean the universe of creatures or the sum of second causes, including man. By including man in nature we do not subject him to the iron rule of natural law, or otherwise pretend that he is something lower than he is. For us, nature is not a machine operated by divine controls; it is a multitude of interplaying forces, sustained in being by the Father of Life. Some natural activities operate in close accord with fixed patterns, others more freely. Nature is not natural because it is bound; it is natural because it is the real operation of second causes, whether they are bound or free. Men are free, or rather, they are just as free as they discover themselves to be; but their actions, in being free, do not cease to be natural; it is their nature to be free, and in exercising their freedom they express their nature. Not that a man is free to be anything you like: he cannot exercise the activities of an angel, nor even the activities of an eagle. He can only exercise his own, those, that is to say, which belong to his nature, and to his place in the total nature.

When we speak, therefore, of God's operation by way of nature, we refer to those activities which he, their first cause, enables the multitudes of second causes to perform, in accordance with the various natures he has assigned them. What happens, then, when man knows God by nature, by his natural reason? We must answer that both the object and the subject of such knowledge are supplied by God; by God, that is, working in the way of nature. Any example will serve to make this plain. Let us take the most hackneyed of all – Aristotle reasoning his way from stellar motions to his Prime Mover Unmoved. (It may well be that his reasoning is wholly invalid: it will still serve for our example.) The object he studies is the stellar motions, and these motions are the activities of second causes, of the energies which compose the bodies of the stars. And they, in moving, express the activity of their first cause, God. So much for the object of Aristotle's study. As to the subject, it is Aristotle's own mind; itself a second cause, exerting a power of speculation continually derived from God, the first cause and archetypal mind. Aristotle, who had, indeed, scarcely the rudiments of what we call theistic belief, chose to concentrate his attention on the activity of God revealed in the stars he studied, rather than upon the activity of God revealed in his own mind as he studied the stars. But in principle either path can be taken. We can ascend from second to first cause either on the side of the subject or of the object. Aristotle was himself aware that the human subject, speculating as he speculated, was exerting an act not so much human as divine.

What do we learn from the example we have taken? That the most aridly theoretical speculation, the typical case of rational theologising, is to be attributed to the divine initiative: to God working by way of nature, God who wills to display himself in the stars, God who wills to elevate a philosopher's mind along the paths of astral contemplation. There is no question of the philosopher's finding God out, as a child may find his father out, unwilling or unaware. God may be in some sense a jealous God, but his jealousy is not this. He is not unwilling to be known, but only (if so) unwilling that, knowing him, we should attribute the achievement to ourselves. In apprehending the Creator through the creature, the philosopher has no cause to boast: he simply consents not to frustrate a principal purpose of his natural being, when the way has opened for him to fulfil it.

But if, in the case we have taken, there is no question of denying the divine initiative, equally there is no question of asserting an action of God outside the bounds of nature. The stars and the philosopher were both exerting their proper forces. There is nothing supernatural about Aristotle's enlightenment.

There are, I know, many people who will listen to a discussion such as this with some impatience. 'When', they say, 'the religious mind insists that God is not to be known without his revealing initiative, it is not to be put off with philosophic generalities about the universal operation of *Deus sive Natura*.[1] To tell us that what we call nature can be called God achieving his ends by way of nature, really alters nothing. What we mean is that God is not to be known by us unless he reveals himself *personally*. Aristotle was, you say, quite unaware of God's personally communicating to him anything. Very well: in that case we shall be inclined to say one or other of two things. We are willing to suppose that Aristotle's mind responded to no personal divine communication, in which case the First Mover he called God will have had no truly divine character, but will be an idol of the philosophic mind. Alternatively we are willing to suppose that Aristotle read the features of true deity into his First Mover; in which case his mind will have at some time responded to a personal divine communication, although he had presumably misunderstood the nature of the communication, through lack of suitable ideas by which to interpret it.'

In turning to consider this type of position, we will fix our attention first upon the phrase 'personal communication'. What does it mean? On the face of it, it suggests that God must speak to us somewhat as we speak to one another. But this obviously does not happen, nor is it going to happen. If I heard a divine voice in the air without, which was no apparition but an actual exterior event, it would still be necessary to suppose that the First Cause, God, was operating through second causes, which would be physical sound-waves: for that is exactly what I should mean by calling the voice exterior and real. If, on the other hand, the voice is not really exterior, but an imagination of my own mind, then the First Cause finds his second or instrumental cause in some working of my natural phantasy. If, again, the voice is a voice by metaphor only, and more properly a movement of thought, then the second cause which God employs is some part of my mental activity; and he employs it to address in his name another stream of my thinking, which is at the moment arrogating to itself the name of *me*.

Now no one, I think, who wished to make Aristotle's knowledge of God conditional upon a 'personal communication' would lay it down that he must seem to hear voices or see visions. Those would not be Aristotelian things to do, and if they are required, then all the Aristotles of this world are damned without remedy. We must take it, then, that Aristotle is to experience the address of God through the secondary causality of his own thought.

I should now like to ask how important it is deemed to be that the philosopher's experience should fall into the form of an inward colloquy, with one part of his thought addressing another as though with the voice of God. I have a special and personal interest in challenging the colloquy-form, because of an obstacle I

---

[1]   'God or Nature' – see further discussion below.

remember encountering in my own adolescence. I had myself (this at least is the impression I retain) been reared in a personalism which might satisfy the most ardent of Dr Buber's disciples.[2] I thought of myself as set over against deity as one man faces another across a table, except that God was invisible and indefinitely great. And I hoped that he would signify his presence to me by way of colloquy; but neither out of the scripture I read nor in the prayers I tried to make did any mental voice address me. I believe at that time anything would have satisfied me, but nothing came: no 'other' stood beside me, no shadow of presence fell upon me. I owe my liberation from this *impasse*, as far as I can remember, to reading Spinoza's Ethics. Those phrases which now strike me as so flat and sinister, so ultimately atheistic, *Deus sive Natura* (God, or call it Nature), *Deus, quatenus consideratur ut constituens essentiam humanae mentis* (God, in so far as he is regarded as constituting the being of the human mind) – these phrases were to me light and liberation, not because I was or desired to be a pantheist, but because I could not find the wished-for colloquy with God.[3]

Undoubtedly I misunderstood Spinoza, in somewhat the same fashion as (to quote a high example) St Augustine misunderstood Plotinus, turning him to Christian uses. Here, anyhow, is what I took from Spinozism. I would no longer attempt, with the psalmist, 'to set God before my face'.[4] I would see him as the underlying cause of my thinking, especially of those thoughts in which I tried to think of him. I would dare to hope that sometimes my thought would become diaphanous, so that there should be some perception of the divine cause shining

---

[2]   Martin Buber (1878–1965), an Austrian Jewish theologian best known for his book *Ich und Du* (1923), translated into English in 1937 as *I and Thou*, which argued that others, including God, should be considered in personal rather than objective terms.

[3]   In the longer citation, Farrer seems to be quoting the Latin text of Spinoza's *Ethics* (1677) from memory. The likely reference is Part II, Corollary to Proposition XI, which says: *Hinc sequitur mentem humanam partem esse infiniti intellectus Dei. Ac proinde cum dicimus, mentem humanam hoc vel illud percipere, nihil aliud dicimus, quam quod Deus, non quatenus infinitus est, sed quatenus per naturam humanae mentis explicatur, sive quatenus humanae mentis essentiam constituit, hanc vel illam habet ideam; et cum dicimus Deum hanc vel illam ideam habere, non tantum, quatenus naturam humanae mentis constituit, sed quatenus simul cum mente humana alterius rei etiam habet ideam, tum dicimus mentem humanam rem ex parte sive inadaequate percipere.* Or, in a contemporary English translation: 'From this it follows that the human Mind is a part of the infinite intellect of God. Therefore, when we say that the human Mind perceives this or that, we are saying nothing but that God, not insofar as he is infinite, but insofar as he is explained through the nature of the human Mind, *or* insofar as he constitutes the essence of the human Mind, has this or that idea; and when we say that God has this or that idea, not only insofar as he constitutes the nature of the human Mind, but insofar as he also has the idea of another thing together with the human Mind, then we say that the human Mind perceives the thing only partially, *or* inadequately.' *The Collected Works of Spinoza, Volume I*, edited and translated by Edwin Curley (Princeton: Princeton University Press, 1985), 456.

[4]   Probably referring to Psalm 16.8, 41.12, and 42.2.

through the created effect, as a deep pool, settling into a clear tranquillity, permits us to see the spring in the bottom of it from which its waters rise. I would dare to hope that through a second cause the First Cause might be felt, when the second cause in question was itself a spirit, made in the image of the divine Spirit, and perpetually welling up out of his creative act.

Such things, I say, I dared to hope for, and I will not say that my hope was in any way remarkably fulfilled, but I will say that by so viewing my attempted work of prayer, I was rid of the frustration which had baffled me before. And this is why, when Germans set their eyeballs and pronounce the terrific words 'He speaks to thee' (Er redet Dich an) I am sure, indeed, that they are saying something, but I am still more sure that they are not speaking to my condition.[5]

To return now to our discussion of a most unhistorical Aristotle.[6] What is it that the personalists demand? Must the philosopher be aware of God addressing him in mental colloquy, or will it do if he should, as St Augustine so vividly did, perceive God as light, shining through his acts of intelligence? Or perhaps what the personalists mean is something different: that it does not matter how God touches the philosopher, whether by mental colloquy, or by shewing through his diaphanous thought, or by falling on him in the splendour of the stars; any of these ways will suffice, so long as they produce the right effect. The philosopher must be brought to realise that the God who so touches him places him in a personal relation to himself. He must acknowledge duties to the supreme worth of divine Spirit, analogous to the duties he acknowledges towards the subordinate worth of the human spirits who surround him; so that for him to say 'Thou, O God' will be no figure, as it might be in the mouth of Horace invoking the Bandusian Spring.[7]

If this is what the personalists mean, they are no longer talking about the way in which God reveals himself to the philosopher, they are talking about the response which the revelation evokes. If Aristotle's mind is so moved by its own operation under God, and by the observed motions of the stars, that it falls into a posture of adoration, of response to an infinite person, it will then be said that God has personally revealed himself to Aristotle, and that Aristotle in consequence

---

[5]   A prize-winning classical student at Oxford with a gift for pastiche, Farrer began learning German as a curate in the late 1920s in order to read the work of theologians such as Emil Brunner and Karl Barth. In 1931 he went to Bonn, Germany, to study with Barth, and in 1932 he went to Zürich, Switzerland, to study with Brunner. 'Er redet Dich an' seems not to be a direct quotation from Buber or another Germanophone writer—although Farrer may have heard it spoken by Barth or Brunner in person—but rather Farrer's parody of this 'personalist' view. That is, he probably chose it over, e.g., 'Er spricht zu Dir', because it sounded more portentous and 'Germanic' to him.

[6]   Farrer later took a more critical attitude to the 'historical' Aristotle and his influence on Western philosophical and theological thinking on causality in *Faith and Speculation: An Essay in Philosophical Theology* (London: A&C Black, 1967), Chapter IX, 'First Cause' (131–41).

[7]   A reference to a famous poem (*Odes*, III.13) by the Roman poet Horace (65–8 BCE) about a cool and constant spring of fresh water to which he offers various sacrifices.

knows something of God. If, on the other hand, Aristotle sees God simply as ultimate being, as mainspring of cause and loadstone of motion, then it will be said that Aristotle does not know God; he knows an idol of his own mind, for God has never spoken to him.

If we have brought the matter to this point, we have brought it to an issue of verbal definition, and nothing else. In either case Aristotle, moved by the First Cause, sees things that are true of that Cause. Above all else it is true that God is the master of our life, but it is also true, so far as it goes, that he is the self-thinking Thought on whom all finite agencies depend. Whichever thing Aristotle thinks, he has been moved by God to think truth of God. Only it is apparently proposed that the name 'God' should be given a restricted use: 'God' is to mean the Supreme Being viewed as the master of our life, personally determining us. In any other aspect he is to be called by some other name. Well, as we said before, let every man use words in such a sense as serves best to make his meaning plain; and there may be contexts in which the restricted sense proposed for the word 'God' would make for clarity. But whatever those contexts may be, anyhow the sober history of philosophical and theological thinking is not one of them.

If we were to ask, as a matter of simple fact, whether Aristotle acknowledged in God the personal master of his life, commanding a personal response on his own part, that, I fear, would happen which so often happens when we apply preconceived definitions to historical instances – we do not know whether to say that they apply, or that they do not. The astral paganism of which Aristotle's theology was so curious a refinement was no mere physical hypothesis, but a genuine, if cool and limited, spirituality. When Aristotle, crowned with evergreen, slew his victim to the highest of astral deities, and said 'Thou, O God', he did not suppose himself to be apostrophising an abstraction or indulging an artificial personification. He was performing an act of homage towards supreme spirit, even though he would have regarded it as a derogation from that spirit's supremacy, if he should deign to hear his worshipper's words. The philosopher knew, in addition, that because God is God, and our minds bear to him some partial resemblance, therefore our highest good must be to practise the acts of godhead so far as in us lies. So much for Aristotle's creed. Whether it constitutes personal response to God, is a question we will leave to those theologians, whose position obliges them to find a *yes* or *no* answer to it.

We should ourselves like to advance, as being at least probable, the following propositions. God, working by way of nature, may lead the human mind to recognise its own supreme cause through its own proper operation. When this happens there are on the human side several degrees of consciousness possible as to what is happening. A man may suppose himself to infer God as the cause of the physical effects he studies, or as the cause of his own existence, without being aware of the divine causality behind his own act in so inferring God. Again, he may be aware of the divine causality behind his own thoughts, but as a general illumination simply, lighting up all his understanding indifferently, so far as he understands: as a candle illuminates all equidistant objects with indifferent rays.

Or, finally, he may see the divine moving of his best thought as the direction of a personal providence, with which he can in a manner co-operate by attending to it. If he has reached this stage, he may be said by personalists to have responded personally to God. But it seems unreasonable, on the face of it, to deny the possibility of other and inferior degrees of consciousness in the natural knowledge of God. Surely God may lead us to the knowledge of himself without our knowing that he leads us, or without our understanding his leading in a 'personal' way. And whichever occurs of the things we have considered, there is no need to seek its explanation in a supernatural act of God: his action by way of nature could suffice.

Nevertheless there is also a supernatural action of God, or so we believe; and we must endeavour now to describe it. Let us begin by placing it in relation with the convenient distinction between the First Cause and the second causes. Not that, if God acts supernaturally, he acts without second causes; but he works through second causes effects which do not arise from the natural powers of those causes. It is by reference to the powers of second causes that events or states are called 'supernatural'. Nothing is supernatural to God, because his nature is infinity, and no action exceeds it. But many acts may be supernatural to man, because many conceivable achievements exceed his natural faculties: to learn, for example, the mystery of Trinity in the Godhead.

It must be understood in this context that by 'cause', 'agent' is meant, as should be evident from the implied comparison between First Cause and second causes. The First Cause is simply a creative agent, and not a cause in any other sense but this: not, for example, a supreme causal 'law', nor a first event upon which other events follow according to causal 'law'. The First Cause is an agent, the second causes are likewise agents or energies. If we understand 'cause' in the Kantian sense, then to talk of a cause being endowed with an efficacy beyond its natural scope, is nonsense.[8] A Kantian may define 'cause' like this: a cause is an event belonging to a class of events, of which it is universally true that they are followed by events of a further given class. If we say that a flash of lightning is the cause of the consequent thunder, we are held to be classing the lightning as an electric explosion, and acknowledging that from all electric explosions sound-waves arise. According to this definition of 'cause', no cause can be endowed with an efficacy above what it has by nature. If an event B follows an event A otherwise than the causal law applicable to A demands, then by the Kantian definition A is not the cause of B at all, and B's cause must be sought elsewhere, in the event C, for example. We might hunt causes for B endlessly.

---

[8]    As a student of metaphysics, Farrer was aware that various philosophers held different understandings of causality (see note 6 above), and in his first book, *Finite and Infinite: A Philosophical Essay* (Westminster: Dacre Press, 1943), very briefly noted that Locke and Spinoza differed on this topic. He continues in that vein here, specifying the particular causal theory he is discussing, in this case, Immanuel Kant's. His point is that Kant's theory of causality rules out Farrer's own theory that natural agents can indeed be supernaturalised – or, as he puts it further below, enabled to exceed their natural power by higher assistance.

If (to suppose an absurdity) we could establish that no cause whatever had caused B *naturally*, we could not conclude that some cause had caused it *supernaturally*, by acting, that is, beyond its natural efficacy; for we have agreed that under the Kantian definition of cause such a conclusion would not mean anything. We should simply have to say that B was apparently *uncaused*.

If we were attempting to be theists as well as Kantians (and after all, Kant attempted it) we might (though Kant would not) attach the event B direct to the causality of God; we might say that it had no second cause, but was an immediate new creation of the First. Such a conclusion may seem at first sight delightful to the pious mind; but a little reflection will shew us that the piety which delights in it must be of the sort to believe the absurd for its own sake. For if we attach the supernatural event simply to the First Cause alone, it is then no part of the existing finite world, having no real connexion with the sequence of finite occurrences: it is a fragment of a new world momentarily interpolated into the old. But that is not (I hope) what we mean by the supernatural. When the supernatural occurs, something in the existing world is supernaturalised, for example, the manhood of Jesus Christ by union with the deity, or, to take a legendary instance, Balaam's ass by being enabled to speak.

The story of Balaam is highly instructive for our purpose.[9] It represents the point at which the magic supernatural comes under divine control. We can easily reconstruct an older Balaam, a figure of pure fairy tale. He is the mighty magician, whose spells are efficacious of themselves. He rides an ass which, in the crisis of her master's destiny – when he is about to collide with an invisible armed magician of power greater than his own – of herself opens her mouth and speaks. Such may have been the original story: but as we have it, it has become something different. Balaam's power of efficacious spell is a supernatural gift from God, and woe betide him if he attempts to use it otherwise than the divine will allows. His ass is no more than an ass, until God gives her a power beyond her asinine nature, that she may be able to warn her master from fighting against God.

I hope it will cause no scandal if I simply confess that the theologising of the magical represents the historical beginning of the supernatural, as we have to define it. In the fairy-tale world it is simply accepted that things and persons act from time to time beyond their determinate 'natures'. The fairy tale takes the world to consist of real active beings which act of themselves – and this at least is as good philosophy as it is good faery. The real active beings of fairyland are of various determinate kinds: men, women, dogs, asses, trees, stones. These beings normally act within the rule of their natural kind, for that is what is meant by saying that they belong to such a kind. On occasion, however, they exert a higher efficacy, developing, as it were, a supernatural margin to the line of their natural act: men ride the wind, asses speak, and rocks obey the human voice. We reach the end of fairyland and pass the boundary-stone which the Balaam-story represents, and such wonders are still said to befall, but only through the supernaturalising of natural agents by God.

---

[9] See Numbers 22.1–35.

I said that I hoped the confession of such lowly beginnings for supernaturalism would cause no offence. I will try now to explain why it need not. I will do this by raising the question, how it is initially possible for the human mind to conceive supernatural action at all. I reply that the possibility derives from the very form of our active existence. We are primarily aware of ourselves as active beings, engaged in interaction with a whole environment of other active beings. We are further aware that we can, of ourselves, vary the form of our activity, from working to eating, from digging to planting. We are also aware that we can, to an astonishing degree, vary the intensity of our activity, from lounging to running for our lives, from day-dreaming to hard thinking. We can also vary the elevation of our act, from eating food like a beast to shaping verse like an angel. All our alternative acts are controlled by the subtle and expansible pattern of our human nature. But within that pattern we have large scope of freedom, and the sense of such freedom easily begets the dream of passing right beyond our nature into supernatural action. What we dream for ourselves, we attribute to others, to dogs, asses, trees and stones, and the world of faery appears.

Yet the idea of unaided supernatural action on the part of any agent is, on the face of it, almost a contradiction in terms; even in the fairy world there is a tendency to attribute the supernatural efficacy of a natural agent to the aid of other beings: beings not necessarily superior in all respects to the agent, but possessing anyhow by nature the type of active power which they are supposed to confer upon him. We say that unaided supernatural action is almost a contradiction in terms. For the 'nature' of an active being, by definition, determines the scope of his unaided action: if *of himself* he acted beyond what he and we supposed his nature to be, we ought to conclude forthwith that we had defined his nature too narrowly, not that he had exceeded it.

The idea of the supernatural is of a finite agent exceeding his natural power by higher assistance. The idea is common to religious thought at many levels: rank superstition, primitive barbarism and high spirituality will all make their own applications of it, for all are concerned with the elevation of man to what lies above him. For us, the typical case of the supernatural is not seen in physical miracles, but in the empowering of the spirit of man by the Spirit of his Creator, to know and to love the supreme and causeless Act, the pure and endless Being, the saving Charity: *to whom therefore, one God in three Persons, Father, Son and Holy Ghost, be ascribed, as is most justly due, all might, dominion, majesty and power, henceforth and for ever.*

# Lecture II:
# The Supernatural and the Weird

O give thanks unto the Lord, for he is gracious; for his mercy endureth for ever.
Who alone doeth great wonders; for his mercy endureth for ever.

Psalm CXXXVI, 1–4

Our purpose here is further to examine the idea of a supernatural act in the human mind, when it knows God by way of revelation.

In the last 50 years the discussion of the supernatural has changed its character. The old critics of the supernatural, the physical dogmatists, thought they knew pretty nearly the bounds of nature, and stubbornly disbelieved anything which appeared to pass them. The new critics of the supernatural are, on the contrary, only too ready to believe in the occurrence of wonders. What they deny is that the bounds of nature can be fixed at all. Nature is so various and so queer, they think, that what were once thought miracles may be perfectly natural occurrences.

We note this particularly in the discussion of uncanny forms of psychical action by our psychical researchers. These people of course admit a rough distinction between the normal and the abnormal in our experience. But those of them who have the best claim to be thought scientific use the axiom that the abnormal is still the action of finite agents, and though not normal, natural. To take the example of telepathy. If a sailor drowning at sea makes an impress on the mind of his wife in harbour, he is held to be exerting a power which belongs to human nature as such, and is available for exercise under conditions ideally capable of definition, however difficult it may be in practice to define them. The song which the psychical researchers sing in our ears is this, that human nature, and the natures of the forces which compose human environment, are other than we had supposed, and infinitely more complex.

It is reasonable to agree with the psychical researchers, so far as the phenomena go which they investigate. But if so, have we any room left to assert the supernatural at all? How, we must ask ourselves, could the genuine supernatural ever be evidenced? How can we ever be sure that any exerted act is beyond the nature of the agent exerting it, if the nature of the agent is so difficult to fix? Must not we conclude that the idea of the supernatural is simply an illusion? Especially since it is so easy to see how the illusion should arise. It is almost inevitable, is it not, that men should misconceive their natural limits, drawing them too narrowly, and ruling out the abnormal. The abnormal occurs, and we falsely suppose that our active power has run beyond the limits of our nature. Such is the first step on the road to superstition. The second quickly follows: we refer our supposed supernatural act to divine influences acting upon us. For since no agent can exert a power he has not got, we look about for some magical agent outside us who has bestowed on us for the occasion the excess power of which we dispose.

The reference of supposedly supernatural acts to a supernaturalising influence from without comes all the more readily, because in many abnormal activities we have the feeling of possession or alien control. His best verses are 'given' to the poet; the fortune-teller cannot predict by a direct volition, but by somehow making his mind expectantly passive, and waiting for images to delineate themselves; and so on. A psychologist will have no difficulty in explaining the appearance of alien control in such cases. It is well known that there are functions of our mind, and indeed of our bodies, which are not controlled by direct will-power, but can sometimes be induced, as it were, to act by ancillary volitions releasing them. Since we identify ourselves with the releasing volitions by the mere fact of making them, we are liable to experience as other than ourselves the action of the functions they release. There is no special mystery about this to a psychologist, but our ancestors were not psychologists, and the phenomenon of apparent alien control must powerfully have helped them to ascribe supposedly supernatural acts to mysterious influences whereby they were enabled to operate.

Such considerations as those we have been entertaining must force a theologian to subject the traditional doctrine of the supernatural to a searching criticism. A test case, for example, will be the healing miracles of Christ. An older and simpler age dogmatically pronounced: as man he hungered and thirsted, as God he healed the lame and blind. In view of the facts of psychological healing now known to us, many of us feel doubt about placing the healing simply upon the divine side. Ought we not to say that powers of psychological healing belonged to Christ's human nature as such? Believers will wish to add that, like other of his human powers, they were enhanced by the taking of Christ's nature into the deity of God the Son: they were, in fact, supernaturally enhanced. But 'enhanced' is not 'conferred': what is now said to be supernatural is not the appearance of such powers, but the degree in which they appear. So a believer may say. An unbeliever, it is obvious, will view this as a position taken up overnight in the course of a theological rearguard action, and not destined to be defended either successfully or for long. We are in full retreat, he will think, towards a wholly non-supernatural religion.

We do not, in fact, view our own predicament with any serious solicitude, nor are we preparing to throw supernaturalism overboard. Let us recur to the definition of supernatural action. It is action which is *above* what our nature allows of. Now psychical research may have left us less clear than we were as to the sideways and downward limits of our natural powers; but it has done nothing, so far as I can see, to raise or unfix the ceiling. We can still speak with confidence about the supernatural, because we know just as much as we did before about the upward limit of our powers. About the *preternatural* as a whole we cannot speak with the same confidence, not being able to fix our limit so clearly in other directions.

The distinction just drawn between the preternatural in general and the more specially supernatural is vital to our argument. It is bound, I am afraid, to land us in considerable complexities of exposition. They will have to be endured, for if we shirk them we shall be unable to say anything of use. To begin with, we shall be called upon to justify the antithesis between an upward limit and a sideways and downwards limit to our faculties. Are any acts we perform intrinsically 'higher' than any others? Do not we call an ability 'high' simply because we are in fact reaching after it with effort, like a man picking fruit from a tall tree? Are not all abilities 'high' in this sense, provided they lie at or beyond the furthest stretch of our powers? Fortune-tellers stretch to obtain premonitions of the future, and mystics to obtain union with their Creator, and scientists to formulate an adequate hypothesis, and statesmen to devise the prevention of public ruin. All these aims are in themselves good or innocent, and all of them are on the tips of the branches. Is one intrinsically 'higher' than another?

We are bound to reply that there is, in fact, a hierarchy of human acts, some higher, or nobler, in themselves than others; this is a first metaphysical truth. If acts were 'high' in proportion to their difficulty, then the gymnastic feat of picking that last apple 'which furthest blushes on the furthest bough' without breaking either the tree or one's own neck – a feat, let us suppose, of fantastic muscular virtuosity – might be as 'high' as the act of finding a fresh solution to a main philosophical problem. It is no use replying, 'Ah, but the apple-picking is a bodily feat', for we do not solve philosophical problems without the instrumentality of our nerves; any more than (conversely) we pick the apple without judgment and resolution. As the action of a frog is a higher form of action than the action of a cog, and the action of a dog than that of a frog: so is human action higher than canine action, and, within the human field, those acts which are more specially human, than those which are nearer to the animal level; and chimpanzees can pick awkwardly placed apples with greater skill than we can.[1]

There is a hierarchy in the order of human acts: we all know this well enough in principle, however hard we may find it to determine the hierarchical grade of a given act. We will assume the principle of hierarchy without more ado, and proceed to relate it to the knowledge of our own upward limit. For we have said that we know our upward limit more clearly than we do our sideways and downward limit. The truth which we hope to make plain is that the knowledge of our upward limit is equivalent to our self-knowledge, for, in a sense, we do know ourselves.

Psychical researchers may try to make our flesh creep by telling us that our conventional idea of our personal being has little if any relation to the truth; that our mind, instead of being limited in space to the operation of our nervous system,

---

[1]　The awkwardly placed apple 'which furthest blushes on the furthest bough' seems to be a reference to Fragment 93 by Sappho (ca. 630–570 BCE), although the translation may be Farrer's own. Dante Gabriel Rossetti (1828–82) translates it as: 'Like the sweet apple which reddens upon the topmost bough,/A-top on the topmost twig,—which the pluckers forgot, somehow,—/Forgot it not, nay, but got it not, for none could get it till now.' *Collected Poetry and Prose*, edited by Jerome McGann (New Haven and London: Yale University Press, 2003), 123. Compare with this more contemporary rendering: 'As a sweet apple reddens/on a high branch//at the tip of the topmost bough:/The apple-pickers missed it.//No, they didn't miss it:/They couldn't reach it.' *A Garland: The Poems and Fragments of Sappho*, translated by Jim Powell (New York: Farrar Straus Giroux, 1993), 12.

and in time to the present moment, and in scope to our conscious acts, is prowling all over the place on its own, ranging into the past and future, and the merest fraction of it deigning to appear in consciousness at all. And the psycho-analysts, with their investigations into the plumbing and the cellarage of our volitional life, may seem to give us much the same impression: the self we know is a mere surface phenomenon floating on an unsounded deep. Yet even if we grant all the particular facts asserted by the psychologists and psychic researchers to be true, we still feel an instinctive suspicion that the negative conclusion drawn with respect to our self-knowledge belongs to rhetoric and not to science.

One of the things which makes us suspicious is that we have heard all this before, in a closely parallel field. As psychic researchers may tell us that we do not know our own souls, so physicists and physiologists may tell us that we do not know our own bodily being. Are not the vital processes of our anatomy complex beyond anything that lay common-sense supposes? And do not those processes organise an infinity of cells, of whose distinct existence we never had the least notion? And does not each cell, in turn, organise an infinity of physical atoms? And has not each atom within it a system of forces of the sort, which, artificially released in sufficient quantity, blew a Japanese city to pieces the other day? Need we go further? Is it not plain that our bodies are each a universe in itself, of which our ordinary bodily consciousness gives us no least idea?

Even under the beating of so many waves of interrogative rhetoric we should none of us, I take it, have much difficulty in keeping our feet. We should readily reply: all this is irrelevant. What I mean by my body is the system of physical motion and sensation in which I live: that is why I call it mine, and why I regard it as a unit. In direct consciousness of having, or being, or using my body, I have an inward understanding of what bodily life is, of what it is to be embodied and alive, which nothing else but simple and direct consciousness can possibly give: anatomy adds nothing to it. I am aware, of course, that the experienced and living form of the body itself uses, permeates, indwells a certain amount of stuff. To speak more exactly of the body, I mean by it the felt pattern of animal life, taken not in abstraction, but together with so much stuff as it directly controls, permeates and depends upon. But in defining the body I do not define the nature of that stuff, I merely state that there is a good deal of it. In the same way, if I were defining a chair, I should assume that it was made of some suitable material, but I should not include oak or mahogany or steel-tubing in my definition. I already know what a chair is before I lift the petticoat of chintz to see what the feet are made of, and I already know what my body is before I begin anatomy or biology or physics. These sciences will tell me a great deal about the subsidiary forms which the form of the living body organises; and in so doing they will tell me a great deal about the conditions which determine the functioning of the bodily form, or even make it possible for the bodily form to function at all. But what I mean by 'human body' is simply the bodily form itself, thought of as organising whatever subsidiary forms it does organise: and the special sciences cast no direct light on what it is to be that bodily form. It is lit up by one thing, and one thing alone – the embodied consciousness of the man whose body is in question. The problem of bodily knowledge is, as we see, solved immediately by the principle of hierarchy. We define the body by its highest organising principle, and, because that remains unaltered, the body continues to answer to the same definition, whatever may be revealed about the subsidiary organisms within it. Even though it turns out to consist of a virtual infinity of distinct real parts, and even though each one of these parts stands in real causal relation with every other element of matter in the whole universe, our body remains, in virtue of its highest form, just what we perceive it to be. We might use the figure of a cone to illustrate the point. If we are looking at a cone whose apex alone is in clear light, we can determine what sort of a cone it is, even though we do not know how far downwards and outwards its base extends into the dark.

To turn now from the body to the mind. The mind likewise is known for what it is by the highest principle in its hierarchic constitution, not by the indefinite multitude of subsidiary elements: by the luminous apex, not by the spreading shadowy base. Mind is known in rational consciousness, where intelligence reflects upon itself, and choice designs the act it initiates. We do not mean by the mind simply this luminous apex, we are dimly aware besides of an obscure psychic mass on which it feeds: all the materials which remain in memory when we are not remembering, all the directions of desire and interest which go on pointing, when we are neither desiring nor interesting ourselves in their aims: and so on. But we should know nothing of all this obscure psychic stuff, if it did not affect consciousness itself from time to time, or if consciousness did not presuppose it: or anyhow we should not regard the shadowy base as any part of the *mind*, unless we perceived that the luminous apex fed upon it.

Now in so far as philosophers or psychologists are really describing the luminous apex of our human spirit, all they can do is to draw to a greater precision what we already know ourselves to be, and if we do not recognise the portrait, we shall rightly reject it. If they want to make our flesh creep or our mouths gape, they must tell us about the shadowy base of the mind, where special techniques and special observations enable them plausibly to establish a great deal about us which never entered into our waking thoughts. But this does not mean that our whole self-knowledge becomes unfixed, for self-knowledge is not a sort of wide statistical generalisation based equally on all the facts discoverable about any and every region of our mind. Self-knowledge has a hierarchical structure: it is the knowledge of the luminous apex of consciousness, taken as supported by such a psychic base as it may be found to have.

Let us now recall the thesis which led us into all this somewhat ambitious effort after philosophical definition. We were saying, were we not, that a serious and a determinate sense can be given to the supernatural, because our human nature has a sharply defined top or apex, so that anything above it must be supernatural to us: whereas we were prepared to admit that the sideways and downwards limits of our nature are all unfixed, so that it is hard for us to feel any confidence that any of the apparently preternatural is really preternatural and not merely abnormal, apart from the truly *super*natural. What we now hope is that the doctrine of the cone may do something to justify confidence in the fixity of our human apex, however indeterminate our lower fringes may be. But we cannot hope to get away with the argument so lightly. We shall be told that however convincing the doctrine of the cone may appear by the light of pure reason, it will not stand up to empirical fact. The doctrine of the cone suggests that our highest act is our centrally human act, by which we define ourselves; and that the obscure and hair-raising matter brought before us by psychical researchers is all related to the lower and subordinate levels of the soul. But this, it may be objected, is simply not true. In obscure abnormal actions which appear to be neither voluntary nor intelligent in the common sense, the human mind performs some of its most godlike feats. By a sort of alienation of consciousness the seer escapes from the bonds of space and time and ranges into the future or to the other side of the planet. And, by unaccountable processes which are certainly not under direct rational control, the poet's mind throws up the golden line to be the corner-stone of the lyric, and the physicist's mind projects the new master-hypothesis. How then can it be maintained that the psychically odd belongs to the bottom of the soul?

We must, in reply, distinguish here. We cannot allow the weird phenomena of clairvoyance, clairaudience, telepathy and prediction to be tied up in one bundle with the noble achievements of inspiration. We must have two bundles and take them separately. Let us take the noble inspirations first. We entirely agree that they belong to the top of the soul, for they are nothing but the specially striking manifestations of a power which accompanies rational consciousness throughout. The excellence of the mind consists of conscious intelligence, but of a conscious intelligence based always upon acute senses and riding upon a vigorous imagination. For although the excellence of the mind is the act of thinking, the act of thinking is not self-sufficient, but has constant recourse to the imagination; and out of such recourse wit and (in the secular sense) inspiration arise. But what springs up though wit and inspiration is not the gratuitous gift of the imagination to the intelligence: the previous labour of the intelligence is thrown down into the imagination as into a cauldron, from which it emerges again fused into new figures and, it may be, enriched with materials from the subconscious sphere, which were never in distinct consciousness at all. Newton's hypothesis and Shakespeare's tragedy were the product of acute and lively intelligence exercised in the appropriate fields. The moments of inspiration may have been apparently passive, even compulsive and as it were invasive: but they would not have occurred but for previous intellectual labour, nor would they have been of any significance if they had not been seized and elaborated by the same intellectual power which had been their remoter cause. In inspired wit a spark leaps from intelligence to intelligence across a field of imagination: whereas in weird abnormal consciousness the spark leaps from the outer dark into imagination itself, providing an image of which the intelligence must make what it can. Inspired wit is a normal part of the life of the mind's conscious apex: without some measure of it we can do nothing but work out sums and syllogisms according to pre-established rules from pre-established premises. It is vain to ask whether wit or reason is the apex of the mind, for neither exists without the other. When inspiration closely accompanies intelligence, we are unaware of it as a distinct power. But when it has a great work to do, it sometimes specializes itself: there is a sort of gap in the intellectual process, a relaxation and suppling of the mind, a throwing of the reins on the horse's neck: presently inspiration strikes into its new path, and intelligence resumes control. Such experiences amaze us, but there is nothing abnormal about them in kind: it is simply a matter of degree. The apex of the mind remains what it supposes itself to be, in spite of the rare experiences of higher inspiration: for the mind does not, in fact, suppose itself to be devoid of wit at any time.[2]

So, then, of the two bundles of mysterious phenomena which are alleged to extend our mental scope above the top of the mind, the one bundle, that of noble inspiration, belongs to what has always been recognised as making up the top of the mind itself, wit and reason. Such inspiration (always using the word in the secular sense) belongs to what is most godlike in the natural man: but it also belongs to what is most centrally human in him. Now to take the other bundle of mysterious phenomena, the weird events that are the special subject of psychical research. They really do fall outside what we commonly take to be human nature: but they are not godlike in the least; they belong to the bottom of the mind. Clairvoyance, clairaudience and foresight would be godlike if such powers were either controllable in their exercise, or determinate and unambiguous in their discoveries: but they are not. It would be godlike if the psychically gifted man could send his mind on a mission, whenever he chose, as Prospero sent Ariel, to sight what was happening to a given person at a given place or time, and return him instantaneously a clear report. It cannot be done. The most the gifted person can do is to let his divinatory power loose, as it were, in connexion with a given person or in the area of a given subject of interest, and see what images it brings back. The images, if they come, carry no guarantee of relevance or genuineness, seldom any clear marks of place, date or circumstance, and,

---

[2]   This paragraph is one of the most important in *The Glass of Vision*. In it Farrer argues for an understanding of 'reason' or rational intelligence that *includes* imagination, 'wit' and (secular) inspiration. That is, he is resisting the common philosophical reduction of rationality to purely logical 'sums and syllogisms' and insisting instead that in all human thought of any significance, deductive reason and intuitive imagination always work together. His use of the term 'wit' is especially crucial in this respect, especially as contemporary usage almost always limits it to clever humour (for example, 'a witty remark'). However, in the chapter on 'wit' in his *Studies in Words*, C.S. Lewis says that in earlier English usage 'wit' was often used to translate the Latin *ingenium* and thus to mean 'the thing which, in its highest exaltation may border on madness; the productive, seminal (modern cant would say "creative") thing, as distinct from the critical faculty of *judicicum*; the thing supplied by nature, not acquired by skill (*ars*); the thing which he who has it may love too well and follow too intemperately. It is what distinguishes the great writer and especially the great poet. It is therefore very close to "imagination"'. See *Studies in Words*, Second Edition (Cambridge: Cambridge University Press, 1967), 86–110, citation from 92. It is this sense of the term 'wit' that Farrer employs in *The Glass of Vision*.

worst of all, no certain rule for their own interpretation. Spinoza coined a phrase for his own use which will exactly fit ours – 'loose experience', *experientia vaga*. For if anything deserves the name, it is the weird experience which we are discussing. It is plausible to suppose that primitive consciousness had it in far greater degree than our more advanced consciousness has it. As though the mind had begun with a small centre of clear intelligence, and a wide penumbra of vague sensitivity to environment, to the near and the distant, the past, present and future, all unplaced, uninterpreted, confused; and that mentality as we know it has been achieved by the suppression of all this *experientia vaga* through the expansion of practical, controlled and determinate intellect, kept workable by close restriction to the present moment and the five senses. The weird experience which we come across in our own day may be more like a primitive survival than a foretaste of higher development. Even so, our whole power to make anything of the weird data depends on our firm grasp of the everyday world through precise, time-bound and sense-bound experience. Normal consciousness supplies us with our mental map of the world, and it is on this map that we place, if we can place, the data of *experientia vaga*. Nobody could make anything at all of a whole world of *experientia vaga* and nothing else: it would be a kaleidoscope of shifting dreams. Only the luminous apex of the mind can do anything with it. *Experientia vaga* belongs to the bottom of the soul.

To say that the psychically weird belongs to the bottom of the soul is not of course to deny that it may be made the instrument of noble acts and purposes. After all, what most of the weird phenomena amount to is roughly this, that whereas we used to think that our minds touched the rest of the world through our own bodies alone, we may now have to admit that they touch it at many other points besides: and especially that our minds touch one another without bodily intervention. If this is a fact, it is just a fact about the way in which the multitude of finite things jostle one another in one universe. As there is nothing specially godlike in the fact that our bodies touch, so there is nothing specially godlike in the fact (if it is a fact) of our spirits touching. Physical contact is nothing godlike, and yet through physical contact a compassionate will can perform those acts which will redeem it from everlasting fire and set it on the right hand of the divine Shepherd – to feed the hungry, to clothe the naked and to visit the captive.[3] So psychical contact will be merely contact, yet of what may not it be made the instrument? Christians believe that their acts of prayer may, under God, assist their neighbours' souls, and it seems likely that the touch of mind on mind has something to do with that. Christians believe also that the charity of departed saints can assist us in this world, and our prayers assist the departed in their purgation: there is an interchange of spiritual act among the members of Christ's body, as though all, in some way, touched one another. There is certainly something godlike here, but it is not the touching, it is what the touching is made to convey – supernatural charity. The exercise of the praying act is godlike, not the contact by which it affects (if it does so affect) another's mind: that is mere mechanics, and might be the vehicle of bad

---

[3]   Matthew 25.31–46.

influence as well as good. We pray with the apex of the mind, with the intelligent will, with what we have always known to be the very principle of our selfhood. And if, in praying, we reach above that apex into what, transcending our nature, is supernatural to us, it is not in touching our neighbours, it is in touching God.

In a sense, no doubt, we touch him by the very fact of our existence, for does not it momently spring out of his creative act? Such a contact, if it is to be called a contact, is not supernatural to us, for it belongs to our nature to be continually created. But if we can rise out of our dependent selves and penetrate the mind of him on whom we depend, then we climb above the top of ourselves and achieve a supernatural act.

Let us consider a little more carefully how far the natural knowledge of God extends, and where the supernatural will begin. I must as a Christian believe that my existence is throughout a two-sided fact. On the one side it is the active being of a second cause, myself, in dependence upon, and interaction with, other second causes. On the other side it is the continual effect of the first cause, God. The total fact is never myself alone, not even myself with the world for its environment, but always my world-environed self, *and God*. My existence has these two active centres always. Not that they can be for a moment placed in equipoise. The centre called 'I' is not a centre at all when considered in relation to God, but more properly a point on the circumference of his action. An impartial view of the double fact of myself and God would simply be God's view, identified with him, operating from his centre. God's view is the view of mind as such, for it corresponds to the real structure of existence. The tendency of any mind, in proportion as it overcomes its creaturely limitations, must be to gravitate towards the divine centre, and share the divine view of things. That is the goal; it cannot be the starting point. So as to be a creaturely mind, a being distinct from God, I must be, and am, the mind of a creaturely centre, closely identified with the operation of a second cause, and viewing things either as they condition that cause, or as it can condition them.

My knowledge is the knowledge of my own active existence. Yet the limitation of my knowledge to the field of my own finitude does not involve me in the supreme lie about it, the supposition that it is *uncaused*. On the contrary: the natural mind may know of God whatever is involved in the perception of its own necessary dependence upon him, as of secondary upon primary being and act. What the finite mind perceives in detail and fullness is always finite existence: what it perceives of God is the bare form of an absolute act, seen as enacting the various multiplicity of finite existence.

Now such knowledge might, in an ideal case, amount to a great deal. If we reconstruct the legendary unfallen Adam, if we give him the intellect of Aristotle, the natural spirituality of St Paul without the gifts of revelation, and the charitable humility of St Francis unenhanced by supernatural faith, we may imagine in such a mind the perfection of mere theism, mere creator-worship. His awareness of God need not be limited to the knowledge of abstract propositions about him and his agency; the divine agency might be read in the creaturely effects, external nature and his own existence might be experienced as the continual work of God.

Especially his own highest acts and desires might be acknowledged as having a source in himself only in so far as he was himself grounded in God. He might practise continual prayer by the continual aspiration to draw the life of his spirit up from the well of infinity, or rather, to open the channels of his mind to be irrigated from that unfailing spring. He might see in God's direction a providence, tending towards the perfection of the natural in all its forms, a fostering charity towards all creatures. This would be much, but none of it need be supernatural, for it would not exceed the perception of God's agency, simply in so far as nature and natural perfections express it. It would interpret God by two things alone: by the created world, and by the general bare idea of first agent cause. Its subjective instruments would be the intelligence and wit of the mind's natural apex, employed upon their natural object, finite existence.

If all this can be natural knowledge (though so much, perhaps, never occurs except by way of accompaniment to knowledge supernaturally given), what knowledge would be distinctively supernatural? Any knowledge would be so, which transposed us, as it were, to the divine centre of activity: which gave us to know, not the bare idea of such a centre, but anything about the way in which the life there lived is exercised and enjoyed at its own divine level: anything which reveals to us the activity of God in God. But it is equally possible to conceive supernatural knowledge about God's activity in the world. Suppose, for example, that God is fulfilling purposes in his direction of finite beings, which are not manifested in the present action and existence of those beings. From the fact that the craftsman is preparing materials you may guess that he is about some work, but it may be impossible for men or angels to infer what the work is to be, without communication with the craftsman's mind: and God's conduct of the universe may be of that sort. Only by shifting our centre from ourselves to him, by communion with his mind, could we know the work of God through nature, in so far as it transcends the purposes of nature as nature; or rather, of nature as what we can apprehend nature to be.

To proceed to examples: the Christian faith claims to possess supernatural truth in both the fields that we have specified. It tells of the life of God in God, and it tells of divine purposes in the natural world transcending nature. It says that in God there is an act of begotten and responsive love, that it is reciprocated, and that it is cemented by a Spirit mutually indwelling. And it says that in the created world there is a work of salvation, whereby mortal spirits are supernaturalised, and drawn into the participation of eternal being. You may think if you will that these mysterious truths are no truths at all: but if they are truths, they are not, in the human mind, natural truths: they are not, that is to say, the fruit of natural human acts, for by no such act could we be reasonably assured of their genuineness. For the life of God in its divine centre is not given me, by nature, to reflect upon. I am not there with him, I am here with myself.

But who exercises the supernatural act by which supernatural truths are known? If you and I suppose we know such things by faith, is the supernatural apprehension ours, or can we borrow the supernatural truths from the supernatural apprehension of an inspired mediator, without ourselves exercising any supernatural act? Let us begin to answer this question by a fictitious simplification. Let us allow ourselves to talk about 'man' set over against God. We shall then have to say that, if any supernatural truth is ever to be known by 'man', God must make 'man' to perform a supernatural act in apprehending God's self-communication. But when we proceed to split up this fictitious subject 'man' into the multitude of believers in one supernatural faith, the distribution of supernatural activity amongst them will not be equal. To Christ's manhood belongs unique supernaturality of act, to the apostles and evangelists their proper grade, and to the saints a higher degree than to us. Yet in our degree we all participate in supernatural act, for we do not receive revealed truth as simply a tale told about God in the third person by others; we apprehend it as assured to us by God himself, or to put it otherwise, the description of divine mysteries ceases to be experienced by us as mere description: in the lines laid down by the description, the mysteries shine with their own light and presence; or rather, with the light and presence of God. Here there is a *guided* supernatural apprehension on our part, but a supernatural apprehension nevertheless. If a child cannot walk unsupported, that is not to say that he is simply dragged, and does not walk at all.

There is a sort of paradox involved in the very idea of a supernatural act. It must be the act of the natural agent, and, to be his, it must surely be absolutely continuous with his natural activity, for it is in virtue of his natural activity that he is himself. If the supernatural act were discontinuous with his natural action, it would be something that happened to him, or in connexion with him, rather than something which he did. On the other hand, if it is absolutely continuous with his natural activity, will not it of necessity be natural itself? This paradox certainly provokes deep reflection: and I must confess that, in the case of such alleged supernatural acts as that of Balaam's ass in addressing the prophet, the paradox defeats me. In what sense can it be said that asinine life, supernaturally enhanced, runs out into the utterance of good articulate speech without, as it were, getting cut off from its natural base, and falling completely out of the subjective unity of asinine action?

The apparent absurdity in the case of the ass is due to the fact that one sort of finite nature is credited with an act distinctive of another sort of finite nature; the ass behaves like a man in a point of behaviour at which the asinine excludes the human. The finite excludes another finite of incompatible nature. But in the serious case of the supernatural, which is at the heart of our religion, we are not concerned with the attribution to man of an act proper to some other finite kind, say to a grade of the angelic hierarchy: we are concerned with the opening of the finite to the infinite. Now it is by no means clear that the finite excludes the infinite in the sense in which one finite excludes another. Every mystery of religion, indeed one may say the very possibility of any spiritual religion, presupposes that it does not. I am enacting my life, you are enacting yours: I cannot enact yours nor you mine. But in some true sense the creature and the Creator are both enacting the creature's life, though in different ways and at different depths: in the second cause the first cause operates. Upon this double personal agency in our one activity turns the verbally insoluble riddle of grace and freewill, or of Godhead and Manhood in Christ's One Person, or of the efficacy of human prayer; indeed there is no issue theologians discuss which is not conditioned by it. There is no question then of the finite excluding the infinite, as the finite excludes the finite. We can, no doubt, state the limiting case: there is a point beyond which infinite God could not divinize his creature without removing its distinct creaturely nature, and as it were merging it in himself: an act which would be exactly equivalent to its annihilation. But, short of this, we can set no limits to the supernatural enhancement God can bestow. He who has by a first act created us, harmoniously extends our operation by a second. There is nothing non-human in what we are thus enabled to do: it is not the act of some other creature tacked on to us; it is simply the act of man enabled to receive divine communication, and not the act of any other sort of being in the world.

Thus, in exercising such an act, we are aware of going into a new dimension, but we are aware of no discontinuity. The act of supernatural faith appears to be only a fresh elevation of the faith we put in other things not brutally evident to sense, for example, our own moral seriousness or other men's genuine care for us. The mysteries of faith must fit into one universe of sense with our natural knowledge of human personality, of history, of the form of nature, of the first principles of being: if they did not, they would not continue to be believed. The judgment upon which faith is based is an *aestimatio* like that used in other fields. Faith leaps beyond it, but that happens too in common life; our faith in the goodwill of a friend goes beyond and leaves behind any weighing of the evidence for it, and becomes a rooted axiom of living. In the case of the friend, such an axiom may be rooted, but not be ineradicable: our friend may disappoint us. As the prophet says, the mother may forget her sucking child; but God will not forget Jerusalem.[4]

*Now therefore to the one unchanging God, the Father, Son and Holy Ghost, be ascribed as is most justly due all might, dominion, majesty and power, henceforth and for ever.*

---

[4]    Isaiah 49.14–15.

# Lecture III:

# Images and Inspiration

Thou hast known the sacred writings which are able to make thee wise unto salvation. Every scripture is inspired of God.

2 Timothy, III.15–16

In the preceding lectures we have considered the mere idea of supernatural action in the mind, and especially in its knowledge of God. Such knowledge bestows an apprehension of divine mysteries, inaccessible to natural reason, reflection, intuition or wit. Christians suppose such mysteries to be communicated to them through the scriptures. In particular, we believe that in the New Testament we can as it were overhear men doing supernatural thinking of a privileged order, with pens in their hands. I wish to make a fresh examination of this phenomenon. For I am not content simply to believe that supernatural thinking takes place, nor simply to accept and contemplate what it reveals, according to my own capacity. I desire to know something more in particular about the form and nature of that supernatural thinking. I may be told that it is sectarian of me to limit my study to the Christian Scriptures. But a man must limit his study to something, and it is as well to talk about what one knows, and what one, in fact, thinks most important. I speak of the Christian Revelation as Revelation *par excellence*, as Revelation simply and without qualification, for such I believe it to be. The degree in which other faiths have something of revelation in them, and the manner in which they are related to Christ's revelation, are matters which I well know to be worthy of discussion, but I beg leave not to discuss them.

No doubt the inspiration of the Scriptures will seem to many people a topic so old and so wearisome that it can be no longer endured. But if so, it will either be because they have no interest in the Scriptures themselves, or because they have not discovered what the Scriptures are good for. Anyone who has felt, even in the least degree, the power of these texts to enliven the soul and to open the gates of heaven must have some curiosity about the manner in which the miracle is worked. And, looking about him, he will quickly realise that interests more vital than those of curiosity are at stake. The prevalent doctrine about Scriptural inspiration largely determines the use men make of the Scriptures. When verbal inspiration was held, men nourished their souls on the Scriptures, and knew that they were fed. Liberal enlightenment claims to have opened the scriptural casket, but there appears now to be nothing inside – nothing, anyhow, which ordinary people feel moved to seek through the forbidding discipline of spiritual reading.

In taking up the topic of Scriptural inspiration, we should like to attach ourselves to the thought of the ancient Church: but this, we are told, is just what we have not to do. For, it is said, pre-modern thought on the subject was vitiated by a single and cardinal false assumption – the assumption that revelation was given in the form of propositions. The sacred writers were supposed to have been moved by it matters not what process of mind to put down on paper a body of propositions which, as they stand on the paper, are *de facto* inerrant. These propositions, interpreted by the light of one another and apprehended through the Church's supernatural faith, gave an account of the saving mysteries as perfect as the condition of earthly man allowed him to receive.

This being the assumption, the question of inspiration could be opened up in two directions. Either one might ask, what sort of control was exercised by the Divine Spirit over the writer, to get the propositions safely down on to the page. Or one might take up the propositions themselves, and ask in what sense they truly signified supernatural realities – whether literally or spiritually; whether univocally or analogically.

It is now impossible, we are told, to get anywhere from here. We now recognise that the propositions on the Scriptural page express the response of human witnesses to divine events, not a miraculous divine dictation. The ancient theory, it might appear, gave a senselessly duplicated account of revelation. The primary revelation, on any showing, was Christ, his life, words, passion, resurrection; and Providence was careful to provide fit witnesses of these events. But now, it appears, the occurrence of the events in the presence of the witnesses is of no practical importance, nor are they allowed to report according to their natural abilities: a few of them are seized by the Spirit, to be made the instruments of a supernatural dictation; and that is what the world will read for ever. It is as though a number of shorthand writers had been solemnly engaged to take down a supposedly extempore oration, and then the orator's secretary were to come round after its delivery and say that as a matter of fact he had got a complete text of the speech in manuscript, and would dictate it to them slowly, so that they could write it in longhand: for his employer had no faith in them, and was convinced from previous experience that they would have jumbled their notes.

Revolting from such absurdities, we say that the revelation was the fulfilment of the divine events in the presence of sufficient witnesses: as for the scripture, it is just the record of the witnesses', or their successors', reaction to the events. It is what St Luke couldn't help fancying someone's having said he thought he remembered St Peter's having told him: or it is the way St Paul felt about what Christ meant to him. As for the terms in which St Paul expressed it – well, there you are – he used any sort of figure that came to hand: he picked up a rhetorical metaphor from a cynic preaching in the market; he turned a commonplace of the synagogue pulpit inside out. He would have been amazed to learn that subsequent generations would make such stuff the foundation of dogmas. We should strip off the fashions of speech; but keep the substance, of course. But what is the substance? It has an uncanny trick of evaporating once its accidents of expression are all removed. Still, let us not acknowledge defeat. At the very least we can safely conclude that Christ had for St Paul a supremely high numinous and ethical value; that he inspired him with new ideals, curing his bad habits, inhibitions and worries. What more does a Christian need to know? Let the modern believer nourish his soul on that. Yes: but to do it, does he really need to read St Paul? He usually thinks not, and it is difficult to refute him.

It does not seem as though the theory of revelation by divine events alone is any more satisfactory than the theory of dictated propositions. At a pinch it will suffice for an account of the historical aspect of Scripture. The events occurred, and we get some sort of usually secondhand report about them with which we must make do. But what did the events mean? It is about this that St Paul and St John have been taken as inspired authorities. The theory we are considering makes them authorities for no more than the way they and their contemporaries were feeling about what God had done. It denies that they were inspired at all, in the technical sense. No doubt they had the Spirit, but then, have not we all? They were inspired as St Francis or St Bernard or John Wesley was inspired. The New Testament is not *uniquely* inspired (though some of its pages may be supreme in this kind). It is, however, uniquely informative, because through it the divine events, and their impact on their age, are made known to us. No other writings can replace it as the channel through which the revealing events come to us.

It does not seem good enough to say that the Scriptures are uniquely informative, but not uniquely inspired, for two reasons. It gives us bare historical events, which by themselves simply are not the Christian revelation, and says they are our only revelation; denying authority to the apostolic interpretation of the events which alone can make them a revelation. And it denies to the text of St Paul and St John the supernaturally revealing character which Christian experience has constantly found in it.

Let us now attempt to construct some account of scriptural inspiration from first principles. This at least in modern thought upon the subject is true: the primary revelation is Jesus Christ himself. When we were talking previously about supernatural knowledge of God, we attempted to define it metaphysically by reference to the primary and secondary causality operative in man's existence. From one point of view, my active existence is exercised by me, its second cause: from another point of view by its first cause, God. My natural mind is identified with the operation of the second cause. In so far as I am made to see things in any degree as from within the operation of the first cause, my mind performs a supernatural act: and this cannot happen by my exertion, but by God's supernaturalising action. Now the Person of Christ, in the belief of Catholic Christendom, is, as it were by definition, the height of supernaturality: for in it the first and second causes are personally united, the finite and infinite centres in some manner coincide; manhood is so taken into God, that the human life of Jesus is exercised from the centre of deity, so far as a human life on earth can be, without ceasing to be a human life on earth: for in him also the general maxim is verified – the supernatural enhances and intensifies, but does not remove nature.[1]

---

[1] This 'general maxim' is a well-known tenet of Thomistic theology: 'grace does not destroy nature, but perfects it' (Thomas Aquinas, *Summa Theologiae*, Part 1, Question

Thus, as a matter of faith, we believe that the revelation of deity to manhood is absolutely fulfilled in Christ himself: in him, man exercises not a supernatural act only, but a supernatural existence, in perfection; he both knows and enacts deity in all his life and thought. To speak so of Christ is to give a deceptively precise description of an unfathomable mystery. We define him, as we define deity itself, by a coincidence of opposites. Deity, for example, is defined as Timeless Life, though with us all life is temporal process and cannot be imagined otherwise, and all that is timeless is lifeless abstraction and cannot be imagined otherwise. In much the same manner we define Christ by the coincidence of supernaturalised manhood and self-bestowing deity, though with us even supernaturalised manhood merely aspires after the infinite transcendence of deity and cannot be imagined otherwise, and even self-bestowing deity is the infinitely distant goal of human aspiration and cannot be imagined otherwise. Christ's Person defeats our intellect, as deity defeats it, and for the same reason, for deity is in it. So the sheer occurrence of Christ's existence is the perfection of revelation to Man, but it is not yet the perfection, or even the beginning of revelation to us, unless we are enabled to apprehend the fathomless mystery which his manhood is.

The first thing to be said of Christ's self-revelation to us is that it is by word and deed, where 'doing' is taken to embrace the action of Christ's will in his *sufferings* also. If we are allowed this gloss, we may be content with St Luke's formula: 'the things that Christ did and taught' are the subject-matter of the gospel.[2]

The actions of Christ's will, the expressions of his mind: these, certainly, are the precious seeds of revelation, but they are not the full-grown plant. Everything that grows must grow from them: but the growth is as necessary as the seed, if here is to be any fruit. It would be abstractly possible to conceive that Christ should have given in his teaching a sufficient exposition of the saving mystery of his being and his act: but even in a context of *a priori* argument we must deign to acknowledge facts. The facts to be considered are two. First, the New Testament itself tells us that the words of Christ in the days of his flesh were not, without comment, sufficient to reveal salvation. Second, our own historical study of the New Testament leads to the conclusion that we cannot separate off from apostolic comment a body of Christ's sayings which by themselves surely and sufficiently determine saving truth. So the apostolic church tells us that we cannot do without what the Spirit revealed to the Apostles: and by study of the New Testament we discover that we are lost, without what the Spirit revealed to the Apostles.

---

1, Article 8, Reply to Objection 2). Farrer's reference indicates his Anglo-Catholic commitments and consequent debt to Aquinas. Farrer's statement that in Jesus Christ 'the first and second causes are personally united, the finite and infinite centres in some manner coincide' is commonly referred to as the 'hypostatic' (or personal) union of divine and human natures in Christ's one person; Farrer is thus observing that in this union Christ's human nature is perfected, not obliterated, by divine grace.

2    See Acts 1.1–2.

Such is the situation. It is often misleadingly expressed in a distinction between 'the fact of Christ' and 'the inspired apostolic comment', as though Christ has said nothing, and the apostles had done nothing. Christ both performed the primary action and gave the primary interpretation: the apostles, supernaturalised by the Spirit of Pentecost, worked out both the saving action and the revealing interpretation of Christ. As his action underlies theirs, so his interpretation underlies theirs. It is not my reading of the biblical evidence that the luxuriant growth of apostolic teaching is impenetrable – that it utterly hides Jesus, the root from which it springs. I will freely confess, for my own part, that unless I thought myself honestly led to recognise in Christ's historical teaching seeds of the doctrine of his divine person and work, then I should not believe. I cannot take these things simply from St Peter and St Paul, as their inspired reaction to 'the fact of Christ'. But I can accept St Peter's and St Paul's inspired comment as the absolutely necessary guide to what I may recover of the Lord's own oracles. Again, if I did not, in my own judgment, consider that the Lord's oracles bore out the apostolic comment, I should not believe. But that does not mean that apart from the apostolic record, I could from the bare oracles make out the apostolic doctrine for myself. I could not.[3]

The work of revelation, like the whole work of Christ, is the work of the mystical Christ, who embraces both Head and members. But, as in other aspects of his work, the action of the Head must be central and primary, it must contain in epitome all that the members fulfil and spread abroad. The primacy of the Head in revelation is seen in two things. First, the self-giving of the divine mind to man is fully actualised in the personal existence of Jesus Christ. Secondly, the communication to mankind in general of the human-divine mind of Jesus Christ is begun by Jesus Christ, who by that beginning lays down the lines of all further development. Development is development, and neither addition nor alteration. The first and decisive development is the work of the Apostolic age.[4]

---

[3] If in the earlier allusion to Aquinas Farrer demonstrates his Anglo-Catholic credentials, in this paragraph he confesses his Reformed status as well, and so stakes out his traditional Anglican *via media*. Although Augustine is not directly named here, Farrer is clearly alluding to his famous statement that – contrary to what Farrer says above – 'I would not believe in the Gospel, had not the authority of the Catholic Church already moved me' (from *Contra epistolam Manichaei*, 5, 6; as cited in *Catechism of the Catholic Church*, Part One, Section One, Chapter Two, Article Three, III: 'The Holy Spirit, Interpreter of Scripture', 119). Farrer would have expected his original listeners to catch this allusion, and also to be amused that 'Austin' (the English form of 'Augustine') was disagreeing with his great name-sake. But also note Farrer's qualification at the end of the paragraph: he is not advocating an individualistic reconstruction of Christianity from the ground up, but rather indicating that he must at least be able to recognise the legitimacy of the apostolic interpretation of Christ. Such apostolic and ecclesial interpretation is not self-justifying, but must still be examined with critical intelligence and historical judgment.

[4] As a third and final allusion, Farrer seems here to be indicating some engagement with John Henry Newman's famous but controversial theory of the development of doctrine ('controversial' partly due to determining what Newman actually meant by it, and whether

   The interpretative work of the Apostles must be understood as participation in the mind of Christ, through the Holy Ghost: they are the members, upon whom inflows the life of the Head. As the ministerial action of Christ is extended in the Apostolic Mission, so the expressed thought of Christ is extended in the Apostolic teaching. Now the thought of Christ himself was expressed in certain dominant images.[5] He spoke of the Kingdom of God, which is the image of God's enthroned majesty. In some sense, he said, the regal presence and power was planted on earth in his own presence and action: in some other sense its advent was still to be prayed for: in some sense men then alive should remain to witness its coming. Again, he spoke of the Son of Man, thereby proposing the image of the dominion of a true Adam, begotten in the similitude of God, and made God's regent over all the works of his hands. Such a dominion Christ claimed to exercise in some manner there and then: yet in another sense it was to be looked for thereafter, when the Son of Man should come with the clouds of heaven, seated at the right hand of Almightiness. He set forth the image of Israel, the human family of God, somehow mystically contained in the person of Jacob, its patriarch. He was himself Israel, and appointed 12 men to be his typical 'sons'. He applied to himself the prophecies of a redemptive suffering for mankind attributed to Israel by Isaiah and Jewish tradition. He displayed, in the action of the supper, the infinitely complex and fertile image of sacrifice and communion, of expiation and covenant.

   These tremendous images, and others like them, are not the whole of Christ's teaching, but they set forth the supernatural mystery which is the heart of the teaching. Without them, the teaching would not be supernatural revelation, but instruction in piety and morals. It is because the spiritual instruction is related to the great images, that it becomes revealed truth. That God's mind towards his creatures is one of paternal love, is a truth almost of natural religion and was already a commonplace of Judaism. That God's paternal love takes action in the gift of the Kingdom through the death of the Son of Man, this is supernatural revelation.

   The great images interpreted the events of Christ's ministry, death and resurrection, and the events interpreted the images; the interplay of the two is revelation. Certainly the events without the images would be no revelation at all, and the images without the events would remain shadows on the clouds. The events by themselves are not revelation, for they do not by themselves reveal the

---

his own thinking on this topic itself developed over the years). Although Farrer is willing to accept that Christian doctrine does indeed develop over the centuries, he apparently is here taking the fairly conservative line that the development is still strictly limited by the original 'deposit' – what is sometimes called 'subjective' or 'intellectual' development – as opposed to 'objective' development in which God's ongoing revelation might lead to any 'addition' to or 'alteration' of the earlier understanding.

   [5]  Farrer's seminal theory of divine revelation through images, here introduced, is also expressed and explored further in his next book, *A Rebirth of Images: The Making of St John's Apocalypse* (Westminster: Dacre Press, 1949), 13–22.

divine work which is accomplished in them: the martyrdom of a virtuous Rabbi and his miraculous return are not of themselves the redemption of the world.[6]

The interplay of image and event continues in the existence of the apostles. As the divine action continues to unfold its character in the descent of the Spirit, in the apostolic mission, and in the mystical fellowship, so the images given by Christ continue to unfold within the apostolic mind, in such fashion as to reveal the nature of the supernatural existence of the apostolic church. In revealing the Church, they of necessity reveal Christ also, and the saving work he once for all performed. For the supernatural life of the Church can be no more than the exposition in the members of the being of their Head. If they understand their life-in-grace, they understand the grace by which they live, and that grace is Christ's saving work. St Paul, for example, sees that his own life in Christ is a continual death and resurrection: and in understanding so his own living exposition of Christ's redemption, he of necessity understands the redemption of which it is the exposition.

In the apostolic mind, we have said, the God-given images lived, not statically, but with an inexpressible creative force. The several distinct images grew together into fresh unities, opened out in new detail, attracted to themselves and assimilated further image-material: all this within the life of a generation. This is the way inspiration worked. The stuff of inspiration is living images.

It is surely of high importance to know what is to be looked for in Scripture. The Mediaeval Scholastic mind, it would seem, was (in theory, at any rate) on the hunt for theological propositions, out of which a correct system of doctrine could be deduced by logical method. If we set about the quest in that way, we close our ears to the voice of Scripture. The modern tendency is to seek after historical record, whether it be the record of events, or of spiritual states in apostolic minds: it is not surprising if it fails to find either the voice of God, or the substance of supernatural mystery. We have to listen to the Spirit speaking divine things: and the way to appreciate his speech is to quicken our own minds with the life of the inspired images.

---

[6] It is likely that in this definition and discussion Farrer has in mind the similar formulation of Archbishop William Temple (1881–1944): 'But whether we think of the unceasing revelation afforded to the whole world-process or of the occurrences which constitute revelation in the specialised sense of the word, *the principle of revelation is the same – the coincidence of event and appreciation*': *Nature, Man and God: Being the Gifford Lectures Delivered in the University of Glasgow in the Academical Years 1932–1933 and 1933–1934* (London: Macmillan and Co., 1940), 315 – emphasis in the original. That definition, so similar in form to Farrer's own, continues immediately with this footnote: 'The appreciation need not be contemporaneous with the event. But till it comes, the event, though revelatory in its own character, is not yet fully revelation. If no one had recognised Christ, the Incarnation would have occurred, but it would have failed to effect a revelation of God'. Clearly, however, where Farrer differs from Temple is with his distinctive emphasis on *images*: Temple sees revelation as the 'coincidence' of event and appreciation, whereas Farrer sees it as the 'interplay' of event and image.

I have heard it wisely said that in Scripture there is not a line of theology, and of philosophy not so much as an echo. Theology is the analysis and criticism of the revealed images: but before you can turn critic or analyst, you need a matter of images to practise upon. Theology tests and determines the sense of the images, it does not create it. The images, of themselves, signify and reveal.

Let us take an example of the way in which a matter of divine truth is contained in Scripture under the form of images. It is a famous question whether, and in what sense, the doctrine of the Trinity is in the New Testament. The answers which we get follow from our methods of putting the question. The old scholastic way was to hunt for propositions which declare or imply the doctrine in its philosophical form. It is possible to make out a case along these lines, but then along these lines it is possible to make out a case for most things. Then there is the new scholastic way, the method of the research-degree thesis. We painfully count and classify all the texts in St Paul or St John in which the Heavenly Father, the Divine Son and the Holy Ghost are mentioned, either severally or in connexion with one another. We inquire whether the texts about the Second and Third Persons talk of them as personally presenting deity, or not: and what is implied of their relation to the First Person and to one another.

This method, since it starts from statistics and lexicography, exercises the usual fascination of those techniques over our minds: but it is false in its assumptions and inconclusive in its results. It is false in its assumptions, because it supposes that St Paul or St John is, after all, a systematic theologian. A very unsystematic systematic theologian, no doubt, too impulsive and enthusiastic to put his material in proper order or to standardize his terminology. Still, what of that? Anyone who has a decent modern education can do it for him: we, for example, will be rewarded a research degree for doing it. We will draw into the light the system which was coming to birth in the Apostle's mind. But suppose there was no system coming to birth in the Apostle's mind at all – not, that is, on the conceptual level? Suppose that his thought centred round a number of vital images, which lived with the life of images, not of concepts. Then each image will have its own conceptual conventions, proper to the figure it embodies: and a single over-all conceptual analysis will be about as useful for the interpretation of the Apostle's writings as a bulldozer for the cultivation of a miniature landscape-garden. The various images are not, of course, unconnected in the Apostle's mind, they attract one another and tend to fuse, but they have their own way of doing this, according to their own imagery laws, and not according to the principles of conceptual system.

The method of the research-degree thesis is inconclusive in its results, because it attempts to find the Trinity as a single scheme behind the many images. But here we break down for lack of evidence. It is obvious, before we start, and without the statistics or the lexicography, that St Paul's several imagery statements speak of personal divine action in the Father, the Son and the Holy Ghost, and, further, that St Paul was not a polytheist. But whether he regards the Son and the Spirit as instrumental modes of the Father's action, or as divine Persons in their own right, can be determined only by a subtle and risky construction of inferences. Just because St Paul writes in images, we fall into absurdity at the first inferential step. Have we not been taught that images can be trusted only to express what he who speaks them intends by them, and that if we syllogise from them in the direction of our own questions which are not his, our process is completely invalid: like that of the man who asks what is the meaning of details in a parable having no bearing on what the speaker has used the parable to say. 'Straightway he puts in the sickle, because the harvest is come'.[7] The reaper is the Son of Man, the corn is the faithful: what does the sickle represent?

A third method of enquiry fastens on the subjective form of religious experience. St Paul's images, after all, it is said, are but the expression in various figures of his existence in grace. Let us try to strip the images down and get to the experience of grace which underlies. Surely, then, we may say, St Paul is aware of the grace of creation – he experiences God as the fount of his being: he therefore acknowledges the Father. He experiences also the grace of Christ – he knows the human-divine life, now ascended, with which he is bound up in one body of supernatural action, as the hand is related to the head. Here is quite a different way of experiencing God – the experience of the Son. But again, there is the experience of holy possession – of being directly seized and filled with the divine life, of being operated by God – and that is the experience of the Holy Ghost. Very well: but here, once more, we break down at the crucial point. Here we have a tri-form experience of God, not the experience of a triune deity. If human existence is a prism which breaks the single ray of divine grace into several colours, that is just what we might expect: for it is universally true that our experience of God and our thought of God resolve the unity of the great Cause in the plurality of his effects.

A fourth method seeks after formulae. St Matthew's gospel requires baptism in the name of Father, Son and Holy Ghost:[8] St Paul once prays that the grace of the Lord Jesus, the love of God, and the communion of the Holy Ghost may be with the Church at Corinth:[9] and he has a tendency, though not a very strong tendency, to print the pattern of God, Lord and Spirit on his homiletical paragraphs. Now this method does at least arrive at apostolic consciousness of a triad: but it does not tell us of what the triad is a triad. Whether it is a triad of Divine Persons or a triad of saving mysteries, we still do not know. Undoubtedly Christians were baptized into the family of the divine Father, centred in the sonship of Jesus Christ, and cemented by the mystery of indwelling: we do not need the formulae to tell us that. But do they tell us any more than that?

If we want to find the Divine Trinity in the New Testament, we must look for the image of the Divine Trinity. We must look for it as a particular image, here or there. Most of the time other images will be occupying the page: we must be content if we can find it anywhere. Our next endeavour, after we have found it, must be to isolate it and distinguish it from other images, not to show that other

---

[7]    Mark 4.29.

[8]    Matthew 29.19.

[9]    Second Corinthians 13.14.

images are really expressed in terms of it, for they are not. The Trinity is one of the images that appear, it is not a category of general application. When we have isolated the image of the Trinity, and studied it in itself, we can then proceed to ask what place it occupies in the world of New Testament images – whether dominant or subordinate, vital or inessential: and how other images are affected by it. After that we can, if we like, go on to ask what metaphysical comment the New Testament image of the Trinity provokes, and which subsequent theological conceptualisations do least violence to it.

But is the image of the Trinity in the New Testament? The image we have to look for is that of a divine Son pre-existing in heaven and bound to his Heavenly Father by the Father's Spirit. Such an image can certainly be found. It is, indeed, a pre-Christian image, except that the Son is neither divine nor really pre-existent, in the pre-Christian form of it. We may start with the eleventh chapter of Isaiah, in which we read of an anointed king, whose anointing is not with oil, but with the Spirit of the Lord, resting sevenfold upon him.[10] Here are the elements of the Trinitarian image. We may take as the next step forward a text which overlays the idea of spiritual anointing with the idea of divine sonship. A famous Jewish writing, known to the principal New Testament authors, is 'the Testaments of the XII Patriarchs'.[11] This book looks forward to a supreme anointed head, of whom it

---

[10]    Isaiah 11.1–3. Note that the Hebrew text has just six gifts of the Spirit resting on the Davidic messiah – wisdom, understanding, counsel, might, knowledge, and fear of the LORD – and that it is the Greek translation of the Old Testament (the Septuagint) – which adds 'piety' for the 'sevenfold' Spirit developed in later biblical tradition.

[11]    *The Testaments of the Twelve Patriarchs* is a pseudepigraphical document, inspired by Jacob's deathbed soliloquy to his sons in Genesis 49, whose date and originating context became a renewed source of controversy after Farrer's Bamptons. In here placing it between Isaiah and Mark, and in claiming that the document was 'known to the principal New Testament authors', Farrer expresses the view, associated with R.H. Charles (1855–1931) among others, that the document is Jewish in origin and was originally written in Hebrew in the second century BCE. According to this theory, passages that are obviously Christian are later interpolations. However, an alternative theory, renewed and defended by Marinus de Jonge in 1953 (five years after Farrer's lectures), is that the document is actually Christian in origin, dating from around 200 CE. As *The Oxford Dictionary of the Christian Church* usefully summarises the debate: 'it can be maintained that if it is pre-Christian, "the book … has achieved a real immortality by influencing the thought and diction of the writers of the New Testament, and even those of our Lord" (Charles). On the other hand, if the Testaments are Christian, "what they illustrate is not the preparation of Christianity but the social and religious life of the early Christian Church" (de Jonge)'. See the entry 'Testaments of the Twelve Patriarchs' in F.L. Cross and E.A. Livingstone (eds), *The Oxford Dictionary of the Christian Church*, Third Edition Revised (Oxford: Oxford University Press, 2005), 1604. Current scholars remain divided on this question, with John J. Collins, for example, arguing that 'the Testaments incorporate pre-Christian Jewish material' but that these Jewish elements 'can only be identified tentatively and with great caution': see his *The Apocalyptic Imagination: An Introduction to Jewish Apocalyptic Literature*, Second Edition (Grand Rapids and Livonia, MI: William B. Eerdmans Publishing and Dove Booksellers,

writes: 'For him the heavens will be opened, and there will descend hallowing upon him, with the Father's voice as from Abraham to Isaac'.[12] The author goes on to set forth the 'hallowing' as the Holy Spirit, in words which are a direct allusion to the eleventh chapter of Isaiah. 'The Father's voice as from Abraham to Isaac' is the voice of the Father upraised in blessing upon an only and beloved Son: 'only and beloved son' being the unforgettable and repeated designation of Isaac in the most memorable history about him. We may now advance into the New Testament itself, to see the whole image become fact in the baptism of Jesus Christ. The heavens are now opened indeed, the voice of the Father audibly designates a divine Isaac as his beloved Son, and the spirit of hallowing descends visibly as a dove.[13]

This is what we read in St Mark. The son is now divine, but is his association with the Father through the Father's Spirit yet seen as pre-existent and heavenly? What St Mark describes takes place at the baptism of Christ: it is an earthly and historical event. Yes: though St Mark, I do not doubt, saw the historical event as the temporal manifestation of a state of things older than the world. But this does not become explicit in his Trinitarian image. For explicit development we must look elsewhere.

There is no doubt, anyhow, that the Son of the Johannine writings was Son before the world began. St John sees him in his Apocalypse like a Lamb standing as slaughtered, having seven horns and seven eyes, which are the seven spirits of God; they are the Holy Ghost, manifested as sevenfold vision and sevenfold strength.[14] There is once more a plain allusion in the wording of the vision to Isaiah's oracle on the prince endowed sevenfold with the Spirit of the Lord. But, what is more significant, St John has himself a few lines before described to us the same sevenfold Spirit of God as a cluster of seven flames burning before the Father's throne.[15] The sevenfold light of the Holy Ghost burns before the Father's majesty, it blazes also in the eyes of the mystical Lamb. The Father's sevenfold plenitude of Spirit is bestowed upon the Son: 'he giveth not him the Spirit by measure'.[16] The Father, the sevenfold Spirit before his throne, the Son on whom

---

1998), 133–43, citation from 136. Farrer's basic argument in this section of the lecture can certainly survive the loss of this textual evidence, but as a point of historical accuracy the question needs to be noted, and Farrer's confident use and dating of the *Testaments* held up to further scrutiny and ongoing scholarly work.

[12]   *The Testament of Levi*, 18.6. For R.H. Charles's translation, which is very close but not identical to Farrer's text above, and which Farrer probably read, see R.H. Charles (ed.), *The Apocrypha and Pseudepigrapha of the Old Testament*, Volume II (Oxford: Clarendon Press, 1913), 314. For de Jonge's more recent and rather different translation, see H.F.D. Sparks (ed.), *The Apocryphal Old Testament* (Oxford: Clarendon Press, 1984), 536.

[13]   Referring to Genesis 22.1–19 and Mark 1.9–11; cf. Matthew 3.13–17, Luke 3.21–2, and John 1.29–34.

[14]   Revelation 5.6. Note that Farrer attributes the Book of Revelation to the same author of the Fourth Gospel.

[15]   Revelation 4.5.

[16]   John 3.34.

the whole Spirit is bestowed – this is the divine Trinity of Names wherewith St John blesses, when he blesses in the Name of God: 'Grace to you and peace from the IS, WAS, and COMETH, and from the Seven Spirits that are before his throne, and from Jesus Christ, the Faithful Witness ...'[17]

St John simply sets forth the image of the Trinity as representing the mystery of divine love into which we are taken up. It is there before we are taken up into it: it belongs, it would seem, to the nature of things. It is plain that the seer does not intend to talk about the form of his own religious experience, but about a transcendent mystery which is simply there. It is because it is simply there, that it gives form to his experience. St John is content to set forth the image. He does not speculatively determine the relation of the Son to the Father. Later theology was to conclude that there is no real meaning in the absolute priority and essentiality of Christ's sonship, if he is himself a creature. He must be himself of the deity. It must be that by an unfathomable mystery, Godhead itself moves round to face in filial devotion the paternal throne of Godhead, and to receive the indwelling of the Father through his inbreathed Spirit.[18]

But that is to go beyond St John, and beyond any New Testament text. We have in St John simply the *image* of the Father, Son and Spirit, placed by relation to us and our salvation in the transcendent place he assigns it. We can argue if we like that it is no more than an hyperbole for the unique spiritual eminence of the man Jesus Christ: we can argue as we will: in any case the image is there, and it is the image out of which the dogma of the Trinity historically grew.

If we wish to determine the sense of the image beyond what it bears on its face, we must no doubt consider its relation to other Johannine images, not of themselves Trinitarian at all. For example, the image of Christ as the Word through whom God made the worlds. We shall have to consider the light thrown by the Word-image on the Trinitarian image, for both belong to the same apostolic mind. But we must, in comparing them, remember that they are distinct images: we must not force them to the pattern of one another. Such forcing was done by the Fathers of the Church, with tragic and confusing effects on Trinitarian speculation. The text about the Word occupies a position of special prominence at the beginning of St John's Gospel. Here, if anywhere, thought the Fathers, Scripture offers us a summary of Christian metaphysics. The Trinity, they argued, is the chief article of Christian metaphysical belief, so the Trinity must be here. What, then, does the text say?

> In the beginning was the Word, and the Word was with God, and the Word was God.

---

[17]    Revelation 1.4–5.

[18]    Farrer later discussed this primary passage from The Book of Revelation (5.6–14) in *A Rebirth of Images*, 225–6. See also 272–80 for a further discussion of what Farrer sees as the Johannine Trinitarian imagery in this book.

He was in the beginning with God; through him all things arose, and without him arose nothing.

What arose through him was life, and the life was the light of men.[19]

This life, which arose through the Word, must clearly be the Holy Ghost, the Fathers thought: and so we have the doctrine that the Holy Ghost proceeds from the Father through the Son. But this doctrine not only falsifies the scriptural image of the Trinity, it also makes any doctrine of an eternal Trinity unintelligible. For by the Spirit Scripture understands only one thing, the life of the Godhead as bestowed. Bestowed, then, on whom? Bestowed *now* on redeemed mankind – 'the life was the light of men'. But that will not give us an eternal Trinity above all worlds, but only a Trinitarian disposition of the Godhead for the salvation of the world. A Spirit eternally bestowed requires an eternal and adequate recipient. According to the Trinitarian images of St Mark and St John, this recipient is the divine Son. The Son is eternally begotten, and the Spirit is eternally inbreathed into him by the lips of his begetter. The act of paternal love is twofold – to beget and to bestow. Such is the divine life above all worlds: when we, by unspeakable mercy, are taken up to partake in it, we partake in both the begetting and the gift. Christ's sonship is extended to us, his spiritual anointing overflows upon us. All this we see in the clarity of the image. But the Fathers, who did not consistently respect the method of images, were bound to force and confuse the sense of scripture. One could not easily find a more telling example of the vital importance of the principle, that images are the stuff of revelation, and that they must be interpreted according to their own laws.[20]

---

[19]   John 1.1–4.

[20]   In this paragraph, the Anglican Farrer seems to side, somewhat surprisingly in 1948, with Eastern Orthodox theology against the Latin West in rejecting the *filioque*, a Latin word added to the Western version of the Nicene Creed in the 6th century. This addition asserts that the Holy Spirit proceeds from the Father *through the Son*. Farrer argues that that such a procession, if understood for the purpose of bestowing the Spirit on redeemed humanity, reduces the Trinity to a purely 'economic' historical activity rather than maintaining an 'immanent' eternal threefold reality. This is identical to the Orthodox case against the *filioque*: according to Geoffrey Wainwright, 'The Orthodox certainly consider the Western declaration that "the Holy Spirit proceeds from the Father *and from the Son*" to be the deepest issue between Eastern and Western Christianity. If the hypostasis [that is, person] of the Holy Spirit is not satisfactorily acknowledged (and that is the threat which the East sees in the *filioque*), then the doctrine of the Trinity falls, and with it the personal character of God. Slowly but surely, the question has been taken up again in the modern ecumenical movement'. See his chapter 'The Holy Spirit', in Colin Gunton (ed.), *The Cambridge Companion to Christian Doctrine* (Cambridge: Cambridge University Press, 1997), 273–96, citation from 292. Farrer's position, while more common among Western theologians today, was precocious in the 1940s.

The theologian may confuse the images, and the metaphysician may speculate about them; but the Bible-reader will immerse himself in the single image on the page before him, and find life-giving power in it, taken as it stands. He reads how we were bondmen until God 'sent forth his Son, born of a woman ... that we might receive the adoption of sons': and how, to confirm our sonship, there was a second mission: 'God sent forth the Spirit of his Son into our hearts, crying Abba, Father'.[21] The Christian who reads this considers the perfection of unique divine sonship, and stirs his heart to gratitude for the amazing gift of a share in it: he awes his mind with the thought that he is possessed by the Spirit of God, and is, in reality and in God's eyes, Christ towards his God and towards his neighbour: he deplores the darkness which commonly veils what now he sees in the clarity of faith, and the sin which falsifies it in act. He throws himself on the love of the Trinity, more patient with him than he is with himself, and silently operative to produce in him even such penitence and vision as now he has. All these motions of the soul take place within the field of the image: they do not pass out of it into the thin upper air of definition and speculation, nor down onto the flat ground of mere penitence and self-management.

Now it will be said, and rightly said, that however vital a place great images hold in the text of the New Testament, they by no means fill it all. Thus, to say that the apostolic mind was divinely inspired by the germination there of the image-seeds which Christ had sown, is not to give a plain and uniform account of the inspiration of the text of Scripture, comparable with the old doctrine of inerrant supernatural dictation. But this, surely, is no blemish. For a doctrine of the unchallengeable inspiration of the whole text is a burden which our backs will no longer bear. What is vital is that we should have such a doctrine of Scripture as causes us to look for the right things in reading Scripture: above all, that we should look for the life-giving inspired word, and make the proper use of it when we have found it. There is a great deal else in Scripture. If we want a single formula to cover the unique value of it all, then it seems we must call it not 'inspired' but 'revealing', in the sense of 'informative about saving facts': for it contains historical matter, and matter which, not itself historical, is of predominantly historical interest to us: for example, St Paul's direct discussion of certain practical problems which have no close analogy in our own world, but cast a vivid light on the primitive community.

Yet, as soon as we have made the distinction between the 'informative' and the 'inspired', we feel inclined to retract it. For the effects of inspiration are widely seen over the historical paragraphs, and anything which suggests the fencing-off of non-inspired areas is to be abhorred. For example, it used to be thought, some 20 years ago, by people who ought to have known better, that St Mark's gospel is informative rather than inspired, that it is a patient and somewhat unhandy compilation of traditions, rather than an inspired interpretation. We know better now. Inspired image and historical memory are so fused in this oldest of our

---

[21]    Galatians 4.4–6.

gospels, that it is virtually impossible any more to pull them apart.[22] Or to take St Paul's discussions of practical problems, now obsolete. How long does he ever remain on the simply practical plane? Do not we, as we read, suddenly perceive that the apostle's feet have gone through the floor and his head through the roof, and that he is speaking in the large dimension of inspired vision? Presently, in the authority and the spirit of a great image, he returns to settle the matter in hand.

It might do justice to the facts as we see them, if we described Scripture as 'a body of writings uniquely informative, and a field in which inspiration works'. And that description may stand, even though we must proceed to take a further distinction within the work of inspiration. Where, we may ask, does the act of inspiration take place? Does it take place in the mind of the biblical writer as he composes, or rather at other times, say in prayer and worship, or even in other men, for example, in prophets and possessors of various 'spiritual gifts'? And if so, is the biblical writer to be regarded as retailing inspiration in the images he employs, rather than undergoing it there and then?

We cannot return a simple answer to this question. On the one hand, we cannot think of reviving the old biblicist error, always, perhaps, more common as an unexamined assumption than as a consciously held belief. We cannot say that the primary instrument of the Pentecostal Spirit was the Bible. No, it was the apostolic Church, of which the apostles and prophets were the sensitive organs. If the biblical books had not been taken to express the apostolic mind, they would not have been canonised: and we shall rightly suppose that the dominant images of the New Testament were the common property of the teaching Church. But it would be mistaken to infer that direct and immediate inspiration played a small part in the composition of the books. It may be that the decisive shaping of the images took place elsewhere. But the images are still alive and moving in the writers' minds, not fixed or diagrammatic. They continue to enter into fresh combinations, to elaborate themselves, to beget new applications. The composition of the books may be on the fringe of the great process of inspired thinking, but it is still inspired thinking, much of it as vivid and forcible as anything one could well conceive.

We have to remember that the business of writing about sacred matters was viewed by the Jew with a solemnity which we cannot easily recover. There was for him only one primary body of writings, the sacred scriptures of the Old Testament: any other writing must be regarded as a sort of extension of Scripture, and he who composed it must attempt to draw out the substance of scripture by spiritual

---

[22] Farrer's very next book after *A Rebirth of Images* was *A Study in St Mark* (Westminster: Dacre Press, 1951), in which he argued for the subtle literary nature of this Gospel's composition. Farrer concludes his Bampton Lectures with a consideration of the ending of Mark's Gospel, which is then further expanded in *A Study in St Mark*. Several of the commentary chapters in this present volume discuss Farrer's theories about 'the poetry of St Mark' as expressed in *The Glass of Vision* and the *Study*. For a recent book-length consideration, see Robert Titley, *A Poetic Discontent: Austin Farrer and the Gospel of Mark* (London and New York: T&T Clark International, 2010).

aid. The New Testament writers are given a position of greater independence through the new revealing acts of God, but that will not alter at once the spirit in which they approach their task. St Mark's and St John's Gospels, and St John's Apocalypse, are, by their very *genre*, sacred writings, mysteries. It is often said that it would have amazed these writers to learn that their books would be viewed as 'Scripture'. I believe this to be true only in so restricted a sense, that it is, if taken without qualification, a pernicious error. They would have been surprised to see their books treated as *primary* scripture, and placed on a level with the Old Testament. But that they were writing books of the *nature* of sacred scripture, they did not doubt: they had no idea of doing anything else. And so it is virtually certain that, if they were men capable of inspired thinking, they did it then, with their pens in their hands.

The case of the Epistles, or anyhow of those Epistles which really were letters written, upon particular occasion to a particular address, is not quite the same: but to suggest that they were simply letters of the sort one writes every day, is grossly absurd. They are at the very least instruments of sacred teaching and authoritative apostolic direction. If St Paul invoked the spirit of prophecy when he spoke mighty and burning words in the congregation, so he might when he composed the letter which was to be read out as his voice's substitute. In fact he records the opinion of some, that he was weightier with his pen than with his lips.[23] Nor would he suppose for a moment that the Corinthian or Philippian Church, after reading his inspired admonition, would toss it into the fire. They would keep it by them (as they did) to be an enduring guide. Many students of scripture might incline to judge that the breath of high inspiration blows more unevenly in St Paul's true Epistles than anywhere else in the New Testament.[24] When it comes upon him, he achieves sublimities nowhere else found: when the mood or the subject is more pedestrian, so is the level of his writing.

The New Testament books may not be at the centre of the process of Pentecostal inspiration, but they are our only direct clue to its nature, and if we neglect the evidence they supply, we shall know nothing about it. It is the constant experience of him who studies the records of the past, that he begins by reading ancient books for the light they cast on the minds of those about whom they write, and then comes to realise that the only mind with which they bring him into immediate and satisfying contact is the mind of their author. We may read the New Testament for what it tells us about prophetic inspiration through the Spirit of Pentecost, in

---

[23]  See Second Corinthians 10.1–11.

[24]  In referring to Paul's 'true epistles', Farrer is expressing the common academic opinion that some of the letters attributed to Paul in the New Testament were written by second-generation Pauline disciples in his name. Paul's unquestioned ('true') letters are Romans, First and Second Corinthians, Galatians, Philippians, First Thessalonians, and Philemon, with the debated letters being Ephesians, Colossians and Second Thessalonians. The three so-called 'Pastoral Epistles' – First and Second Timothy, and Titus – are in a separate category, with a strong scholarly consensus that these are late and non-Pauline.

the hope of constructing some account of the phenomenon. But what we learn is little but externals: that the Spirit appeared to act compulsively, that prophets had difficulty in withholding their utterance until suitable occasion, that they supposed themselves to be the heirs of the Israelite prophets and imitated their behaviour, that it was taken for granted by all that they were really possessed, that tests were applied to prove whether their possession was of God or Beelzebub, that some of their utterances were particular predictions, and others of them rebukes which laid bare the innermost thoughts of their hearers. All this is of interest so far as it goes, but it does not tell us what sort of yeast it was that worked in those exalted minds: indeed, we are tempted to complain that the primitive Christians were too much impressed by the froth. No doubt what they called prophecy was often frothy enough. But the true substance of inspiration was surely everywhere one: the most histrionic of the prophets, if they had any breath of real inspiration in them, were under the pressure of supernatural mysteries speaking through living images. If we want to know anything of the nature of the process, we must see how the minds of the sacred writers are moved as they write, in their passages of high inspiration.

Through the secret act of God by which the Apostles were inspired there came upon us in imaged presentation the shape of the mystery of our redemption. It possessed and moulded their minds, it possesses and moulds ours: we are taken up into the movement of the life above all creatures, of the Son towards the Father in the Holy Ghost. *Now therefore and always be ascribed as is most justly due all might, dominion, majesty and power to the Unity indivisible, the Trinity of sovereign love.*

# Lecture IV:

# The Metaphysician's Image

And God said unto Moses: I am that I am.

Exodus, III.14

We have concluded that divine truth is supernaturally communicated to men in an act of inspired thinking which falls into the shape of certain images. We have now to consider a further point: how it is that the images are able to signify divine realities. The images themselves are not what is principally revealed: they are no more than instruments by which realities are to be known. The inspired man may not reflect on the instrumental function of the images, but whether he reflects on it or not, he makes an instrumental use of them. He does not think *about* the images, but about what he takes them to signify. When a man speaks metaphorically without being aware of it, he is always attending to what the metaphor means, never to the metaphor. Conscious attention jumps the metaphor, but that does not make the role of the metaphor any less vital. Metaphors may mislead us or send us right, without our observing it. It is therefore always a question for a philosopher, whether a man using a given metaphor can be thinking to any purpose with such a metaphor about such a subject.

Suppose, for example, I were to say to you: 'It stands to reason that the stronger of two desires must prevail with me, unless a third force of some kind intervenes.' Would you not retort with one voice that I am abusing a metaphor? That I am symbolizing the will as a physical field in which commensurable forces of ascertainable strengths collide: that the metaphor has its uses, but is childishly inadequate, and that the inward experience of ourselves nowhere shows us such commensurable and determinate forces of desire: that the conclusion I draw follows from the structure of the symbol I use, not from the structure of the reality it symbolizes. And if I cry out for mercy, and say I was not even aware of using any metaphorical symbol at all, you will pitilessly insist 'So much the worse: if you had criticised your images, you would not have talked such nonsense'.

Thus the fact that St Paul or St John is inspired through the working of images to think divine mysteries under the images, does not foreclose the question, how thinking of such a type can express truth, or why we should accept it as true. We have not here merely the common risks of metaphorical discourse to reckon with: we have a special difficulty which is far worse, and of which the nature is fairly obvious. For we suppose in general that the applicability of images is to be tested by looking away from the images to the things they symbolize, as in the difficult example we were considering just now. It might be hard, by self-analysis, to see how the lure of any desire operated, but anyhow there was hope of our being able to make out enough of even so baffling an object, to decide whether the gross physical analogy of measurable impelling force applied or no. So far so good. But in the case of supernatural divine revelation, nothing but the image is given us to act as an indication of the reality. We cannot appeal from the images to the reality, for by hypothesis we have not got the reality, except in the form of that which the images signify.

But have not we got the reality? Does God feed his saints with nothing but figures of speech? Does he not also operate in their souls the supernatural action to which the figures refer? St John is inspired to think of the incarnation under the figure of a word of power clothing itself in flesh and blood. But along with the figurative declaration of the incarnation, does not God breathe into him the substance and act of the incarnation? Is not God's incarnation operative in the members as well as the head, in John as well as in the manhood of Jesus Christ? Does not John exercise supernatural virtue, does not he pray in the heart of Jesus Christ, is not his charity carried and moved by Christ? And if so, can he not refer the figurative description of the incarnation to the experienced act of the incarnation, and judge the adequacy of the expression by awareness of the thing expressed?

The question we have asked does not admit of a yes-or-no answer. On the one hand it must be admitted that apart from the presence in the soul of a foretaste or earnest of supernatural life, revealed truth is dumb to us. We may hear and read the verbal declaration of divine truth for years, and not apprehend the thing signified; when a motion of supernatural life stirs within us, then we have thing as well as word, and begin to apprehend. But on the other hand it is an absurdity to suggest that the supernatural action we exercise is the adequate real counterpart of the divine truth we believe. There is no sort of proportion between the two. What is, as an exercised act, the least kindling of supernatural charity, the slightest uplifting of the heart towards God, is interpreted by faith as the extension of God's Incarnation, the indwelling of the Godhead in the Person of the Holy Ghost, the effect of an eternal predestination, and the beginning of our everlasting divinization. Are all these mighty mysteries adequately expressed in our supernatural act? Are they expressed there at all?

We are faced here with as delicate an issue of definition as any that is ever likely to meet us. In trying to deal with it, we shall probably find ourselves beginning from spatial metaphor, as we commonly do. We shall say something like this: 'The total object in which we believe is a vast divine process, in the Godhead, in the manhood of Christ, in the whole mystical body of Christ. A part of this process takes place within any one believer at any given time: but how infinitesimal a part! It bears no proportion at all to what takes place outside him. To suppose that we can judge of the whole by the infinitesimal part is absurd: our picture of the whole must be supernaturally imprinted on us, and supernaturally interpreted to us: we cannot interpret so much from so little, the whole blaze of divine action from the faint spark it kindles in ourselves.'

Such a line of reflection may carry conviction while we entertain it: but presently it will provoke a reaction. What is this ungodly nonsense, we exclaim, about areas of divine process outside us and within us, as though the proportion between them were to be taken in square yards? Is not our faith precisely this, that the *whole* Christ is active in associating our life with his, and that the Holy Ghost personally indwells us? Is Christ divided?[1] Can the Person of the Spirit be parcelled out? The whole mystery, not a part of it, is active at each point. To apprehend that single point, then, is to apprehend the substance of the whole mystery. And so there is no reason why the supernatural act wrought in us should not suffice as the real and directly known object, to which the revealed figurative description may be referred.

Very well, and the conclusion is proper enough so far as a complete view of the facts is concerned. The divine mind could construe the whole saving mystery from the single supernatural act in any soul: but then the divine mind does not need to, for it also sees the whole operation of the mystery direct, for it sees all things. But, for our minds, a curtain hangs between the divine agency and its effect in us. We may be directly aware of the supernatural in the form of our own supernatural act: but we are not in the same way aware of the divine agency effecting it in us. Though the divine agent be nearer to our act than the fleshly body our act indwells, a subtle veil secludes him, of no thickness, yet impenetrably dark. Were it to rend, that would be the Day of Judgment, for we should see our Creator.

Yet on further reflection we shall rebel against the veil-image too: it is as misleading as any other. How, we shall ask, can our supernatural act be so utterly secluded from the knowledge of its divine context? For if it were, it would not have the subjective form of a supernatural act. The act by which we love God is an intentional act, and intentional acts take their natures from the objects upon which their intentions are directed: and the intention cannot be directed unless the object is known. The supernatural act of love is not merely directed upon God, for in that case a natural apprehension of God might suffice, without revelation. It is directed upon God revealed in the act of his incarnation. Our supernatural act is precisely the love of a God revealed: and so the veil is done away, for we cannot love him unless we know him.

Yes, but we can love a God whom we know by faith alone; and therefore the veil remains. All we have to say is that the veil, however impenetrable, is not blank. It is painted with the image of God, and God himself painted it, and made it indelible with his blood, when he was nailed to it for us men and for our salvation. We know him through the image, and by faith: our supernatural acts take their intention and form from a revealed description of the saving mysteries. Thus, to say that we perceive in our own supernatural act the reality to which the revealed figures refer, is an absurdity: our act embodies in itself the form of the mysteries, but only by believing in them through the revealed figures. Faith must recognise in the supernatural human act not the reality of which she apprehends the image, but a fresh reflection of the image of herself: charity is faith reflected into action. Yet again the figure misleads us; for as compared with the images faith perceives, our supernatural act of charity is not more shadowy, the shadow of a shadow: it is more substantial, the process of the retranslation from shadow into substance has begun. The act of believing charity is a real supernatural effect, a part of the great mystical action and a foretaste of the beatific vision.

---

[1]    First Corinthians 1.13.

It is unnecessary for us to carry the dialectics of faith and knowledge any further. What we have said is sufficient to establish what we have to shew. The supernatural act in man is a foretaste of the whole substance of the saving mystery, as he will behold it in the beatific vision, but it is no more than a foretaste: and if we set it alongside the figures of revelation, we must say that there is a huge overplus of sheer promise in what the figures express. The paradox remains. How can we receive and understand a promise, unless we know by experience the things promised? We need not, of course, know just those things, but things of the same sort, we surely must know. The child has never been to the party where you promise to take him but to parties he has been. We have not 'seen' God at any time.[2] How, then, can we understand the figures that speak of him?

The question which the paradox drives us to ask, is this: can metaphorical images be understood in no way but by getting behind them to a non-metaphorical understanding of fact? Can it be that images themselves and by themselves are able to illuminate us? The suggestion appears at first sight logically scandalous, but we are reduced to such straits that we must examine it, however unpromising it may appear. After all, we may fairly doubt whether our commonsense logical assumptions really do justice to the part played by images in our thinking.

If we are to consider this question, we shall not be wise to take it up at the level where we are now standing, that is, the level of revelation and faith. Revelation may present the extreme example of irreducible imagery, but it will scarcely present the most manageable example. Rational Theology will be a more hopeful starting-point: and we seem to remember having heard that the rational knowledge of God comes to us wholly by way of analogies: and what are analogies but sober and criticised images?[3]

Shall we start our enquiry, then, from Rational Theology? That may be an awkward thing to do, for '(Rational) Theology is accounted a part of (metaphysical) philosophy', and its method will presumably be no more than a special case of metaphysical method. We had better examine first the role of images in metaphysics. Even this will be no comfortable starting-point, for anyone who knows how the name of metaphysics sounds now in philosophical ears will realise into what a thicket of thorns we have run.[4]

---

[2]    John 1.18; but cf. First John 1.1–4.

[3]    The emphasis on analogy and analogical knowledge of God is typically associated with Thomas Aquinas, and so provides yet another example of Farrer's Thomistic sympathies. Rather than *univocal* descriptions (one-to-one correspondence) or *equivocal* descriptions (no correspondence at all), Aquinas held that we can only speak of God *analogically* or *metaphorically*. Thus, if we say that 'The Lord is my rock' (Psalm 18.2) we mean that God is like a rock in some ways, but in not others. That is, God provides strength and shelter but is not made of granite and so on.

[4]    Farrer was writing during a time in England when logical positivism had excluded the entire discipline of metaphysics as, strictly speaking, meaningless. See, for example, A.J. Ayer's *Language, Truth and Logic* (London: Victor Gollancz, 1936; second edition, 1946). Farrer, however, was convinced that metaphysics was both possible and necessary, and devoted his first book, *Finite and Infinite: A Philosophical Essay* (Westminster:

When a subject has become extremely perplexed, it is sometimes useful to draw back out of it, to view it as from a distance, and to speak of it with the greatest possible simplicity. And this is what I shall try to do about the matter of metaphysical philosophy. I listen to the debate which the philosophers sustain about the very possibility of metaphysics, and I try to strike a balance. The extreme enemies of metaphysics deny that any metaphysical proposition has any factual significance: the friends of metaphysics defend it as a meaningful way of thinking, but for the most part abandon the old account of it as a science in which exact problems about the real world arise, and obtain exact solutions. After listening to the debate, I feel that the ground of metaphysical thinking really is shifting. The world is not going to be persuaded that the whole business of metaphysics is without factual significance: but neither is the old 'science' of metaphysics going to be reinstated. What I shall advance in the following pages is little better than a parable. In such a matter as this, can a parable cast more light than it causes misunderstanding? Anyhow, let us take up our parable and speak.

There are, properly speaking, no metaphysical problems and no metaphysical solutions. There is, for example, no problem in finite causality to which the postulation of a divine First Cause is the solution. The business of metaphysics is not with problems but with mysteries, and mysteries are not to be solved, but (always inadequately) to be described.[5] The so-called problems of metaphysics are difficulties of description: that does not make them either unimportant, or easy to manage. On the contrary, they may be quite agonising; nor are any questions of greater importance to a mind which desires to understand the nature of its real world. There is no finality about the descriptions offered by metaphysics for the mysteries of existence, but there is advance in apprehension of the mysteries by the refining of the descriptions.

I shall now explain the difference between problems and mysteries, for the purposes of the present argument. The mysteries I shall speak of will not include all mysteries – not, for example, supernatural mysteries; but only the mysteries of our natural existence. And the problems I shall speak of will not include all problems, not for example, practical problems; but only the sort of problems most likely to get confused with natural mysteries. I will take problems first.

A problem arises in so far as we approach the world with a fixed measuring instrument, whether of the literal and physical, or of the conceptual sort. Let us

---

Dacre Press, 1943; second edition, 1959) to its defence, specifically to the question of whether *substances* existed – an issue that Ayer had dismissed: 'The metaphysical question concerning "substance" is ruled out by our criterion as spurious' (Ayer, 40). Here, in this chapter of *The Glass of Vision*, Farrer reflects upon the enterprise of metaphysics as such, in light of such critiques.

[5]    As acknowledged in the preface, Farrer has drawn this distinction between 'problems' and 'mysteries' from Gabriel Marcel's *Être et Avoir* (1935), published in English the year after *The Glass of Vision* as *Being and Having*, translated by Katharine Farrer (Westminster: Dacre Press, 1949).

begin with the physical instrument. If I approach my physical environment with an actual yardstick, problems arise about what the measure in yards of each thing is, and how the yard-measurement of one thing stands mathematically related to that of another. I know exactly what the problems are, and how they are in principle to be solved, even though I cannot solve some of them here and now; for example, I cannot measure a given line because it is an irregular curve, and my yardstick is fixed and straight, or I cannot measure the height of a tree, because I cannot climb to the top of it. Such difficulties as these give rise to a new sort of problem – the problem of perfecting the instrument of measurement. The problem of measuring the irregular curve may be solved by the brilliant invention of a tape-measure, and the problem of measuring the tree by an instrument recording an angle, taken from the ground by eye at a given distance from the tree. Here, then, are two sorts of problems: problems about elements in environment arising from, and solved by, the use of the instrument; and problems about the instrument, which arise from its inadequacy to an observed need, and are solved by its development or variation. To the first sort of problem there is always *the right answer*: the measurement of a given plank in yards is just what it is. To the second sort of problem there is *a* right answer – several different instruments might do the job, but anyhow, here is one which will do it.

The same two sorts of problems arise if I approach the world not with a tangible, but with a conceptual instrument, for example, a determinate idea of physical cause. This gives rise to any number of problems in environment, for it leads one to ask, what is the cause of each particular physical event. Again, it leads to problems about the instrument: in the attempt to fix particular causes we are driven to formulate general causal rules, and so the instrument is elaborated. Not only may it be elaborated, it may be revolutionised: in using her causal concept, science comes to see that a fundamentally different concept will be more fertile in its application: and so cause itself comes to mean something different from what it did.

The field of the problematic is the field in which there are right answers: and it is the field of what is commonly called 'science'. The sciences are distinguished from one another by the different conceptual instruments they severally employ: and the real subject-matter of any science is whatever in our environment is amenable to measurement by the conceptual instrument of that science. The sciences yield real information about the world, but only in terms of their conceptual instruments. It is only the relation of real things or events to the instruments that is disclosed: it is only the relation of the size of things to a yard-measure which is discovered by the use of a yard-measure, and only the relation of the structure of real processes to the formulated pattern of causal uniformity, which is discovered by the use of the formula of causal uniformity. The information which we get is real, for all magnitudes bear a real relation to a yardstick, or we could not measure them by it: and physical processes have an aspect which genuinely corresponds to our concept of causal uniformity, or we could not interpret them by it. The information which we gain is real, but it is highly abstract or selective. When I approach my environment, yardstick in hand, I do not ask the general question 'What have we here?' or even 'What here is most important?' but always the narrow question 'What will my yardstick tell me about the things that are here?'

The true scientist is justly credited with a supreme respect for fact, that is to say for the real world upon which he makes his experiments. He will stubbornly refuse to record what his yardstick does not bring to light, or to construct in defiance of any least thing that it does. This is rightly called respect for fact: but it can scarcely be called respect for being. The scientist may feel the deepest respect for being also; he may go in constant amazement at the mysterious nature which the world must be supposed to have in itself, so as to be the sort of world which yields such complex and orderly responses to his yardstick method. But this amazement, this almost religious awe, does not find direct expression in his scientific activity; in so far as he entertains such feelings, he is more of a metaphysician than a pure scientist. That is only another way of saying, that as well as being a scientist, he is a man: and indeed, most scientists are human.

If we have to suppose a state of exclusive preoccupation with the yardstick business itself, to the exclusion of all sense for real being, we must view such a state with the gravest disquiet; it portends the death of the soul. For religion is based on respect for being – for God, yes, but only because God is seen to be uniquely worthy of it by a mind open to respect for being in general. Now if our experiencing of things and persons is limited to the trying on them of pre-arranged tests devised by ourselves, full respect for their being is excluded from the first. If we respect any being, we allow it to make its own impression, and, as it were, to formulate its own claims upon us. Just as a man confessing his sins cannot choose what he will confess, and what he will hide, but must confess all, because he is not making a judgment, but submitting to judgment: so a man who feels respect for any being cannot choose what he will explore and what ignore in the object of respect, but must give to his thoughts the most self-denying adaptability, ready to apply or improvise whatever thought-forms the nature of the object may require, if the aspects it insists on presenting are to be appreciated. He cannot even be content to appreciate every given aspect; he will endeavour to integrate the aspects in the unity of their being, for it is being, not the abstracted aspects of being, which is properly to be revered.

Where the attitude of almost passive respect combines with a rigorous demand for understanding, metaphysical activity will appear. Since no ready-formulated tests are to be applied, and no yardstick is presupposed, no determinate and soluble problems arise for the metaphysician: to his enquiries there are no 'right answers'. He is not faced with the limited and manageable relation which arises between a conceptual instrument and the object it is applied to: he is faced with the object itself, in its fullness: and the object meets him not as a cluster of problems but as a single though manifold mystery. His purpose is to understand it as well as he may. Since the human mind understands in the act of discourse, and not by simple intuition, to understand will be to describe. The metaphysician seeks to understand his mysteries in seeking to describe them.

But, you may object, here the preconceived verbal yardstick immediately returns after all. For nobody, attempting to describe an object, makes up a new vocabulary for the purpose there and then. I may invent a new term to *designate* an object of which I am already sufficiently aware, but by assigning it this new-fangled name I do not either *describe* it to myself, or help myself to get hold of its nature. So it is only by means of preconceived terms that the metaphysician will be able to describe: he must approach his object with a whole cupboardful of yardsticks.

Yes, certainly: but the way in which he differs from the scientist is in the way he uses them. The scientist insists on his chosen yardstick, the domain of his science is just whatever that stick can be used to measure. It is true that, as we saw, the scientist does modify his instrument to make it more serviceable, but always so as to extend or refine its actual use. He will go forward with his method: that is what makes him a scientist in any one science. But the metaphysician must not predetermine his choice of conceptual instrument: he must be willing to use such terms as his object appears to demand. He cannot, of course, approach the object and hold out to it a tray of words and ask it kindly to pick out its own description. His approach to the object means his being already talking about the object in whatever terms he has chanced to begin. But his endeavour to comprehend the object means an endeavour to improve on his description, to find better terms. In fact, the metaphysician's method is to keep breaking his yardsticks against the requirements of real truth. The method which thus aims at the comprehension of the reality of things is that method of which Plato said that it and it alone proceeded by smashing the suggestions it put forward. By continually breaking and bettering and breaking his descriptions the metaphysician refines his understanding of that which he tries to describe.

The mysteries of which the metaphysician discourses are all of a high generality, but each is unique. An example of such a mystery is the relation of a knowing act to the thing it knows, or the relation of the mind to the body. Each of these relations is of the highest generality – every cognitive act provides an instance of the relation of knowledge to its object, and every human act or state whatsoever provides an instance of the relation of mind to body. But each of these relations is unique – it is fairly obvious that the relation of a knowing act to a thing known is not an instance of any other sort of relation: it is its own sort. So also with the relation of the mind to the body. What can be said, then, about the unique? Can the unique be described? We do not have to sit idly asking whether it can be described, for we are describing it instinctively, before we begin to reflect. I do not need to read philosophers, or to philosophise myself, before I begin thinking of the knowing act as a sort of intellectual sight. That is to say, I describe the knowing intellect by the analogy of the seeing eye. Or to take the other example – I think of my mental self as the inhabitant of my body, as the possessor and manipulator of my body, as a specialized activity of my body's, as simply identical with my body. All these conflicting descriptions occur to me at different times, and all are analogies. The man's mind is to the man's body as the whole man is to his house –

but it cannot be, for the relation of man to house is a relation of body to body, and how can the mind-body relation be like that? And so on with the rest.

What, then, does the metaphysician do? He does not simply reject all the analogies equally. He rejects the casual and fantastic, and holds fast those which seem most illuminating and natural. Into any analogy that he retains, he will gradually introduce more and more artificial modifications, for the purpose of suiting the analogy to the mysterious reality it is being used to describe. For example, the Aristotelian philosophy plainly describes the relation of the knowing act to the object known, by analogy with the relation of the exact replica of a thing to the thing of which it is the replica. We really begin with the formula, that for our act of intellect to know a mountain, is for it to *be* the mountain it knows, so that there is perfect correspondence between the known and the knowing of it. But so gross and violent an analogy would scarcely pass as a masterpiece of metaphysical description. The philosophers of the Aristotelian school show their wit in breaking down the analogy by a series of modifications. The knowing mind is the mountain – but not all of the mountain. It is the form of the mountain without the matter. For there are general aspects of the rocky mass in virtue of which we call it a mountain, and it is these aspects alone that the mind understands when it understands 'mountain'. So we have no need to import all those tons of variously veined actual granite into the mind. After all, the eye, from a distance, may be said to take the form of the mountain: and what the eye takes seems a highly etherealized and insubstantial sort of thing: so let us say that the form of the mountain, which the knowing mind 'becomes', is something like that. It still corresponds to something in the mountain, for the mountain really has the form. Yes, but it will never do, either, to say that the mind 'becomes' the *visible* form of the mountain, for then the mind would be the sense of sight, which it is not. It must become the *intelligible* form of the mountain, and that will be something still more subtle and immaterial. The visible form of mountain is always the form of one particular mountain: but the intelligible form is common to all mountains worthy of the name. When we have reached this point we have reached the point of metaphysical crisis. We have so whittled away and subtilised our original analogy, that it seems if we could subtilise a little further we should express the very mentality of mind: but on the other hand, if we did subtilise any further, we should run the risk of getting completely out of touch with the analogy from which we started: our pipe-line of analogical fuel would be drawn so fine that no substance of analogy would pass down it; in further refining the analogy we should be refining nothing, our refinement would mean nothing and would describe nothing. Thus, if we want to proceed further than the last stage of refinement our analogy will bear, we can only do it by standing on the extreme tip of our tapering spit of analogical description, and pointing out to sea. We say 'We are getting towards the nature of the knowing act, but still this isn't it: it is just itself, and lies beyond'.

Such dumb pointing is not, of course, the only resource of the metaphysician who has stretched his analogical tether to the limit. He may take up an alternative analogy for the same mystery, and work that out in a similar way; he may attempt a composite picture out of several analogies: there is no end to the things he may do. Nevertheless, in principle, the method remains what our sketch indicates: the description of natural mysteries by the criticism of analogies. And 'analogies' is only another name for sober and appropriate images.

When I talk thus about the business of metaphysics, I have my eyes fixed on the great metaphysicians of the past and consider what they have in fact been at: not what they say they have been at, but what I see them to have been at. If someone now wishes to give the name of metaphysics a new sense, he is no doubt free to do so: let him confine metaphysics to the criticism of our own intellectual presuppositions, and exclude it from pronouncing on the truth of things. It will remain that the great metaphysicians of the past wrestled to describe the real; he who admitted himself to have nothing to say about reality acknowledged himself to be no metaphysician.

But, by this very test, that is, by the practice of the great metaphysicians, is not our own account of metaphysics refuted? It might fairly be objected that what we have hitherto discussed under the name is not metaphysics at all, but something else – let us call it desultory dialectic, or free existential description. For, so far as our account has gone, metaphysics might be a gallery of miscellaneous analogical pictures representing each a separate 'mystery', and each worked out in a distinct technique, according to the requirements of its subject. Is this metaphysics? Surely metaphysics begins with the endeavour to unite the several pictures into one panorama, one interlocking system of all the mysteries.

If he is to achieve the unity of system, the metaphysician must select certain analogies of supreme common usefulness and apply them everywhere, not, of course, with the yardstick uniformity of scientific concepts, but variously broken down and qualified to suit the several spheres of their application. It was this that Aristotle was in fact doing when he interpreted the knowing act as an event in which the mind becomes the form of the object known. When we discussed this example just now, we talked as though Aristotle had adopted his terms of description in an unprejudiced attempt to appreciate the knowing act on its own merits: that is to say, we talked as though Aristotle were engaged in free existential description. But he was not: he was working within a system of which the analogical conventions were already fixed before he approached the mystery of the knowing act: they had been already fixed by his analysis of physical being and physical change. There was no question of his abandoning these basic conventions: the only question was, how they must be broken down and manipulated to express the special character of the knowing act.

At the first glance, it may seem folly for the metaphysician thus to tie his hands. If his business is to describe the mysteries of existence, surely he would do better by leaving himself free to choose whatever analogies best fitted any one mystery. And it must be admitted that there is truth in this contention: systematic metaphysics must sacrifice something in the matter of appropriateness to any one given mystery. But anything the description of each mystery thus loses in appropriateness it more than makes up in what we may call a fullness of analogical overtones. For the peculiar quality of each mystery will be so expressed as to relate it to the whole system of other mysteries: the common analogical convention is a common measure which relates each to all. The Aristotelian system is, once more, an admirable example of this. It provides a common metaphysical grammar in which everything in heaven and earth can be more or less adequately expressed. To express anything in this grammar is immediately to feel its due relation to everything else that we have hitherto expressed in it. It is this fact which chiefly explains the sway still exercised over theological minds by the Aristotelian system; even now, when it is cut off from the logical and physical roots from which it grew. Logic and physics move on and use other conventions, but the theologian is tempted still to use the Aristotelian metaphysical language, because he above all other men has an interest in seeing all the mysteries of existence in their relation to a single unity. And since the break-up of the Aristotelian-Christian system at the Renaissance, no one has had the genius to construct so variable, so supple, so extensible and consistent a metaphysical language.

Let it be granted, then, that nothing properly to be called metaphysics appears until we have system and comprehensiveness. Yet, if we are not to be simply the slaves of a system, if we are to be able to criticise and reform it, or even to remind ourselves that reality is something more various and vital than the system can express, then we must step outside the conventions of the system and have recourse to free existential description, that is, to the description of each mystery in any analogical terms which may appear expressive. Free existential description is really prior to metaphysical system, it is the soil out of which it grows: and it is for the health of systematic metaphysics that there should always be minds in revolt against what they esteem its sterile dogmatism, and devoted to the free play of uncontrolled existential description.

Metaphysics undertakes the whole complex of natural mysteries, free existential description takes them piecemeal, and the use the two methods make of analogy differs according to their aim and scope: but both use analogy, and in essentially the same way, that is, descriptively and critically. It does not concern us here to pursue the distinction between them, but rather to exhibit their common form: and for the appreciation of this, the examination of free existential description is perhaps more immediately illuminating.

Let us now recall the question which led us into this perfunctory sketch of metaphysical procedure. What was puzzling us was the function of images in revealed truth. The scandal appeared to be, that we cannot point away from the revealed images to any imageless or 'straight' truth which the images signify. So we decided to consider the use of images outside the special province of revealed truth, and took up the broader province of metaphysics. Well, and what have we discovered? Can the metaphysician point away from the analogical statements he uses to a non-analogical truth which they state? We cannot answer yes or no to that: the question is ambiguous: the reply depends on what you mean by the non-analogical *truth*. If by 'truth' you mean a piece of true *thinking*, the answer is No: the metaphysician cannot point away from his analogically-expressed thoughts about the natural mysteries to some non-analogical thoughts about them, which mean all that the analogical thoughts mean. He has not got any such non-analogical thoughts: analogy is the proper form of metaphysical thought, in the realm of *thought* there is no getting behind it.

If, on the other hand, by 'truth' you mean the existent reality which the metaphysician is talking about, then indeed he can in a sense point to a truth outside his analogical statements, which they are designed to state. For he can point to the natural mysteries. Without analogising he can do no more than point to them, or at the most name them: he cannot express or describe them. He can, without analogising, say 'There is what I call myself, and there is what I call my body, and the two have something to do with one another'. But what it is they have to do with one another can only be stated in analogies. The relation of self and body is *there* in our act of existing, and it is that to which our analogical discourse reacts: but it does not get *expressed* in any parallel and non-analogical reaction.

Is this fact of irreducible analogising so odd after all? It appears to be a simple consequence from the most obvious characteristic of all thinking whatsoever. Thinking is mental discourse, and no act of discourse can be performed without at least two terms. The sentence, not the single word, is the proper expression of thinking. A single word may express a thought, but only because further terms are taken as understood. If we say MURDER, we either mean 'Murder is going on here' or 'What so-and-so committed was nothing less than murder', or 'Murder so-and-so' or, if we are bloodthirsty enough, 'Murder away, never mind whom'.

All thinking, then, is a movement, passing, as it were, from term to term. The relation stated between term and term may be any conceivable relation: spatial collocation, temporal succession, effect and cause. But suppose we do not want to relate anything to anything else; suppose we want to consider its *nature*: for that is the proper business of the metaphysician. Certainly he deals with relations, but of them too he enquires what their *natures* are. How can we simply consider the *nature* of anything, if considering means passing from something to something else? The ordinary form of speech informs us how we can do it: we do not ordinarily ask 'What is its nature?' but 'What is it like?' To describe a thing is to compare it with other things. So, then, we express the nature of a thing by assigning it its place among the comparable natures of other things.

In comparing one thing with others, in saying what it is like, we can either use straight classification, or we cannot. Fido is like Toby, for both are dogs. Dogs are like cats, for both are mammals. But metaphysical discourse does not deal with the classifiable: the 'natural mysteries' it attempts to describe are each unique, or anyhow it is what is unique in them that it attempts to describe: and here classification lends no aid. I suppose we can say, if we like, 'the relation of person to body is like the relation of captain to boat, for both are relations', but if we do say this, we shall not be thought to have contributed much to metaphysical discussion. No: we cannot classify, and so we are condemned to sheer irreducible analogy, the attempt, never really possible, to express one thing in terms of another thing which it somehow resembles, but from which it is nevertheless diverse throughout. We try to understand the correspondence (so called) of thought to thing in terms of the correspondence to a thing shewn by its replica: but there is no point of absolutely identical form in the two relations, except what is purely trivial and metaphysically quite uninformative, for example that each is a two-term relation, or that in each pair the second term (thought or replica) comes into existence with a view to the first.

In order to understand, then, why metaphysics is irreducibly analogical, we need only to recognise (i) that thought requires plurality of terms; and (ii) that metaphysical thought attempts the expression of the unique.

We will return to the comparison between the function of metaphysical analogy and the function of revealed images. We can see at a glance how far more favourably placed the metaphysician is than the scriptural theologian. Neither of these men, it is true, can get behind the imaged form of statement, but the metaphysician's object of study is absolutely given to him in his own existence and in its environing conditions: it is about these things that his analogical statements are made, and he has such an awareness of the realities he describes as to be able to feel the relative adequacy of different analogies to them. Not so the scriptural theologian. He has got *something*, indeed, of given reality to which some of his statements refer, that is to say, the work of grace in his own soul. But not even with regard to this is he in the same position as the metaphysician. For the work of grace in one's own soul, taken as something simply given, and apart from the transcendent realities to which it is believed to be related, is not even recognisable as the work of grace. So the theologian cannot simply feel the adequacy or inadequacy of the revealed images to the object they describe: for he has not that object. He cannot criticise the revealed images from his acquaintance with their object: he can only confront them with one another.

We have not room in this lecture to take the next step forward, and follow the fortunes of imaged discourse out of metaphysics into rational theology; so we will turn aside from chasing the images, and conclude with a brief digression on the spiritual importance of metaphysical thinking itself.

Obviously (to begin with) the healthy-minded man does not need to be a metaphysician, any more than the believing Christian needs to be a theologian. The believing Christian does the sort of thinking which the theologian criticises and regulates, and the healthy mind does the sort of thinking which the metaphysician criticises and regulates. Since men, or anyhow some men, are speculative animals, there will always be theology as long as there is religious thinking, and in the same way there will always be metaphysics while there is ordinary healthy thinking about our natural existence. When theology is exploded, it is because the validity of religious thinking is denied: and the vindication of religious thinking then becomes the business of theology. And where metaphysics is repudiated (as it now is) it is because the ordinary healthy thinking which metaphysics criticises is denied validity. And this is a very serious state of affairs.

What, then, is the ordinary healthy thinking of which metaphysics is the systematic elaboration? It is just contemplative thinking. Whenever the mind contemplates the deep mystery of what it is to know or to love, or to be an embodied spirit, or to be subject to the form of time, and yet able to rise above the temporal stream and to survey it: whenever we consider the vitality and the richness, the inexhaustible individuality of the being whom as wife or friend we love: when we aspire to ask of the forces of nature, not how they work simply, but what in themselves they are: when we advance from curiosity to admiration, and stand upon the brink of awe: then we are thinking in the form from which metaphysical philosophy arises.[6]

It is useless to say, 'We can contemplate indeed, but we cannot metaphysicize'. For either our contemplation holds something real in view, or else it is a mere sensuous enjoyment, or a mere emotional attitude. If contemplation attends to what is real, then the nature of that real must be the most serious subject of intellectual enquiry: to deny this is to deny that we can think in a serious or rigorous way at all about what meets us as most real in all our experience. It is an ancient axiom that the perfection of intellect is to grasp what is: and it should be fairly evident that if we recede from this position we make all serious religious belief impossible, for when we know God we know him on whom the reality of things is founded. If we surrender metaphysical enquiry, we shall vainly invoke supernatural revelation to make up for our metaphysical loss of nerve. For if our cravenheartedness surrenders the ground of metaphysics, it will have surrendered the bridgehead which the supernatural liberator might land upon. Get a man to see the mysterious depth and seriousness of the act by which he and his neighbour exist, and he will have his eyes turned upon the bush in which the supernatural fire appears, and presently he will be prostrating himself with Moses, before him who thus names himself: 'I am that I am'.[7]

---

[6]    This paragraph describing the contemplative origin of metaphysical thought bears a strong resemblance to a passage in Farrer's posthumously-published essay 'Poetic Truth', probably written sometime between *Finite and Infinite* in 1943 and *The Glass of Vision* in 1948: 'The chief impediment to religion in this age, I often think, is that no one ever looks at anything at all: not so as to contemplate it, to apprehend what it is to be that thing, and plumb, if he can, the deep fact of its individual existence. The mind rises from the knowledge of creatures to the knowledge of their creator, but this does not happen through the sort of knowledge which can analyse things into factors or manipulate them with technical skill or classify them into groups. It comes from the appreciation of things which we have when we love them and fill our minds and senses with them, and feel something of the silent force and great mystery of their existence. For it is in this that the creative power is displayed of an existence higher and richer and more intense than all': Austin Farrer, *Reflective Faith: Essays in Philosophical Theology*, edited by Charles C. Conti (London: SPCK, 1972), 37–8. Douglas Hedley discusses this passage in 'Austin Farrer's Shaping Spirit of Imagination' (on page 203 of this volume).

[7]    Exodus 3.14, the verse used as the opening biblical text of this lecture-sermon. Farrer is here speaking out of the ancient Jewish and Christian tradition, inherited and developed by Aquinas, which saw Exodus 3.14 as a divine revelation of God's name and nature as self-subsistent or necessary Being itself. For a brief discussion, see Fergus Kerr, *After Aquinas: Versions of Thomism* (Oxford: Blackwell, 2002), 94–6. Farrer is thus also criticising what he understood to be the 'cravenhearted' Barthian rejection of this 'ground of metaphysics' in favour of supernatural revelation alone.

To reject metaphysics is equivalent to saying that there are no serious questions for the human mind except those which fall under the special sciences. We can ask historically why the crucifixion of Christ came about: physiologically, whether he died of heart-failure or by some other cause: psychologically, what train of thoughts and feeling induced him to put his neck into the noose: morally, how his action squared with a copy-book of ethical imperatives. But we cannot consider what in itself, in its intensity and elevation of being, in its divinity, the voluntary passion of Christ was. We have a first interest in keeping this road unblocked, the road by which a serious and realistic wonder advances through the contemplation of Christ's manhood into the adoration of his deity, that it may lay hold upon the Eternal Son, who, hanging on the Cross, is enthroned in Heaven; who, lying in the sepulchre, lies in the bosom of the Father; and standing in the upper room, breathes forth from the heart of all being the Paraclete, the Holy Ghost. *Now therefore to the indivisible Trinity and social Unity, one Godhead in three Persons, be ascribed as is most justly due all might, dominion, majesty and power, henceforth and for ever.*

# Lecture V:
# The Rational Theologian's Analogy

The Heavens declare the Glory of God, and the firmament sheweth his handiwork. There is no speech nor language, neither are their voices heard among them. Their sound is gone forth into all the earth, and their words to the end of the world.

Psalm XIX.1–4

The heavens declare the glory of God, their voiceless words sound in the ear of an attentive reason; so a natural knowledge of God is acquired from his handiwork. We have now to consider this natural knowledge of God from a particular point of view – we have to describe the part played in it by images. After that we will look at the even more mysterious part which images play in the supernatural and revealed knowledge of God.

In the last lecture we prepared the ground for the enquiry we have now to undertake. For, seeing that God's existence is one of the topics of metaphysics, we spoke generally of metaphysical method. Now we must narrow the field, we must isolate the question of God's existence from all other metaphysical questions, and study it by itself.

The first thing to be explained is that God's existence is one of the mysteries of metaphysics, not one of the puzzles of metaphysics. Let me explain what I mean by the distinction between mysteries and puzzles.[1] The metaphysician studies mysteries, mysteries of our natural existence, which are simply there in any case, whether we metaphysicise about them or not. We simply have a personal identity, for example, and we simply have a physical body; but the nature of these two realities, still more of the relation between them, is highly mysterious. Such mysteries the metaphysician wrestles with; he attempts to describe them by means of analogies. In his attempt to describe, puzzles are certain to arise – puzzles interior to the particular analogical description he chooses to employ. Since no analogy ever fits perfectly, the adaptation of any analogical description to the object described must create puzzles. How is the description to be made either consistent or suitable? For example, the Aristotelians took in hand to describe the mystery of the knowing act. Under the descriptive conventions proper to their system, they found it necessary to distinguish between the active and the receptive

---

[1]  As acknowledged earlier, Farrer derived the distinction between 'mysteries' and 'problems' from Gabriel Marcel's *Être et Avoir* (1935), published in English the year after *The Glass of Vision* as *Being and Having*, translated by Katharine Farrer (Westminster: Dacre Press, 1949). He continues in that vein here, although 'puzzles' differ from 'problems' in that puzzles themselves arise within particular metaphysical theories.

powers of the intellect. When they had done this, the puzzle arose, how the active intellect and the receptive intellect were to be related to one another in one mind. This is a puzzle of the Aristotelian system; it is not a mystery of existence. We can be rid of the puzzle at a single stroke by refusing to be Aristotelians. If we do not choose to use their conventions or talk their language, the puzzle is no puzzle for us. But the mystery of existence remains. We may not wish to talk about the mysterious character of the knowing act in Aristotelian terms, but the mystery of the knowing act is still with us. We may adopt a convention of speech which makes it impossible for us to talk about the mystery of knowledge – that is quite easy: I dare say the Hottentot language would save us from discourse upon this and other metaphysical mysteries. But the mysteries do not vanish because we talk Hottentot, and they will catch us out one of these days, constraining us to speak of them in some language which will allow them to get a foothold in our minds.[2]

The believer in God must suppose that the mystery of God's existence is no mere puzzle, but a genuine mystery, presented to us by the stuff of our own existence: whether we describe it well or ill, whether we speak of it or ignore it, it is still there. For God appears in our thoughts as the name of a real being we attempt to describe, not as a convenient analogical term used by us in describing something else, in describing the moral conscience, for example. We cannot abolish every question in which the name of God occurs at a single stroke, simply by refusing to talk the special language of this or that philosophical system. 'God' is not a factitious term, like Aristotle's 'active intellect'. So believing philosophers say: not so the unbelieving philosophers; in fact, this is the very point where we part company with them. We say to them: 'Though you reject one description of transcendent being, you still have the mystery of transcendence on your hands to describe.' They say to us: 'There is no mystery of transcendence. There is, in the working out of certain metaphysical systems, the puzzle of transcendence. We take no interest in those systems, nor in that puzzle.'

Now the most serious philosophical task that I could undertake would be to go on with the debate from this point. It is the business of believing philosophers

---

[2]    'Hottentot' is a European term for the Khoikhoin people of southwestern Africa. It is now considered offensive by many, and Farrer's casual use of it here and elsewhere is typical for his time and place in 1940s Oxford. Clearly, however, he is not using it to refer specifically to this particular people-group with its distinctive language or culture, but rather to any 'primitive' society, assuming without question that such indigenous thought-forms were incapable of metaphysical sophistication. In a review of Ann Loades and Michael McLain (eds), *Hermeneutics, the Bible and Literary Criticism* (New York: St Martin's Press/London: Macmillan, 1992) – a book containing several essays on Farrer, three of which are included in this volume – George Pattison, no doubt with *The Glass of Vision* in mind, comments negatively on Farrer's 'condescending asides about Germans and Hottentots which somehow conjure up all that was most insular about English theology in mid-century': see *Literature and Theology* 7 (1993), 103. Having said that, however, Pattison later accepts 'the continuing need for the kind of clarity of logic and language and the quality of religious passion and conviction which, alongside sensitivity of imagination, characterize the best of his writing'.

to show reason why God's existence is a genuine mystery, not a factitious puzzle. I cannot undertake so momentous a task here, nor is it the business we have in hand.[3] Meanwhile, just to keep our courage up, let us observe that the mystery of transcendence is not got rid of at a stroke by the resolution to talk a language which ignores it. Like nature, it keeps on turning up: *expellas furca, tamen usque recurret.*[4] Rationalism must exorcise it again and again with bell, book and Bunsen burner: and then there it is, haunting us once more. Please do not think that I consider this a decisive consideration: there are some superstitions which die extremely hard; theological belief might be one of those.

Believing and unbelieving philosophers differ as to whether the mystery about God's existence is a mystery at all. Is not this something of a scandal to start with? One might think that philosophers would disagree in their *descriptions* of the natural mysteries, but would at least agree as to which the natural mysteries are. There may be a scandal here: but if so, it is not a scandal peculiar to the question about God's existence. There is a disagreement about other natural mysteries also, as to whether they are genuine mysteries or not. To many of us human free-will appears the most pressing and unescapable of natural mysteries; yet some people think it to be a factitious puzzle; and there is a sect of people who allow there to be no natural mysteries at all.

To accept the mystery about God's existence as a genuine mystery may be to beg the chief of all metaphysical questions. Nevertheless, since we are here speaking from within our Christian faith, let us beg it, and advance to a fresh point. Supposing that the mystery about God is somehow just *there*, let us ask in what way it forces itself upon our attention.

If I were asked in general how the natural mysteries present themselves to the metaphysician's attention, I should be inclined to make a simple classification of them into two groups, 'me' and 'not me'. Some natural mysteries are parts of the form of my own active existence – my free-will, for example, or my embodied state. These are the 'me' group, and I become aware of them in attending to my own action. The 'not me' group are presented by the environment with which I interact: I become aware of them in attending not to my own action in itself, but

---

[3]    This 'business' was, however, precisely Farrer's task in his first book, *Finite and Infinite: A Philosophical Essay* (Westminster: Dacre Press, 1943). For a summary and analysis of Farrer's argument in this book, see Robert MacSwain, *Solved by Sacrifice: Austin Farrer, Fideism, and the Evidence of Faith* (Leuven: Peeters, 2013), 113–39. In this chapter of *The Glass of Vision*, 'The Rational Theologian's Analogy', Farrer presents a less detailed and more accessible explanation of how our minds can rise from the finite to the infinite, stressing the role of images and analogies. He thus seeks to build on the 'contemplative' foundation identified at the end of the previous lecture.

[4]    Horace, *Epistles*, Book 1, Epistle X, line 24: *Naturam expellas furca, tamen usque recurret* ('You may drive out Nature with a pitchfork, yet each time she will speed back'). Farrer's ironic point is that, like nature itself, transcendence cannot be driven out as easily as the logical positivists of his day thought. They are the 'sect of people' he alludes to at the end of the next paragraph, who in denying 'natural mysteries' deny metaphysics.

to the field in which it plays. Such mysteries are: the nature of merely physical bodies, or the relation of other finite minds to mine. Into which of these classes shall we try to put the mystery of God? Hardly into the 'me' class – God cannot be the form of my existence, surely; still less can he be one part or detail of the form of my existence. It seems more hopeful to try to put the mystery of God into the group of mysteries that are not me: unless, that is, I have decided to be a pantheist.

Let us consider, then, the way in which the realities that are not me shew to me their mysterious existence. On the level of common-sense, of course, we take physical bodies and other people's minds for granted: we take it that they are simply there. But presently some of the well-known puzzles of philosophy perplex us, and we begin to wonder whether the beings which compose our environment are what we had taken them to be. Our first reaction to this doubt is to say: 'Well, there is *something* out there, and it is really impinging on me with causal force. But perhaps my mind and my senses have been wrongly interpreting the nature of this mysterious energy which plays upon me from without.' I may assist my imagination by using the figure of a spider's web, of which the threads are lines of physical relation. The centre, where all the threads run together, is the focal point of my existence. But it would be the focus of nothing, unless the threads of relation ran in all directions towards other centres of being. At any moment any of the threads may be pulled, and it may be pulled from either end. It is pulled from the centre of the web, when an action of mine has an effect on somebody or something else: it is pulled from the circumference, when somebody or something else so acts as to have an effect on me. It is out of the pulling of the thread, we think, that our exterior knowledge arises. Our senses directly react to the trembling of the thread: on the basis of it, they give us sensual signs of that other something or somebody, and on those signs we found an immediate intellectual supposition of that other's existence. If, then, the suggestion comes to me that my suppositions about that other are inadequate and bewildering, that its real being is a mystery, my first reaction is this. 'Anyhow', I say, 'there is the fact of active relation. There is the spider's web, and the threads really tremble, they are really attached at their outer ends: their tremors express something that really happens at their outer termini. It may be, however, that my senses and intellect combined give a highly mythical account of the real activities out there to which the tremors of the threads respond.' I do not say that such a line of reflection is very profound: I simply say that it is how my thoughts immediately arrange themselves, when the suggestion is made to me that my knowledge of finite beings is a mystery.

I observe something further. I observe that if it is suggested to me that my knowledge of God is a mystery, I am inclined to transfer my account of the mystery of finite knowledge to the mystery of knowing the infinite. I say 'Yes, indeed: God must be all unlike what I suppose him to be. But anyhow, I may believe that my suppositions about him arise out of my active relation to him. That at least may be solid fact. There is the thread of my relation to him trembling with his action upon me: from that tremor my mind, by whatever secret and baffling processes, makes her conjecture of God.'

This is what I all too readily suppose. Further reflection shows that it will not do: my relation with God is not an environmental disturbance on which a particular act of my consciousness can be based. My existence does not *come under* God's causal influence, so that I may be aware of the shock. To his causality my existence itself is due. A shock is administered to me by my being flung into water, but no shock is administered to me by my being flung into existence, for to feel the plunge into water I must be there before I plunge, but before I am plunged into existence I *am not*. According to the Freudians, we can in a dim manner experience being born, but not even the most precocious of us can experience being conceived, still less can we experience being created: and it makes no difference to this conclusion, that whereas our conception was an event in the past, our creation continuously and timelessly underlies our being. It remains that we are there to act and suffer simply in so far as our creation takes effect. We do not therefore suffer it, or react to it. Our relation to our Creator is real enough, but what arises on the basis of it is not a particular state or act of our conscious existence, but our whole conscious existence.

When I think of myself in active relation to environmental energies I take both my existence and their existence for granted, and ask what I do to them, or they to me. If I try to think myself in active relation to God, I do the same thing. I take my existence as well as his existence for granted, and then ask, perhaps not what I do to him, but anyhow, what he does to me. But the answer is 'nothing'. Once I have taken my existence for granted, I can find nothing that my Creator does to me. What he does to me is to cause my existence; but I was not there to experience that, I can only exercise experience once I am created.

The process of my creation is neither an action nor a passion of my existence. Not an action, for I can do nothing about it; nor a passion, for I am not there to undergo it. It is simply the act of God's existence. It has not two focuses, one in God and one in me: its focus is simply in God. I cannot first be aware of my creation as something impinging on my focus, and then proceed to interpret it as something arising from God's focus. If I am aware of it at all, I must be aware of it in him from the start. I must be simply aware of the divine or infinite act which is God himself – not, certainly, of God in all the aspects of his infinite active being, but God in that aspect of his action which looks towards my creation.

But this, it may be objected, cannot be true and is not true. I am not aware of God's creative act unmediated. I am only aware of it, in so far as it is mediated to me by my own created existence, or by some other created existence. Yes: but to say that, is not to determine the nature of the mediation which the created existence supplies. We have so far only dismissed the suggestion that the creature mediates knowledge of the creator by undergoing his creative influence. It may mediate knowledge of him in other ways, for example, by offering material for a shadow or image of him. Somewhat as though my eyes and my hands were by some necessity wholly employed in a field of finite relationships outspread in front of me, so that I was unable to have direct awareness of a current of creative power which continually sustained and supplied me from behind. Yet the vast shadow of my Creator himself might fall over my shoulder into the field of finite things before my eyes. Then the visibility of the shadow to me would depend on the substance it found on which to print its figure. A shadow may fall for ever imperceptible through empty air, but even mist or smoke on the motes in the sunbeam will embody it, better still a solid surface, a shining surface best of all. So perhaps our awareness of the infinite Act depends on the materials for a shadow of him presented by finite existence: perhaps that sheerly given metaphysical mystery with which rational theology wrestles is the shadow of the Infinite in finite being.

All this, as you will be quick to point out, is pure metaphor, unworthy to find a place in philosophical discourse. True, but metaphors are sometimes the dawning of intelligence: whether they are or are not we do not know, until we have decoded them. Let us see what we can do with this figure of the shadow.

The problem of our knowing God, we will say, is never a problem of his being made present, but always of our being able to apprehend his presence. A star in the Milky Way needs to be made present to me by the passage of light from it to me; if it is small enough and distant enough it may be impotent to achieve effective presence with me. As between God and me, this sort of question does not arise. True, the *mode* of his presence to me is as yet a mystery: it is not, for example, by way of particular and variable causal influence. But if we are prepared to consider the possibility of his being known at all, we may simply concede his presence, in whatever fashion. The problem will be, not about his presence to our minds, but about our minds' receptivity for him. Will he pass through us completely, as perpendicular light through a pane of perfect glass, or, to change the metaphor, will he find nothing to illuminate in us, like a ray passing into a hollow sphere lined with velvet black?

Our minds, in fact, are neither mirrors nor containers: their receptivity depends on what they can *do*, on their ability to busy themselves with their object, to express it in discoursing on it. But it seems that our minds are impotent to discourse on God, to express God. No doubt once we have obtained knowledge of him, we may assign to the object of our knowledge a name coined for the purpose, for example, the name 'God' itself. But that is after the event; our ability now to use the name 'God' significantly casts no light on the act of discourse by which we first made God's idea a part of our mental existence.

Let us consider our predicament. We can only know God in expressing God: and we can express him in no other terms than such as are already significant to us, terms we already have in familiar use. Such terms will be terms descriptive of finite existence, for hitherto we are supposed to know no other existence. Therefore our power of knowing God will depend upon the resources of our finite experience. Only in proportion as our experience of finite existence affords analogies in terms of which God can be discoursed upon, shall we be able, in discoursing on God, to actualise an apprehension of God: for without discourse there is no intellectual apprehension.

From such a statement as this we may readily form the picture of Nature presenting to the human mind a colour-box of analogies, and saying to her, 'Here are your colours: now go ahead, and paint the portrait. Take a touch of spirituality from human virtue, a touch of sublime changelessness from the mountains, a tint of bright ubiquity from the light, and paint the image of God.' 'Ah', our mind would have to reply, 'but unhappily I cannot see the subject I am trying to paint. It was only in painting that I was to see him, and until I have painted I do not know how to begin, how to lay the colours, or indeed what colours to choose.'

What is the way out of this *impasse*? There is no way out of it, because it is not really an *impasse* at all. For the same situation confronts us in all knowledge, and not only in the knowledge of God. It is always absurd to ask how the human mind can voluntarily set about thinking of something, the like of which it never thought about before. All our voluntary thinking is ultimately the development of involuntary thinking which has already occurred in us. How do our first thoughts about ordinary physical things arise? Are they not part and parcel of the involuntary process of sense-perception? It is only by the refinement and development of these involuntary thoughts that we can think *at will* of physical nature. In the same way our first thoughts about ourselves are part and parcel of our conscious behaviour; and we begin to behave before we choose to behave. We first find ourselves behaving, and only at a second stage reflect at will upon ourselves as the subjects of the behaviour. By this analogy we might expect that our first thoughts about God must be involuntary, too: only when we had begun to think about God could we elaborate and refine at will our mental picture of God.

But what should make us begin to think about God in an involuntary way? As a drowned man breathes by being dragged through the motions of breathing, so our thought about *physical* things begins by our being dragged through the acts of physical thinking: the dragging being done by brute sensation. So too in the case of thought about self: we are dragged through the first motions of it by our animal behaviour. But what is to drag us through the first motions of thought about God? Nothing simply happens to us in this connexion: we do not suddenly perceive God through the senses without, we do not find him suddenly functioning as a factor of our existence within. God is perceived neither by the sense-bound acts of mind, nor by the mental acts which are tied to behaviour. Is he then perceived by the simple mind? But the simple mind has no organ for perceiving anything, unless we allow the name of 'organ' to her act of discoursing about a thing. If the mind begins to perceive God involuntarily, it must be that acts of discourse about God are forced upon the mind.

But what can force upon the mind an act of discourse about God? Nothing, presumably, unless it be an experience of finite existence. Again, how can elements of finite existence force a discourse about God upon the mind which experiences them? Only in one way that I can conceive: in getting themselves taken by the mind as an embodied discourse about God, as symbols or shadows of God. If, for example, I were to be meditating upon my own acts of knowledge and will, knowledge which is never a tenth part adequate to the real nature of anything existing, will which is always nine parts bound; and if I were suddenly to find myself taking them as reduced or confused or adulterated instances of sheer will and knowledge, things in their essence perfect and absolute: then my own existence would have presented to my thinking mind the shadow of absolute spirit, which is the shadow of God.

Before we go on with our proper business, which is to consider the shadow of God in finite being, we must pause to explain ourselves about one of the phrases we have used. Finite objects of experience, we have said, *force* the mind to take them as shadows of absolute being, or *drag* the mind through the motions of thinking the absolute in thinking of them. This, surely, is nonsense. How can the objects of finite experience exercise such a compulsion on the mind? We will agree immediately that *dragging* or *compelling* are, in such an application, very violent metaphors: their merit is simply to emphasise the difference between voluntary thinking such as that done by a philosopher thinking out his natural theology, and involuntary thinking, such as happens to him when he finds himself instinctively taking his own spiritual acts as finite, that is, as limited instances of something intrinsically infinite. But it is not really proper to talk about involuntary thinking on any level as happening under exterior compulsion. To take sense perception, for example. It is proper, no doubt, to think of the mind as being abundantly active throughout the process: the mind is, as it were, out for experience, and in co-operating with sensation follows its own bent and exercises its own energy. It is not forced or dragged by sensation, it exploits the occasion which sensation offers. But in exploiting it, it acts by nature rather than by choice: in fact it acts like the digestion. Digestion seizes and assimilates any suitable matter, of its own vital motion indeed, but not by deliberate choice: if the suitable matter is given to it, the digestive process simply does act. So with involuntary thinking: the mind simply does act when the sensation gives it the occasion: it does not choose whether it will or no.

So the mind which first takes some finite object as a shadow of the infinite, acts involuntarily in the sense that it acts by nature, not by choice. The mind must be thought of as placed between two presences: the simple presence of the infinite, and the changing and various presence of the finite. It has a natural tendency to become aware of both presences: but it cannot become aware of the infinite except by symbolising it in terms of the finite. When finite objects happen to have been brought into such a mental focus that they are capable of acting as symbols of the infinite, then the mind's power to know the infinite leaps into actualisation, seeing the finite in the infinite, and the infinite in the finite.

The event that we are speaking of is a double event: two things are happening. First, there is an ordinary pedestrian act of the mind, appreciating some aspect of finite existence. Second, there is a sublimer act, by which the finite object is itself appreciated as a symbol of the infinite. Of these two acts, the former and more pedestrian is unambiguously directed towards a finite object: the second and sublimer act is ambiguous in its direction; it bears both on a finite and on an infinite object, for it treats the one as a symbol of the other, and so seems to hang between earth and heaven. This being so, we shall naturally expect the first act to exercise an attraction upon the second and pull it in the earthwards direction.

Let me explain what I mean by this perhaps not very well-chosen language. What we are talking about is an act of mind in which something finite serves as a symbol for the infinite. The mind which performs such an act will be bound to tip in one of two directions: it cannot hold the balance even. Either it will take itself to be thinking about the infinite being, or it will take itself to be thinking about the finite being. Suppose, for example, my own act of knowledge or will is the finite symbol to be employed. Then one of two things will happen: either I shall be saying, 'God's existence is the absolute expression of such knowledge and will as these of mine': or I shall be saying, 'This knowledge and this will of mine are but limited, cramped, adulterated expressions of sheer knowledge and sheer will, activities intrinsically infinite and divine'. In the first case I shall be thinking of God by the light of myself: in the second case I shall be thinking of myself as a partial ray which falls from the full brightness of God.

There is nothing to choose between these two forms of the symbolising act so long as we think of that act apart from any particular context. But, in the present argument, we have got a particular context for it. We are not thinking of any men at any time symbolising the infinite in terms of the finite. We are thinking of the special case of a man who, for the first time, takes a finite thing as a symbol of the infinite in the process of thinking about the finite thing. Now this man, by hypothesis, is thinking about the finite, not about the infinite, when the sudden and mysterious act of symbolisation takes place. It is fairly certain, then, that this man's act of symbolisation will take the form of a thinking about the finite under the light of the infinite, not a thinking about the infinite through its expression in the finite. He will see himself as thinking primarily about the natural object, not about God. The natural mystery which is the starting-point of rational theology is the finite manifesting itself as the shadow of the infinite.

As Descartes pointed out, once we have arrived at a certain level of conceptual clarification, it makes no odds which way round the act of symbolisation takes shape. The intelligent appreciation of the finite as finite involves the appreciation of infinity, and it matters not the least on which of the two our attention is first focussed, we shall shift it to the other directly. But this is only so when a certain conceptual clarification of the mystery has been achieved or accepted. At an earlier, more inchoate stage it is of course of huge practical importance that what we are labouring with appears to be located in the finite, not in the infinite. To the theistic philosopher it seems that people are everywhere wrestling with the mystery of the shadow of the infinite, but that they have often no notion that the shadow of the infinite is what they are wrestling with: their knowledge of God therefore remains purely implicit and they are unable to bring it into explicit consciousness.

I shall now swing the argument still further in the direction in which it has been moving. We have so far talked as though the mind's real concern throughout were to know God in terms of the creature, not the creature in relation to God. We have thought of the mind as being in the presence of God always, but unable to see him until she finds a mirror in created existence which will in some measure reflect his image. We do not normally contemplate reflections in mirrors for the purpose of obtaining information about the properties of looking-glass: we look at them for knowledge of the face reflected there. On such an analogy we should suppose that the mind's vision of the shadow of God in the creature was solely for the sake of the knowledge of God. But such a suggestion is false. God alone is primal being, and the relation of any other being to him cannot be left out of account, if we are to know that other being fully. Thus the fact that my own existence is a limited and fragmentary shadow of divine existence is just as important a truth about me as about God. In one sense it casts more light on my existence, in another sense, more on God's existence. If we consider that I know nothing at all of God's existence except through his finite image in my existence, then it may seem that more light is cast by that image on his existence than on mine; for I do at least know that I exist without observing God's image in me, but I do not even know that God exists without observing his image in me. On the other hand, if our test is adequacy to the nature of the object known, we must say that more light is cast on my existence than on God's: for my being a fragmentary finite image of him is an infinitely poor clue to his infinite being, whereas the fact that, being what I am, I am a finite shadow of the infinite reality, is a tolerably good clue to my metaphysical status.[5]

By this line of argument we work our way back to a formula which we used some while ago – natural knowledge of God is primarily the knowledge of existence at our own level, including the knowledge that it is existence of a secondary or dependent kind. For in such a knowledge of our own existence there is some knowledge of God involved. It is because God's infinity is shadowed forth in finite existence that the knowledge of God as absolute being is natural knowledge to a finite mind, in the sense in which we have defined natural knowledge.

Let us, by way of conclusion, collect an answer to the question with which this lecture began: what is the function of images in the natural knowledge of God? The natural theologian is a metaphysician, and the metaphysician, as we have seen, is condemned to use analogical or imaged statement in any case: but the metaphysician has the compensation that the natural mystery he strives to describe is actually present in his own existence, so that he *feels* the applicability or inapplicability of his proposed analogies to the object they should express. Is the rational theologian simply a case of the metaphysician, or is there something peculiar about his predicament?

There is certainly something peculiar about his predicament, because there is something singular about his object. God's creative act is present to us in so singular a manner that we do not know whether to say that it is present or absent. In the case of other mysteries we can at least name them without analogising: for

---

[5]   This evocative paragraph seems key to Farrer's decision to title his Bampton Lectures *The Glass* ['Mirror'] *of Vision*—see the note on the volume's epigraph for the deliberate ambiguity of 'glass'. This paragraph and the one below it also summarise the basic argument of his *Finite and Infinite: A Philosophical Essay* (Westminster: Dacre Press, 1943).

example, we have seen that I can say, 'There is my moral person and there is my body, and the two have something to do with one another'. It is only when we go on to describe this something that we must analogise. But in the case of knowing God we cannot name him until an analogical act of mind has taken place: it is only in being aware of something finite as an analogy of God that we begin to be aware of God at all.

From this extraordinary conclusion we might be tempted to infer the corollary that the analogy used in rational theology functions in the same way as the image used to convey revealed truth: for neither in revelation nor in rational theology can we point away from the image to that which the image signifies: in both we must be content to refer to the reality by understanding what the image tells us. Nevertheless, rational analogies and revealed images concerning God do not function in the same way: and we can express the difference by saying that the rational analogies are *natural* images: the revealed figures are not, in the sense intended, *natural*.

The rational analogies are natural, first of all, in the sense that they may be, and originally are, spontaneous: unless finite things put themselves upon us as symbols of deity we can have no natural knowledge of God. Revealed images do not do this: they are authoritatively communicated. The stars may seem to speak of a maker, the moral sense of a law-giver: but there is no pattern of being we simply meet, which speaks of Trinity in the Godhead or the efficacy of the Sacraments. Many symbols, indeed, suggest the Trinity and the Sacraments to a Christian, but they are the product of faith already accorded to a revelation already received: they are not just there, like moral reason or the Milky Way.[6]

Rational analogies are natural in a second sense: the analogy which the natural symbol appears to bear to God is founded on a real relation in which it stands towards God. Suppose, for example, I take my will as a symbol of God, because it seems to be a limited instance of something intrinsically infinite, sheer creativity. In such a case the symbolical relation corresponds with a real relation: in making me a voluntary being God has made me to participate in his own creative energy; my will symbolises God because it participates of God. Whereas revealed images are commonly just parables. For example, I am taught the mystery of Christ's mystical body in terms of physical organism. But there is no real and causal relation between natural organisms and Christ's mystical body: bodies, by being bodies, do not really participate in the mystery of saving incorporation. I do in fact participate in Christ's mystical body, but not by being a natural bodily creature: I participate in Christ's body by a supernatural and imperceptible gift; and this gift is no part of the figure by which revelation teaches me about the body of Christ.

---

[6]   An allusion to Immanuel Kant's famous statement: 'Two things fill the mind with ever new and increasing admiration and reverence, the more often and more steadily one reflects on them: *the starry heavens above me and the moral law within me.*' *Critique of Practical Reason* [1788], translated and edited by Mary Gregor (Cambridge: Cambridge University Press, 1997), 133 [5:161].

On the contrary, I need the revealed figures just as much to teach me about my supernatural gift as I need them to teach me about the divine body in which, by reason of the gift, I partake. Only the figures are revealed, and the figures are simply parables. Let us quote St Paul. 'As the body is one, and has many organs, yet all the organs of the body, being many, are one body, so is Christ.'[7]

Rational analogies are, by contrast, natural, but in being natural they come no nearer to being adequate. They speak of a God everywhere immediately present, but everywhere deeply incomprehensible, no less in the manner of his presence, than in the nature of his existence. May he who is so near to our being and so far from our conceiving forgive our belittling speech concerning his inviolable majesty, and assist us rather to praise, in words he has himself revealed, the One God in three Persons, Father, Son and Holy Ghost: *to whom be therefore ascribed as is most justly due all might, dominion, majesty and power, henceforth and for ever.*

---

7    First Corinthians 12.12.

# Lecture VI:

# Archetypes and Incarnation

And the Word became flesh and dwelt among us.

John, I.14

We cannot but be interested in what is most near and most real to us: and if I have hitherto dwelt disproportionately upon the natural knowledge of God, it will be because of its place in my mind. I know there are those who can readily enter into the apprehension of divine mysteries by the direct road of revealed Truth; and to such men it often seems that all the labour of the philosophers to establish a natural knowledge of God is a vain endeavour, since believers have no use for it, and unbelievers cannot be constrained to acknowledge it. But have not the believers a use for it? Those are happy, no doubt, who can enter directly into the promised land of Christ by the invocation of his Name. But such will not wish to forget that there are others, men who often find it best to climb the ladder from the bottom, proceeding through the natural to the supernatural knowledge of God. Are those Christian minds really so rare whose nearest gate into the invisible world is a simple awe at natural fact? I need but to consider that I am able from moment to moment to draw my breath; to live by an act which is my very being, yet is not mine, for I do not breathe by choice or will, still less by my own devising; and then to consider what is more fully mine, my act of thought, an act which aspires to identify itself with the objective truth of things, to see all beings, and myself among them, impartially, as though from a great height, as though from the steps of a heavenly throne: my thought which is nevertheless momentary, precariously seated in a tremor of my cerebral nerves, and embodied in the trifling act of stringing together words, or the imaged ghosts of words; when I see how much of being and of truth is somehow balanced on the absurd pin-point of my perishable moment, I step into the contemplation of him who does not alter or pass, who possesses and masters all he is or knows.

These thoughts are real to us: from the simple appreciation of our finitude we pass to the consideration of the infinite Being. And afterwards, in a reflective hour, we wish to know by what process our thought has moved, and in what sense we can ascribe validity to it: and we call this enquiry rational theology, the enquiry into man's natural knowledge of God.

But is it the enquiry into *man's* natural knowledge of God, or merely into ours? Can we reasonably take the spontaneous reflections of modern men, of Christians, even of would-be philosophers, as typical of those original apprehensions by which man has seen the shadow of God in nature? No, we cannot take them as typical; but we are bound to take them as standard. There are certain fields in which the typical gets us nowhere, and we always do think by standards. No one thinks of virtue or excellence of any sort in terms of Gallup polls. All species of mammals are equally mammalian, but not all wise men are equally wise: we are bound to think of wisdom proper as a true or perfect wisdom, and men as wise in so far as they approach to it. Now natural religion seems to be a sort of wisdom. No doubt an uninstructed Hottentot can be as *religious* as a Christian philosopher, in the sense of being as whole-hearted about the religion he has. But his religion is not so high a wisdom, and we only call his beliefs beliefs about *God* in so far as they approximate to some standard theistic belief. And what is our standard belief? It must be what we believe ourselves: it is nonsense to pretend to believe and at the same time to pretend that a belief other than our own is our standard of what should be believed. Some students of the religious history of mankind, for certain limited purposes belonging to their art, have attempted to find flat-rate definitions of theistic belief, equally valid for all instances: the results are depressing. What are we to say if we are to keep the Hottentot on board without crowding the Christian into the water? Shall we call the divine 'A non-natural power able to help or harm and open to conciliation by ritual practice'? One sees the Christian on his toes to dive out of the ship which sails under this device: and if you can keep him on board, it is only by exploiting the shameless ambiguity of the formula. The Christian does not mean by 'conciliating' God what the Hottentot means, nor does he mean the same by 'non-natural power', nor, to start with, has he the same ideas about what is natural and what is not.[1]

Indeed, the search for flat-rate definitions in religion is an unprofitable exercise: and if we let our thought take its natural course, instead of making it hobble down pseudo-scientific alleys, we shall all think of 'religion' as covering the religion we believe, together with other systems of belief in so far as they approximate to that. For the moment we are discounting supernatural revelation, and considering natural religion: by which we are, therefore, bound to understand our own apprehensions of God through nature, together with those of the Gentiles, so far as they participate in or approximate to the form of our own. Men have always been apprehending the shadow of God in Nature, but in many partial aspects and under much confusion of mind: the first apprehensions were not the best: *quasi pedetemptim intravimus in cognitionem veritatis.*[2]

---

[1]    See note 2 in Chapter V for comments on Farrer's use of the term 'Hottentot'. In this paragraph, however, Farrer seems to have something more specific in mind than mere 'primitive religion' – namely, animism and a certain theory of propitiating nature deities. Perhaps less contentiously, then, Farrer is here exploring the difference between philosophical theism and animistic polytheism. Given Farrer's quotations from Alexander Pope's *Essay on Man* later in this chapter, it is interesting – if somewhat disconcerting – to note the similarity between Farrer's 'Hottentot' and Pope's famous 'Indian': 'Lo, the poor Indian! whose untutor'd mind/Sees God in clouds, or hears him in the wind;/His soul proud Science never taught to stray/Far as the solar walk or milky way;/Yet simple Nature to his hope has giv'n,/Behind the cloud-topp'd hill, a humbler heav'n.' See *The Poems of Alexander Pope, Volume III, Part 1: An Essay on Man*, edited by Maynard Mack (London: Methuen, 1950/New Haven: Yale University Press, 1951), Epistle I, Section III, lines 99–104 (page 27).

[2]    'It is as it were step by step that we have entered into understanding of the truth.' Here Farrer is apparently citing from memory Thomas Aquinas, *Summa Theologiae*, Part I, Question

The apprehension of God as infinite being and first universal cause may be the quintessence of natural religion, but it lies deeply hidden in the confused thinking of primitive men. They are little aware of the mystery of sheer creation: they are more concerned with particular manifestations of creative power, in the growth of their crops or the child-bearing of their wives. We were saying in a previous lecture that there is only one relation between the creature and the Creator, the single fact of being created: but this single relation is a channel which sometimes runs water, and sometimes runs wine – indeed, what passes through it allows of an infinite variety. We cannot ask 'Does God do nothing for us but create us?' for in our creation all else is comprehended. God never ceases to create us, and he creates us thus or thus. Every distinct act that I perform – for example, my endeavour now to understand and to speak – rests on a distinct intention in God's creative act: everything that flows out in the stream was first in the hidden and inviolable fountain, except the mud which the current scoops up from its bed.

This being so, it is natural enough that the divine cause should be first seen in particular effects, and even thought of as a plurality of particular causes: the spirit of growth causes growth, the spirit of birth causes birth, the spirit of love causes love and so on. And more especially God was seen as the archetype and cause of crucial human functions which were performed with difficulty. The fact that my act of trying to speak or understand reposes on God's creative intention for me does not remove the necessity of effort on my part: but that effort is made more fruitfully, I trust, and with fuller confidence if I remember the creative act on which it is founded. And so I, because it is my business, if I can, to think, must specially concern myself with the figure of God considered as archetypal wisdom.

In primitive societies in which the tradition of learning and the rule of discipline were imposed by paternal authority, the father saw himself as the representative of a divine and archetypal father, who might, in fact, be an actual or supposed human ancestor, clothed with the functions of ultimate and creative paternity. When human kings arose, invisible divine kings stood behind their thrones. Indeed, kingship worthy of the name is distinguished from mere leadership by the divinity which supports it. Now, if kings arose with divine support, we might suppose that the divine king was already known: for how can the human king be clothed with divine authority except by a divine king already acknowledged? But then, on the other hand, until men have seen human kings, how can they know what a divine king would be? In fact, the human king and his divine archetype arise at once, they are inseparable: each makes the other. *Caelo tonantem credidimus Jovern regnare: praesens divus habebitur Augustus …*[3]

---

44, Article 2, Answer: *Dicendum quod antiqui philosophi paulatim et quasi pedetentim intraverunt in cognitionem veritatis.* Ralph McInerny translates this as: 'It should be said that the ancient philosophers little by little, and, as it were, haltingly entered into a knowledge of the truth.' See Thomas Aquinas, *Selected Writings* (London: Penguin Books, 1998), 363.

[3] Horace, *Odes*, III.v: 'When Jove thunders in the sky we are accustomed to believe that he reigns there; Augustus will be accounted a visible deity …' (lines 1–2). David

The divine King establishes human royalty: a new divine archetype stood behind prophecy. Prophecy, in its greatness, involved the endeavour to comprehend and to fulfil historical destiny. The prophet saw himself frankly as a magician, able to predict by the spirit, able also to make and destroy by the powerful breath of his word; but there stood behind him the divine prophet, the cosmic magician, whose word was of such power that its mere utterance had shaped the world out of chaos, its blessings and curses changed the destiny of nations as clay vessels are marred and made under the potter's finger. It was only by communion with the omnipotent master of spells, and in unquestioned obedience to his word, that Isaiah could preach the Assyrian host back from the defences of Jerusalem, or Jeremiah, under a more cruel obedience, could shake down the guilty walls of Zion in face of Chaldaean assault.

The kingly archetype had its origin at a time, a few thousand years before Christ: the prophetic archetype burst on the world in the recorded history of Israel. An archetype of great and still unexhausted power shone upon us in the later Renaissance, when along with the human physicist there appeared the divine physicist, the God of deism, the God of Descartes, who had imposed on the universe by a creative *fiat* that very regularity of iron law which the scientist set out to discover under God's guarantee.

The believer will surely find it an impressive fact that our family, our state, our sense for world-history, our all-conquering science, were brought to the birth under the inspiration of divine archetypes. It is testimony to the power and naturalness of religion, that men have not been able to have confidence in great developments of human function, unless they could apprehend in their working the presence and authority of God. Yet it is an equally impressive fact that the family, the state, history and science, once they have established themselves must be naturalised. Perhaps only a father with supernatural awe to clothe him could have created the civilising patriarchal family, but a father clothed with supernatural awe is a domestic tyrant and a pillar of barbarism: the family must be humanised if civilisation is to proceed. Only a king who ruled by divine right could establish a state on something wider than the ties of blood, and something less cruel than force: but kings are not, in fact, 'earthly gods' nor magical persons: political power is human, and intelligible, and politics must be rescued from stultifying hierarchy. Nothing, perhaps, but the prophets' dramatic attempt to predict and wield the destiny of peoples in the name of God could have created the sense of history as an intrinsically meaningful forward movement: but prophetism must be got rid of before scientific history can begin, for the dynamic of historical process is not rightly estimated by intuitions of a moralistic divine teleology in battles and famines.[4]

---

Brown observes that the third line continues '… when the Britons are added to the empire and the formidable Parthians'. That is, Horace here anticipates further military successes on the part of Augustus, confirming his 'divine' status.

[4]   In *Metaphorical Theology: Models of God in Religious Language* (Philadelphia: Fortress Press, 1982), Sallie McFague writes: 'Austin Farrer, the sensitive analyst of

The most interesting case for us is that which stands nearest to us, the case of physical science. Professor Collingwood, in the most paradoxical of his writings, calls on us to rally round the Athanasian Creed and save scientific civilisation.[5] His reasoning seems to me to contain two serious mistakes – first as to the connexion between Christian theology and scientific deism: second as to the connexion between scientific deism and science itself. The emergence of scientific deism was certainly conditioned, historically, by a long tradition of Christian theologising, but scientific deism was not for all that itself a Christian phenomenon, but an expression of natural religion, emerging as the ground of a purely natural activity, viz. scientific enquiry. Then as to the second error: the connexion between deism and science was not logical, but historical and dynamic. Deism supplied the dynamism which set science afloat, but science can now proceed, like politics or history or family morals, under its own steam, and without any winds of theological magic to fill its sails. Those who prove that science cannot be irreligious in spirit by appealing to the original connexion between deism and science are making things too easy for themselves.

The reason why archetypes become dangerous is that they favour dogmatisms. The father-God archetype, understood in the patriarchal sense, attaches an absolute value to paternal discipline which it does not possess. It suggests that God acts more through a patriarchy exerted over us than, say, through any light inwardly directing us: a doctrine which is as theoretically indefensible as it is practically stultifying. And the divine archetype of scientific deism suggests that God is specially concerned with flat-rate general laws, and leads in the end to a soulless physicalism, a contempt for individuality and a denial of providence.

> The first almighty Cause
> Acts not by partial, but by general laws,

---

religious imagery, nonetheless reveals his "false consciousness" in the following statement in which he appears to recognize neither his masculine bias nor the human construction of social realities: "Perhaps only a father with supernatural awe to clothe him could have created the civilising patriarchal family." From a feminist perspective the creation of the patriarchal family is man's work and has not proved "civilizing" for either men or women' (151). However, two things must be said in reply. First, McFague misleadingly cites only the first half of Farrer's sentence: the second half fully acknowledges her concerns, and is indeed rather progressive for 1948, as is what follows in subsequent paragraphs regarding the dangers of idolising these various archetypes. Second, McFague reads Farrer's use of the word 'patriarchal' according to its later derogatory feminist meaning, whereas Farrer (rightly or wrongly) means simply the actual primitive social units from which (for better or worse) our human civilization gradually emerged.

[5]   Robin George Collingwood (1889–1943), an English philosopher and archaeologist who made important contributions to 20th-century discussions of aesthetics and the philosophy of history. He was Waynflete Professor of Metaphysical Philosophy at the University of Oxford from 1936–41. Farrer is referring to his book *An Essay on Metaphysics* (Oxford: Clarendon Press, 1940).

is, taken strictly, blasphemous nonsense.[6] General Law has no theological privilege. The action of the finite forces of which the world is composed has an aspect of uniformity, and equally an aspect of particularity: each aspect of the creature's functioning is based on a corresponding intention in God's creative act. Indeed the only security against the false suggestions of the archetypes is the reduction of them to creative intentions. God is not intrinsically the principle of general law, he simply intends the uniformity which is proper to his creatures, along with everything else he intends for them. Nor is he intrinsically the principle of paternal authority: he simply wills that it should play that part which it has to play in the perfecting of mankind.

The reduction of the archetypes to creative intentions is only possible to us if we have a highly philosophical, some would say, a highly rarefied, conception of what God is in himself. If he is not to be tied to any of the archetypes, if he is not to be essentially this or that, he must be simply pure and infinite essence. And so a natural apprehension of God which begins by seeing him as the archetype of this or that natural function, is driven by its own practical dangers into the 'natural theology' of tradition. It must come to know God as simply that infinite creative Act which underlies all finite acts.

Let us say, then, of the archetypes that they have a purely historical justification. At a certain time in history God's creative will for man seems specially directed towards family discipline or kingly rule or scientific construction, and then his special creative intention finds a response in his creatures through the projection of the corresponding fatherly, or kingly, or 'scientific' archetype. The archetype then plays the part of a useful rhetorical exaggeration. Kingship is better supported by the doctrine that God is essentially king, than by the doctrine that kingly rule is a thing he approves and intends, a way among many ways for preserving and extending the cosmic order he creates.

We may call the archetypes just rhetorical exaggerations; but the exaggeration they employ has huge spiritual consequences. For once we see God as essentially king, father, cultivator or whatever it may be, then the human counterpart to him becomes a revelation of God, and what he achieves becomes visible and particular divine action. If Isaiah is God's prophet, his word is a divine intervention; if David is the Lord's Anointed, his victories are the hand of God; the astonished eyes of man may watch the act of naked omnipotence, when the Philistines fall before him. If we reduce the archetypes to creative intentions, then nothing in the world (it would seem) is any more a revelation of God than anything else: it is not the king, the prophet or the sage who reveals God: any finite or created being can point us to the infinite and increate; and God must be credited with a special creative intention equally in respect of every creature. God intends the man, he also intends the microbe who kills the man. But if the whole of nature and everything in it is equally sanctioned by the divine will, then by contemplating God we shall learn nothing of practical use which we could not derive from contemplating nature. It sounds very grand and large-hearted to declaim of him:

------

⁶    Pope, *An Essay on Man*, Epistle I, Section V, lines 145–6 (page 33 of edition cited in note 1).

> Who sees with equal eye, as God of all,
> A hero perish, or a sparrow fall,
> Atoms or systems into ruin hurl'd,
> And now a bubble burst, and now a world.[7]

How enjoyable it is to profess our enlightened acceptance of that cosmic will which,

> Lives through all life, extends through all extent,
> Spreads undivided, operates unspent,
> Breathes in our soul, informs our mortal part,
> As full, as perfect in a hair, as heart,
> As full, as perfect in vile Man that mourns
> As the rapt seraph that adores and burns.
> To him no high, no low, no great, no small:
> He fills, he bounds, connects, and equals all.[8]

These are fine sentiments incomparably expressed: but what is the practical conclusion?

> Hearing this descant on omnipotence
> 'So what?' interpolates our practic sense.
> Wisdom replies: Presume not God to scan,
> The proper study of mankind is man.[9]

Precisely. If God is everything, we can make our bow to him, and get on with the business of being something.

Is this the inevitable progress of theology? Must man begin with a fertile but superstitious idolatry of archetypes, reduce the archetypes to creative intentions in one supreme will, and then agree to know nothing about him, except that everything expresses him? We have certainly got to move forward from archetypes to universality, but is the negative road the only road that can be taken? There is another road, and Scripture describes it: it is the road by which God himself has been pleased to lead us. Let us consider it with the greatest possible brevity; and let us, for that purpose, go back again to the beginning of the road, the place where the archetypal images stand.[10]

---

[7]   Ibid., Epistle I, Section III, lines 87–90 (24–5).

[8]   Ibid., Epistle I, Section IX, lines 273–80 (48–9).

[9]   Parodying Pope's *Essay on Man*, Epistle II, lines 1–2 (53).

[10]   In note 63 on page 206 of *Metaphorical Theology* (cited in note 4), Sallie McFague argues that while *The Glass of Vision* is 'impressive' it nevertheless results 'in an absolutism of images and a profound ahistoricism'. She is probably thinking of this chapter in particular. Obviously, Farrer's various proposals are problematic for many contemporary theologians, including some feminists, and are discussed thoroughly in Part II of this volume.

The archetypes, however heathenish they look, hold the promise of revelation. Of Jehovah the King, King David is the instrument; then David's righteous acts are as the acts of God: and if God manifestly acts, that is revelation. David's kingdom failed most evidently to express either the holiness or the power of the God whom Israel knew. This being so, several developments were possible. Crass heathenism would have reduced the image of God to the scale of David. Enlightened rationalism would have abandoned the kingly archetype, and cut the thread connecting God with the throne. The soul of Israel, in the end, did neither: it saw in David the foreshadowing of a holy and universal kingdom in which the Kingdom of God should be adequately expressed. Religion became faith, and looked forward.

But how could that which faith hoped for possibly be realised? The divine King revealed in the kingdom of David would not do, because the kingdom of David was simply a part of nature; it was a thread in the woof of history, and history is a cobweb in the enormous edifice of the world. But suppose that God should act in another way; suppose he should introduce a shining thread into the web, a new David, whose existence should be no mere part of nature, but the supernaturalisation of a natural life, by the taking of it into God? God broke the old kingdom of David through the folly of the kings, the stubbornness of the tribes, and the sword of Nebuchadnezzar, and out of great tribulation he brought a new David, the Son of Man.

If we set out from the place of the old archetypes, there are only two roads we can follow. If human reason is our guide, we must take the negative road, reduce the archetypes to creative intentions, and merge them in the creating mind. This is as much a retreat as it is an advance: an advance in reason and liberty, a retreat from the hope of seeing God. An unequivocal advance does not lie in our power, but only in the power of the God our faith desires to see. An advance from the place of archetypes is only possible by the enhancement of the archetypal relation to a relation of identity. Thou shalt not make to thyself a graven image:[11] God cannot be revealed in picture or in effigy, whether the effigy be a golden calf under Sinai or David enthroned at Jerusalem. No half-measures are possible: only if the image comes alive, if the pictured deity steps down from the golden frame, if God is incarnate, can we say with St John: we know that the Son of God is come; this is the true God, and eternal life; my children, keep yourselves from idols.[12]

When we, from our cool place of historical detachment, study the world of primitive religion, we may speak of the archetypal relation between the God and the king. But to the primitive believer the relation is always more than archetypal, there is a real identity there, at least an identity of action. The Lord's anointed is a present God, or the hand of God. The archetypal relation must be pressed in the direction of identity: it is not good enough to say that the Lord's heavenly throne is the archetype of the mercy-seat in the temple: we must say that in some manner he is enthroned on

---

[11]    Exodus 20.4.
[12]    First John 5.21.

Zion, or the cultus becomes an absurdity. There are, in fact, only two ways in which the archetypal relation can be treated as a dynamic identity: either God must be naturalised, or his expressive instrument must be supernaturalised. God cannot be naturalised, man can merely feign it. But God's instrument can be supernaturalised, for God can effect it. To naturalise God is idolatry: for God to supernaturalise his instrument is incarnation. The religion of Israel was neither idolatry nor incarnation, but a suspense between the two. The religion of the Gentiles tends also to hang in suspense: not so often, however, between idolatry and incarnation, as between idolatry and theistic rationalism. And in so far as modern Judaism loses the Messianic Hope, it must conform, in this respect, to the Gentile type. Let us not, however, be too ready with that reproach, since much that passes for Christianity is in the same predicament, poised between pure rational theology, and a superstitious reverence for a supposed human author to the Sermon on the Mount.

Where there is paganism, genuine mythology can flourish. God being finitized, finite images can properly express both him and his doings. The acts of the archetypal and divine king are the enlarged shadows of what his human image performs. Sometimes they coincide; when David assails the Philistines, the God of battles descends and leads the van. At this level, speech about God involves no philosophical problem. If the divine archetype is reduced to his human image, why should he not be described in human terms? If we take the negative road and move in the direction of pure theistic rationalism, there is no great difficulty, either, in seeing what will happen to the mythology: it will become Platonised. The archetypes have now been reduced to creative intentions in the divine will. David reigned, and God willed David to reign. Whatever is real or positive in David's kingly rule will, no doubt, express a preceding divine intention: what the intention was can be most usefully studied in the effect. We shall, no doubt, view the providence which underlies history as something more than the history; but for the theistic rationalist to form a positive conception of this providence, to give content to this divine thought, can never be a wholly serious exercise. He will be more or less knowingly relapsing into the old finite archetypal theology. He will do so, not because he supposes that the result can have any proper truth, but because (let us say) he wishes to adore the divine providence behind history. But you cannot adore a bare notion, you cannot adore the fact that there is (presumably) providence. Providence must be bodied forth, it must be made *visible á la fantaisie* if it is to be made *sensible au coeur*:[13] so the worshipper of historical providence will allow himself the luxury of a model which is not an idol, an imaginative realisation without claims to particular truth.

The real philosophical problems about mythology arise when we take the other road, and advance under the leading of God from archetypes to incarnation. For here we shall be asserting in all seriousness that God, the true, the infinite God, is both intending and performing particular acts. How can his acts be seen, known, conceived or uttered? If the Lord acted through David his anointed, David's act was natural – the overthrow of Philistia – and God's act was the enlarged shadow

---

[13]   'visible by the imagination'/'sensible to the heart'.

of the natural and earthly act, projected upon the clouds. If God is, in Christ, reconciling the world to himself,[14] there is not even a natural *starting-point*: for Christ's act in reconciling the world is not a natural action. He does the reconciling, indeed, by death, and the death of a man is certainly natural enough: we can all die presently, we need no more than leave off food and drink. But Christ's human death is not, of itself and in itself and as a natural event, the reconciliation of the world: what reconciles the world is an act of God fulfilled through the passion of man. This divine action is the supernatural thing. It is for us as vivid and particular and real a divine action as anything ever conveyed by mythology to a primitive mind. Did God descend from heaven to visit Baucis and Philemon?[15] God visited no less particularly when he entered the virgin's womb. But while Jupiter had only to step down from a definable place above the glassy floor of heaven, the Eternal Word must be gathered from all immensity and begin in Mary to have a place. Even so to speak is to materialise eternal godhead: immensity is not gathered into Mary, but he who is neither immense nor measurable nor in any way conceivable by spatial extent takes place and body, when the Word of God is made flesh.[16]

The ineffable thing happens: for why should not God do that of which man cannot speak? But man must also speak it; or how shall it be known and believed? Man cannot conceive it except in images: and these images must be divinely given to him, if he is to know a supernatural divine act. The images began to be given by Jesus Christ; the work was continued by the Spirit of Christ moving the minds of the Apostles. It was possible for Christ and the Apostles to use the images meaningfully, because the old archetypes were there to hand, already half transformed under the leading of God in the expectant faith of Israel. Christ clothed himself in the archetypal images, and then began to do and to suffer. The images were further transformed by what Christ suffered and did when he had put them on: they were transformed also by their all being combined in his one person. What sort of victorious David can it be, who is also the martyred Israel and the Lamb of sacrifice? What sort of new Adam can it be, who is also the temple of God? And what sort of living temple can it be, who is also the Word of God whereby the world was made?

The choice, use and combination of images made by Christ and the Spirit must be simply a supernatural work: otherwise Christianity is an illusion. Pagan superstition can believe crass mythology, and platonic myths can be handled with discretion by the poetical rationalist, but only God can make the figured representation by which is known for the first time 'what eye hath not seen nor ear heard, what hath not entered into the heart of man, whatsoever God hath prepared for them that love him'.[17]

---

[14]   Second Corinthians 5.19.

[15]   A story from Ovid's *Metamorphoses*, Book VIII, in which the poor and elderly couple Baucis and Philemon offer generous hospitality to two strangers, who turn out to be Zeus and Hermes in disguise.

[16]   John 1.14.

[17]   First Corinthians 2.9.

The Apostolic minds which developed and understood the images of faith performed a supernatural act: but supernatural acts, we remember, are continuous with natural functions, of which they are, so to speak, the upward prolongations. The boundary between the two need be neither objectively evident nor subjectively felt. The apostle would find himself to be performing a sort of activity well-known to the Rabbinic Jew, the activity of seeking fresh insights by the comparison and fusion of sacred images. Only now the images cluster round the central figures of Christ's self-revelation, and the insights sought from them are insights into Christ and his saving work. In his curiously mixed act of thought, half-poetic, half-expository, the apostle might feel himself to be seized by the pentecostal Spirit and to undergo a control not his own. Yet such a seizure was neither the guarantee nor the condition of inspiration: not the guarantee, for compulsive thinking is of itself a purely psychological phenomenon: not the condition, for God can supernaturally mould the thought of the saints apart from it. Inspiration is not a perceptible event.

The images are supernaturally formed, and supernaturally made intelligible to faith. Faith discerns not the images, but what the images signify: and yet we cannot discern it except *through* the images. We cannot by-pass the images to seize an imageless truth. Does this mean that our minds are simply given over to the images, bound hand and foot? Can we in any way criticise the images? Have we, outside them, any rule by which to regulate our intuition of what they mean?

Certainly we have a rule, a rule of a highly general kind, in the conception of God supplied to us by natural theology. The subject of the revealed figurative sentences is God: they must, then, be so understood that God can be the subject of them: and natural theology supplies us with a notion of God, itself analogical, it is true, but, as we said in a former lecture, composed of natural, and criticised, analogies, so that it can be settled and defined by a rational process. When we use this idea of the supreme being as a canon to interpret revelation, we are not importing into revelation something which was originally absent from it. On the contrary: guided and assisted by revealed insight, the apostles plainly did exercise that apprehension of the infinite creator through the works of nature which is the substance of natural knowledge. Had not Christ himself preached the God of nature to them from lilies and sparrows? The apostles were not, indeed, philosophers: but the philosophy of natural knowledge presupposes the knowledge it analyses and refines, and that natural knowledge, in abundant measure, the apostles had. What God bestowed on them through Christ was revelation of God's particular action. They had not known before that God would send his Son for us men and our salvation,[18] but they had known that God was God; and what they now learnt was not that some superhuman Father had sent his Son, but that God had done so. Natural theology, then, provides a canon of interpretation which stands outside the particular matter of revealed truth.

---

[18]  A phrase from the traditional English version of the Nicene Creed in The Book of Common Prayer: faith is professed 'in one Lord Jesus Christ ... who for us men and for our salvation came down from Heaven'.

Again, within the field of revealed truth, the principal images provide a canon to the lesser images. The reduction of the lesser images to terms of the greater is a theological activity, and we see it already proceeding in him who first earned the title of theologian, the 'divine' St John. Christ, the Church taught, must come to be our judge. But, says St John, his judging can be reduced to his coming: the light has only to come into the world, and it shows up the dark patches: and men's judgment is effected by their turning their back on the candle of the world. But when judgment is thus reduced to advent, it is not got rid of. If men are judged by seeing the face of God, they are judged, and their judgment is an additional truth to the truth of the vision, though now subordinated to it. St John is not reducing everything to a confused simplicity. The images which he 'reduces' to terms of others no more disappear or lose their force, than do the whole body of images, when we remember that they are no more than images, and so reduce them to the one ineffable simplicity of God's saving love. All is denied, and all is affirmed: what the Christmas hymns say of God's descent to earth is the stammering of children's tongues, and nothing of it in accordance with the truth of that unspeakable mystery; and yet it is what God has taught us to say, when out of the mouths of babes he would establish praise.[19] We speak because silence is impossible, and when we speak this is how we speak:

*Behold the great Creator makes*
*Himself a house of clay:*
*A robe of virgin flesh he takes*
*Which he will wear for ay.*

*Hark, hark, the wise eternal Word*
*Like a weak infant cries:*
*In form of servant is the Lord*
*And God in cradle lies.*

But now the high celestial throne
Ascribe we as is meet
To him, the Father's only Son,
Who breathes the Paraclete.[20]

---

[19]    Psalm 8.2; Matthew 21.16.

[20]    Farrer here quotes the first two verses of a well-known hymn, with words by Thomas Pestel (ca. 1586–1660), but then concludes with a doxological verse of his own composition.

# Lecture VII:
# Prophecy and Poetry

> O Lord, thou art stronger than I, and hast prevailed. If I say, I will not make
> mention of him, nor speak any more in his name, there is in my heart as it were
> a burning fire shut up in my bones, and I am weary with forbearing, I cannot
> contain.
>
> Jeremiah, XX.7–9

We have been trying to think about divine revelation, as we may see it happening in
St Paul or St John, and we are driven back again and again to the same conclusion.
The moving of these men's minds, or of any men's minds, by divine direction
is in any case a profound and invisible mystery, as is the whole relation of the
creature to the creator; but if we turn from the unfathomable depth to observe
the surface, the perceptible process in the inspired mind, the psychological fact,
then we may say that it is a process of images which live as it were by their
own life and impose themselves with authority. They demand to be thought in
this way or that, and not otherwise. Now such an account inevitably suggests
a comparison with the inspiration of the poet; and to this comparison we will
now turn, though with fear and trembling; for we all know what are the dangers
lurking here. If we fall into doctrinal heresy we shall receive indulgent correction
from the theologians, but if we attempt to define the poetic fact we shall wither
under the scorn of those who show, both by teaching and example, that the Muse
is in the melting-pot.

The Muse is in the melting-pot, and in what shape will she emerge from it?
In her own shape rejuvenated? But has she a shape of her own, or is she a female
Proteus, and unconfined to any special form? If so, is it any use talking of what
she is, let alone comparing her with apostolic inspiration? If, when we begin to
get our fingers round her feline elusiveness, she slips through them in a fish, a
flame or a fountain, can we ever hope to hold her? Shall we ever compel her back
into her proper visage, shall we ever wring oracular truth from this Old Woman
of the Sea?

Is there, indeed, such a thing as poetry, or is every school and age of poetry,
perhaps every poet, a distinct nature? The question is a perfectly possible question
to ask. Theology, by hypothesis, is unchangeable in essence, for in spite of its
various historical manifestations, it has to do with an eternal fact, the relation of
the creature to the creator. But is there any deep and invariable necessity why men
should spin verses, or why, if they do spin them, they should use them always for
the same expressive purpose? Is poetry, like football, just what it happens at any
time to be? For if football was first played in the streets of a town by unlimited
numbers of boys, with rules based on the particular lay-out and hazards of the

pavements and buildings, then football was not what it is now. All football, no doubt, is based on certain invariable facts, such as the aptitude of inflated bladders to bounce and to roll, and the tendency of immature males towards mimic conflict; but these invariable factors do not of themselves determine the nature of football. And poetry appears to be a free play of the mind, and a delight: and if some people have taken it in deadly earnest, what of it? Some people have taken football in earnest, and some people never grow up.

Poetry, like football, rests on certain invariable facts. Man expresses himself by language, and language, being repetitive noise, is capable of musical arrangement. Again, a man cannot apprehend anything without an act of imaginative creation. From these two invariable facts arise the two possibilities of playing freely with the musicality of words, and playing freely with imaginative creation; and out of these two possibilities flows the third joint possibility of making the musical game the expression of the imaginative game. Such a joint form of game may not seem any more inevitable than other mixed forms, say opera or polo. And even granting that men will mount upon the crests of verbal rhythms to play at imaginative creation, it is, again, in no way inevitable that anything serious should come of it; or that if it does, it should fulfil one spiritual function rather than another.

If we compare apostolic inspiration with poetry, it is no doubt with great or serious poetry that we shall compare it. According to some of our most admired contemporaries, 'Sing a Song of Sixpence' is poetry of the purest water; but it offers no useful analogy to the Gospel of St Mark or the Revelation of St John. If only we were concerned with 'Sing a Song of Sixpence' we might claim to be dealing with the eternal essence of poetry, for this sort of thing has been going on since men and blackbirds first began to sing. It is precisely the serious poetry that is so time-conditioned. If I ask myself about the nature of serious poetry, I shall very likely find myself reflecting on what the English poets were doing from Spenser until some time after Keats, from the Renaissance, that is, until the Renaissance Muse began to feel desperately used up, and ready for a plunge into Medea's pot; where they are, let us hope, cooking her up into a fresh youth.[1] But is the spiritual function of great poetry from Spenser to Keats the spiritual function of great poetry, or just the spiritual function of great poetry from Spenser to Keats?

We can, of course, compare what St John was doing with what Shakespeare was doing, but that will not be to compare the essence of inspiration with the essence of great poetry, it will be to compare St John and Shakespeare, a comparison which may have a limited interest. If I do talk about comparing the essence of apostolic inspiration with the essence of great poetry, I am suggesting that one might compare the inspired writing St John produced with the great poetry he might have produced if he had been the recipient of a different sort of gift. Here indeed is a fascinating speculation: let us indulge it a little.

---

[1]   A character in several Greek myths, Medea had a cauldron that was used both to restore youth and cause death.

St John is to be a poet; shall he write in Hebrew, or in Greek? Since we are ignorant of Hebrew, let us plunge for Scylla and shun Charybdis by all means; he shall write in Greek. What medium did the Greek of his time offer to such a poet? The Classical Greek convention was then far more certainly used up and spent than the Renaissance convention is now. If it is now difficult to write heroic lines without appearing to parody Dryden or Pope, it was far more difficult then to write hexameters without parodying Homer or Hesiod. The convention of language limited the subject-matter: if one wrote the old measures, one refined on the old themes. To such a man as St John, standing outside the academic Classical culture, and in the shadow of the synagogue, the composition of Homeric hexameters could scarcely be the vehicle for great poetry; if you want to see the sort of thing likely to result from the attempt, you may read, if you do not fall asleep in the middle, a page of the Jewish pseudo-Sibylline Oracles. What, then, could he do? He must presumably begin a new poetry out of the rhythms of prose. And here he would be more fortunate, for the popular rhetoric of his period had developed an ornate and musical style, with clauses carefully balanced in cadence and length. And these rhythms would easily combine in his head with the balanced clauses of the old Hebrew poetry, as that poetry could be felt even through the jagged barbarity of the current Greek version. What sort of thing, then, should we expect him to write?

> These are they • that issue
>      from the great • tribulation:
>           Who have washed • their garments
>                and who have • whitened them
>                     in the blood • of the Lamb.
>
> Therefore are they • in presence
>      of the throne • of God:
>           And do him • service
>                both by day • and by night
>                     within his • sanctuary.[2]

In any case St John's poetry would have to be a rhythmical prose; the lines need scarcely have differed from the loftiest phrases of his actual prose writings. So much for manner; now for the matter. For however an inspired apostle and a poet may coincide in style, their functions are surely very different. Well: but so far as matter is concerned, St John is decisively attached to the Jewish tradition, and not the Greek. If, then, an Israelite wrote great or serious poetry, what was it like? An Israelite might certainly write simple love-ditties, or simple dirges, or drinking songs. But great poetry, I take it, is supposed to express something more complex than a simple emotion of love, grief or pleasure: it is supposed to express

---

[2]   Revelation 7.14–15, as translated and arranged by Farrer.

the texture of human existence, or the predicament of man. Could the Israelite do this except by way of psalm, or prophecy, or prayer, or devout meditation, or theological epic? Is great poetry, in the sense in which Shakespearian tragedy is great, conceivable in Israel, otherwise than as sacred utterance? And is Israel singular in this regard? Can one suppose that any really primitive people could have a great and deep poetry which was not religious? If not, we may wonder whether we have been asking the right question. Should we ask what is the relation between religious inspiration and great poetry, or should we not rather ask how the inspiration of great poetry ever came to be secularised?

As a mere fact of historical process, we can see the secularisation take place under our very eyes. In the pagan classical culture, mythological epic and ritual drama were progressively humanised. Gradually the poets cease to write about the gods as real persons who govern or intervene, and must be served and propitiated: they become names for the aspects of human destiny. Aphrodite is no longer anything but the passion of love itself. But in so far as this passion is still personified and divinised, a common essence is felt to be expressed in all loving. This gives the poets something to write about. They are not novelists, elaborating the simply particular: they are poets, expressing a common essence extending through multiple experience. The Christian and Renaissance poets clung to the figures of the classical gods, which, though theologically unreal, were real poetically, since they expressed the essences which were still the subject of poetry. Keats wrote an ode to the god Autumnus, not a description of an autumn day; the personification holds together the various autumnal features in a single essence which, without the personification, would fall to pieces. Shelley invents an endless new mythology, the spirit of this, and the spirit of that: soberer minds have been content with a single goddess, Nature.

Now in our day, perhaps, the Olympian gods who suffered a theological death 1,600 years ago, are undergoing poetical death, their last dissolution. This may be a fact of higher importance than appears. Whether the poets have now got any essences to write about, and whether, in the lack of them, they will be driven either into prose, nursery rhymes, or true religion, I would not venture to suggest. The Muse is in the melting-pot, and I cannot see what is happening to her: though I do seem to catch glimpses of some severely theological shapes forming here and there in the molten mass.[3]

Those of us who are not quite up to the guessing-game around the melting-pot, form our instinctive opinion of poetry from the happy post-Renaissance period, so let us return to that. It seems that the great poets of this period wrote with an implicit faith, of which they might be wholly unaware, in human existence as something infinitely deep and rich, and as having a common essence throughout. One took up some symbol which for any reason obtruded itself, whether the figure

---

[3]   Farrer is perhaps alluding here to T.S. Eliot (1888–1965) – the 'Mr Eliot' referred to in the final lecture – as his religious poems *Ash Wednesday* (1928) and *Four Quartets* (1936–42) had been published by this point.

of a dead god or the story of a Danish prince, or some more common object of natural experience, and one set it moving by poetical incantation. It moved, it controlled the words, it insisted on acting and expressing itself in one way and not another. The resultant verse had a certain inevitability: that was the thing. One reads it and says that it is right, or true. Right or true about what? Not simply about the particular object, whatever it may be, of the poet's imaginative experience – when we say that it is true we are not simply saying that something has really been imagined, and that the imagination has really been expressed. We are saying that, no doubt, but we are saying also that the expressed imagination has great and wide symbolising power. It is a sort of focus into which is drawn together much that seems to us most important in the common essence of our human existence. The phrase which is just right has infinite overtones: or it awakens echoes in all the hidden caves of our minds.

The problem of the meaning of such poetry cannot be understood in independence of the problem of meaning in general. How any word succeeds in meaning anything is a mystery which almost defeats philosophy on the threshold of her enquiry. A word is, of itself, simply a sound in my mouth or the shadow of a sound in my brain. Yet I use it with significance – because, we may think, the imaginative representation of that to which the word refers accompanies the word. But this simply is not true. Even if I say something simple, like 'dog', I am not commonly aware of any imaginary dog trotting in the field of fantasy; and if I use the name of something highly complicated, like 'post-Renaissance poetry', there is no question of a corresponding object being represented in imagination. What I feel inclined to say is that when I use the expression I pick up, as it were, a complicated knot, in which are ready tied together threads running to all that variety of ideas for which 'post-Renaissance poetry' is the shorthand expression. Thus, if I say the expression and know what I am saying, I have got all the threads in my hand; and I can easily follow any of them I like back to the idea to which it leads. And this is true; having used the expression, I can follow it up by looking at one after another of the particulars to which it refers. But my power to take up, in further acts of thought, the references of a word, does not explain in any way how the word is significant now: the fact that I could perform further acts of thought (but may not actually trouble to do so) cannot explain the nature of the act of thought I am performing now. It seems necessary to swallow the mystery, and to say that the things the word means are sufficiently present to our minds to put meaning into the word, but not sufficiently present to clutter up our mental vision with a mass of distinct detail. They are fully present, in fact, through and in our act of using the word, not alongside of it.

In the case of our ordinary practical or logical thinking, it may indeed be hard to say just what threads of meaning any word touches, but anyhow our object is to limit and define meaning: words with vague and indeterminate suggestions are liable to be a nuisance. But it would seem that the words of a poem have an opposite purpose, and are intended to arouse all possible echoes. Of course the poetical line must have a *prima facie* meaning which is fairly simple and determinate like any other sentence: according to the *prima facie* sense we are listening to Hamlet talking about waking and sleeping. But according to a secondary or symbolical significance, the line suggests the repulsion and attraction of death to Hamlet, and Hamlet, placed as he is and feeling as he does, becomes the symbol of heaven knows how much.

Those who revolt from any suggestion that poetry has a symbolical sense are revolting, principally, perhaps, from the suggestion that the symbolical sense can be *stated*, in a number of sentences other than those of the poem itself; and with this objection we may agree. What the poem presents to us is simply two things – first, the literal and obvious sense, whatever that may be, and second, whatever echoes of human nature or destiny or the like the poetry does in fact evoke. But it is with the poetical words as it is with any other words – what they primarily signify is expressed in them, not alongside of them. It is in the act of discourse or of understanding discourse that we apprehend. Though what we apprehend is not the words, what we apprehend is stated in the words; there is no getting behind that mysterious fact. So if I read the words of Hamlet it is in reading those words that I apprehend, first, the imaginary person and predicament of Hamlet, second, whatever of human existence is focussed in Hamlet. It is with the second and vaguer apprehension that we are concerned when we are talking of the high inspiration of great poetry. The mind apprehends life in talking about it, and for the most part we talk about it piecemeal and with some exactitude, and that is the most useful way of apprehending our life for practical purposes. But in talking the language of Hamlet we may grasp our existence or the possibilities of our existence over a wide area and in a richer and more confused way. If we ask just *what* we are grasping, we are returning to the prosaic form of thought and the poetry vanishes.

I know the appalling rashness of such generalisations as that which I have just thrown out; and no doubt it is true, if at all, about some of the significance of some great poetry, and has no right to pass as a general description. Still, if we are trying to compare the inspiration of our apostle with the poetry of a post-Renaissance poet, we must generalise in some way about the poetry, and here is the generalisation we have thought fit to make.

Let us now advance a step further, and ask what must have been happening in the poet's mind if he is to produce poetry having the sort of power which we have attempted to describe. Consciously, perhaps, he is only setting images in motion by rhythmical incantation, and then appreciating a certain way in which they 'ought' to develop and to express themselves. It is this 'ought' which is the heart of the riddle. The poet does not know what sort of an 'ought' it is, except that it is the 'ought' with which his craft is concerned, and that he is able to feel and acknowledge it. But what the poet assumes, the philosopher investigates. We need not here, perhaps, take the investigation very far. It may be enough to say that since, by our hypothesis, the poet is going to produce a symbol powerfully expressive of a deep quality in human existence, what he must feel in the 'ought' is the quality of human existence clamouring for expression and, as it were, pressing upon his mind and directing the manipulation of the poetical symbols. The poet's imagination is responsive to the possibilities of destiny in general as well as to the particular possibility of destiny realised in Hamlet: that is why he sees that he ought to make Hamlet speak as he does, and not otherwise.

Let us say, then, that the post-Renaissance poet is responsive to qualities or patterns of human existence. But here the theologian or even the metaphysician within us is likely to awake, and to say that the actual quality or pattern of our existence is determined by our place in a system of being which transcends ourselves: that in all our existence we are conforming to or falsifying the relation of a creature to its creator, we are denying or actualising a nature which has been assigned to us, we are either pretending to be angels or trying to be beasts, in one direction or another we are forcing the clauses of the charter of our creation. If the poets are sensitive to the qualities of existence, are they or are they not sensitive to all this? Everyone knows the answer: for the most part they are not, or anyhow not directly. There is a subjective bias about post-Renaissance poetry; that to which the poets are responsive, that of which their great poetry is the effective symbol, is life as it is lived and felt by a sensitive and capacious mind. Theological symbols may be found in it, but all they show us at the most is how men think or feel about their destiny in the crises of it: what they say about their relation to God, and not what that relation really is, nor even how what they say compares with the theological truth.

This subjective or human bias is so strong that even poets who have the will to be theological and objective cannot bring it off. Milton ought, according to his own lights, to be showing us two things about Satan: first, how Satan, the proud and rebellious will, thinks of his relation to God, second, how what Satan thinks compares with the truth of his relation to God. And Milton tries to do both things: but according to the experience of most readers, he does not succeed in making such poetry of the second thing, as he does of the first. Satan, the rebel, is a tragic hero, expressing what sort of reaction an indomitable will both beaten and in the wrong can make; which is, further, a particular expression and symbol of the quality of the human will at all times. So much is great poetry: but the true relation of a created will to the creator, and the way in which Satan falsifies that relation, these matters are eloquently stated by Milton, but they do not live with the same poetical life. The mind which reads the poem does not tingle with a sense of the invisible cord binding creature to creator, a cord which we can throttle ourselves by struggling with, but can never break. What the reader's veins do tingle with is the titanic quality of Satan's will.

People say habitually that poetry is not moral, still less theological, truth, it is just life; and we can see well enough what the remark means when it is applied to post-Renaissance poetry. But then we could almost have known *a priori* that it would be so, for the post-Renaissance culture was as a whole devoted to the intoxicating task of exploring the length and the breadth, the depth and the height, of the microcosm man.[4] If the poetry of such an age is 'just life' in the

---

[4]  Alluding to Galatians 3.18–19.

sense intended, it hardly follows that the poetry of every other age will have to be 'just life', too. It may well follow, indeed, that those who have made the post-Renaissance attitude their own will not be able to feel the poetical force of any other poetry, or will only be able to feel it in so far as they can humanise it: but that does not prove that only humanistic poetry is possible, nor that all non-humanistic poetry is really aiming at humanism, even though it has not arrived there.

The speeches of the Almighty in *Paradise Lost* are not great poetry, and one feels about them as one feels about the little heavens appearing in the right-hand top corners of baroque pictures – they are not the principal thing. But the speeches of the Almighty in the Hebrew prophets are the principal thing, in fact they are the whole thing: some of them have a claim to be great poetry, and it is very difficult to humanise them or to say that they are 'just life'. The unreclaimed humanist in all of us may bathe in the court-history of King David, and when we came to 'Would God that I had died for thee, O Absalom, my son, my son', we feel that we are getting our familiar food.[5] But we must also have a faint awareness that we are being allowed a holiday from the proper business of the Old Testament Muse.

But what is the humanist going to do with this?

> Wherefore I will yet plead with you, saith the Lord; and with your children's children will I plead. For pass over to the coasts of Kittim, and see; and send unto Kedar, and consider diligently; and see if there hath been such a thing. Hath a nation changed gods, which are yet no gods? But my people hath changed their glory for that which profiteth not. Be astonished, O heavens, at this, and be horribly afraid; be utterly desolate, saith the Lord. For my people hath committed two evils: they have forsaken me, the fountain of living waters; and hewed them out cisterns, broken cisterns that can hold no water.[6]

According to the humanist formula these lines must presumably express what it feels like to be the member of a people which, falling into bad luck, experiences a superstitious remorse about its neglect of the tribal God. But to say this is to twist Jeremiah's lines. Shakespeare knew that he was writing about human life: Milton tried to go higher, but could not always; then he failed by an inward and strictly poetic test. But Jeremiah is not, in his own intention, writing about human life, but about the Lord God of Israel; and he does not fail by the inward test, we do not see him slipping off the point; we see no evidence of a painful and unconvincing effort to keep the image of God in the centre of the picture. On the contrary, there is a painful effort from time to time to obtrude Jeremiah's private hopes, fears, and recalcitrances; but they are forced back, trampled, annihilated by the Word of God.

If we permit ourselves to think of Jeremiah as a poet, as a man who sets images moving by musical incantation, and allows them to arrange and express themselves as they *ought*, then what are we to say about his *ought*? Partly, like any

---

5   Second Samuel 18.33.

6   Jeremiah 2.9–13.

poet's *ought*, it will be a matter of right musical arrangement, of consistency and force in the images themselves: but that will not be all. The post-Renaissance poet, we suppose, experienced in the *ought* of his craft the pressure of life – what it is to be a man, and alive, and up against destiny, and so on. If it is not 'just life' which presses Jeremiah, then what is it that presses him, and constrains his images?

It is impossible, I am afraid, to answer this question without betraying some definite metaphysical assumptions. If we accept Jeremiah's own assumptions, all is plain. What constrains his images is the particular self-fulfilling will of God, perceptible in the external events of history and nature which God controls, perceptible also in a direct impact upon Jeremiah's inspired mind. If we are not prepared to believe in the perceptibly expressed particular divine will, we can still make some sense of Jeremiah's poetry, so long as we grant an eternal creative act from which the creature cannot escape. If we grant that the self-will of the creature can be experienced by the creature as a straining of its bond with the creative act, then we can say that the prophet dramatises the ineluctable hold of the creator, and the self-punishment of our rebellions; he casts into personal and mythological form the ever varying revenges of eternal Truth upon our restless infidelities. But if we will not concede even this: if there is no ineluctable nature of things except, let us say, economic and political realities, against which Israel rebels: if the only forces of destiny are soulless and lower than man himself, if that from which Israel turns away is not, in any case, a fountain of living waters: then we must say that Jeremiah's poetry corresponds to a visionary and fanatical idolatry only: and if the negations which our lips profess are operative in us at an imaginative level, we shall not even begin to experience Jeremiah's lines as great poetry.

So far we have been stretching the name of poetry as widely as we can: we have attempted to think of Hebrew prophecy and post-Renaissance poetry as coming under the same general description as two varieties of poetry: only, we have said, what presses on the poet, what makes his 'ought', differs in the two cases. But the difference between the two controlling pressures is enormous, and it has such important consequences, that when we have taken them into account we may no longer wish to retain prophecy as a species of poetry.

Let us note first that the control of reality over the post-Renaissance poet, just because it works subjectively, is infinitely elastic. If we are responding to the quality of human existence, subjectively considered, we can imagine and devise the freest of fictions: we can place Miranda in her magic island, and see what she must do and say in such conditions.[7] There has to be a 'must' or there can be no great poetry, but the 'must' merely tells us what the imaginative experiment in human existence *must* be, to be human. It stops us making our invention inconsistent or frigid, it does not stop us inventing. And this fact has given poetry its name: the poet is a 'maker'.[8] Whereas Jeremiah is not in any sense a 'maker'.

---

[7]   A reference to Shakespeare's *The Tempest* (c. 1610–11).

[8]   The English word 'poet' is derived from the Greek word ποιητής (*poiētēs*), which means 'maker'.

He is not stretching this way and that the elastic possibilities of human nature. His objective control does not limit the evolutions of any puppets freely made by fancy: his control tells him exactly what to say, for he is not responding to the quality of human life, he is responding to the demands of eternal will on Israel as they make themselves heard in the determinate situation where he stands.

We do meet the self-conscious poet, the 'maker', in the Old Testament – and we find him somewhat incongruous. 'My tongue is the pen of a ready writer', he declares: 'I recite the things I have *made* upon the King'.[9] He is, in fact, a laureate who has made up a piece of jewelled rhetoric for the marriage of some Ahab to some Jezebel. He is a *maker*, as truly as was any loyal Elizabethan sonetteer; but there is nothing great about the performance. For greatness we may turn to Jeremiah: and there is the greatness, but it is not a 'making'. The Old Testament will supply us with mixed cases, halfway between the 'making' of the psalm *Eructavit* and the prophecy of Jeremiah, for example, the book of Job: but it is the pure case we can most profitably study.

To take now a second difference. We said some while back that we cannot distinguish in post-Renaissance poetry between the symbol, that is, the expressed poem, and its 'message', as old-fashioned people used to say. Qualities and possibilities of human existence, vaguely felt or anticipated in many parts of our minds, find expression in the poem. The poem expresses whatever of the infinite aspects of human existence it does express: what it does not express, it leaves unexpressed. One can never say 'The poet ought to have been saying so and so, but he has only succeeded in saying this'. There is nothing that he ought to have been saying except what he has said. All life is open to him: let him say what the Muse prompts him to say. He may not say much, or he may not say it well, but he cannot say the wrong thing. And what he says is said in the poem: it cannot be put into other words, for other words would evoke different echoes, and would be an expression of different qualities of existence (if of any).

The case of the prophet is not, anyhow, this. What he has got to say is determinate and particular, it is what the Lord God declares and requires on the day on which he speaks. It is designed to evoke not an exquisite and contemplative realisation of human existence, but particular practical responses to God. For this reason it can be put into other words: whether we say 'They have deserted me, the fountain of living waters, and hewed them out cisterns', or say 'They have turned their back on the living God, and made to themselves graven images' the same essential truth is expressed; even though the poetical evocations of 'the fountain of living waters' are infinite, and that expression is far more moving than the

---

[9]   From Psalm 45.1. The opening words of this psalm in the Vulgate, or standard Latin translation, are *Eructavit cor meum*; the Authorized Version of 1611 translates them from the original Hebrew as 'My heart is inditing' but the Revised Version of 1885 translates them as 'My heart overfloweth'. The Book of Common Prayer designates psalms both by their number and by their opening words in Latin, hence Farrer's reference to '*Eructavit*' below.

other. Indeed, the prophet's message might be translated into the flattest of prose, without completely evaporating: though almost nothing that the prophets say in God's name is flat prose. Still, if the prophecy can be put into prose and the poem cannot, does not this seem to show that the poetical character of the prophetic utterance is immaterial – that the prophet is really just a rhetorician, who knows what the substance of his message must be first, and then colours it up with the flowers of speech to make it effective? No, if anything can be known about the prophets at all, this, anyhow, can be known to be false. It is the other way about: poetry, for the prophet, is a technique of divination, in the poetic process he gets his message.

The prophets used, at various times, several divinatory techniques; the more primitive and dramatic of them were handled with great understanding and knowledge by a recent Bampton Lecturer.[10] The prophet divined from what he saw when he looked out of a window, he divined from chance words overheard. An investigation into such divinatory practices is of the highest interest, but it leaves us always with one unsatisfactory reflection. Even the great prophets used these devices from time to time: Jeremiah himself divined from the chance sight of a budding almond, and of a boiling pot. But for the most part the great prophets used no such methods: they simply had their minds charged with the word of God. But in such a case, what happened? Is not the answer really obvious, that poetry itself was the method of divination? Whatever signs or omens set the incantation of shapely words moving in the prophet's mind, it went on moving and forming itself with a felt inevitability, like that of a rhapsodical poetry which allows for no second thoughts: it formed itself under a pressure or control which the prophet experienced as no self-chosen direction of his own thinking, but as the constraint of a divine will. As the prophet speaks his own person is lost, and the person whose utterance the words express becomes the person of the Lord. If this had not been the prophet's experience he would never have dared to give his words as the words of a God who avenged falsification with death, nor would he have been so utterly shattered when what gave itself to him as the Lord's word appeared to be refuted by the event.

What the prophet shares with the latter-day poet, then, is the technique of inspiration chiefly: both move an incantation of images under a control. The controls are not the same, and therefore the whole nature and purpose of the two utterances go widely apart: the poet is a maker, the prophet is a mouthpiece.

Everything that we have said, either about the poet or the prophet, will be likely to cause the psychologist nothing but quiet amusement. He will say something of this sort. When we control our speech by logic and common-sense and constant reference to practical experience, we can keep it objective, but when we set going an imaginative incantation and let what will control it, then the

---

[10]   Alfred Guillaume (1888–1965), whose Bampton Lectures of 1938 were published as *Prophecy and Divination Among the Hebrews and Other Semites* (London: Hodder & Stoughton, 1938).

psychologist knows what will happen. The control will be exercised by the non-rational forces of the unconscious or subconscious mind. This objection opens the door on an endless discussion in which I am neither willing nor competent to engage. I must content myself with forcing the door to again with a single philosophical generality. Our psychological make-up is admittedly an instrument of the most baffling complexity, liable to all sorts of disorders, and certain to colour whatever passes through it. There will be something for the psychologist to study in Shakespeare and in Jeremiah: and indeed the province has not been neglected. But are we to conclude that the waywardness of our psyche prevents reality from exerting any real pressure or constraint upon us, except in so far as we bully and regiment her by hard logic and hard practicality? Does the reality of our friends not shine through our free emotional reactions to them? Do we see men most really when we let ourselves love them, and even poetise a bit about them, when we let our minds free to respond to them, or when we take them to pieces with analytical exactitude? If there is objective reality in the poetising of love, in spite of all its riot of subjectivity, then there seems no reason why the apparent greatness of Shakespeare's poetry should not have something to do with realities of human existence pressing and constraining his fictions: nor is the question of the reality of the divine constraint on Jeremiah's mind excluded by anything we know.

We have been driven into an examination of Hebrew prophecy, because we wanted to know what sort of poetry St John would write if he wrote it. We thought it would be more in the nature of great Hebrew poetry than of post-Renaissance poetry: so we examined the great Hebrew poet, and found him to be a prophet, and therefore, not properly a poet at all. Shall we say, then, that St John is a prophet? If we do, we shall receive confirmation from St John's familiar angel. I am a fellow-servant, says this angel, with thee, and with thy brethren that have the testimony of Jesus: for the testimony of Jesus is the spirit of your prophecy.[11]

No one, surely, can talk about such mysteries of the mind as we have discussed without knowing that he is talking nonsense. There is no question here of proper and exact statement, of a theory of poetry or of prophetical inspiration. All we can do is to distinguish certain real differences, and evoke the inscrutableness, even in our own minds, of the making word. What then shall we say of that word whereby the world was made, or of that utterance more high and more divine, of which the effect as well as the begetter is Almighty God, whereby that Son is constituted in being, of whom it is written, 'His generation who shall declare?'[12] *To whom, therefore, with the Father and the Holy Ghost, be ascribed, as is most justly due, all might, dominion, majesty and power henceforth and for ever.*

---

[11]    Revelation 19.10.

[12]    Isaiah 53.8; also read and cited by the Ethiopian eunuch in the New Testament in Acts 8.33.

# Lecture VIII:
# The Poetry of the New Testament

The voice said, Go, take the book which is open in the hand of the angel that standeth upon the sea and the land. And I went unto the angel, bidding him to give me the book. And he said to me, Take it, and devour it.

*Apocalypse, X.8–9*

In this last lecture we must try to draw several threads together and say what we have to say about the movement of inspiration in apostolic minds. We have compared the inspiration of the New Testament with the inspiration of the ancient prophets and with the inspiration (so called) of great poets. We have said something about the prophets and the poets, but about the apostolic writers almost nothing at all. It is in the apostolic field that we need now to apply and work out the comparison.

Let us start by tidying up an apparent inconsistency. A good way back we said about St Paul and St John that they reveal divine truth to us under the form of certain master-images: we gave the example of the Trinity. It was this observation which sent us off on a wide detour, examining the function of images in metaphysics, rational theology, poetry and prophecy. And while all the suggested comparisons proved relevant, the comparison with prophecy was obviously the closest: indeed, we quoted St John's own testimony to show that he regarded his own inspiration as prophetical. What, then, is the inconsistency? It is this: we thought of the divine control over St Paul or St John as developing the images in his mind: the images were the matter of revelation. Whereas in talking of Jeremiah we suggested that the poetical and imaged form was rather a technique of divination than the matter of revelation: in fact, we said, one could translate from image to image, or even into cold prose, without destroying the content. Here, then, we seem to have got prophets whose images are inessential to their message, and prophetical apostles whose images are the substance of what they reveal. But, if this is really so, then the comparison between prophet and apostle cannot be so close as we supposed, and the distance which opens between them touches the very point which is most vital to us, the quasi-poetical movement of images in the inspired mind.

For light upon this difficulty let us return to Jeremiah. We used as our example one of those oracles in which the divine voice pleads with Israel. 'They have deserted me, the fountain of living waters'.[1] The substance of the reproach, we said, could be alternatively expressed, and, we might add, does receive in the prophets a great number of equivalent expressions. Yes, but behind all such alterable images there remain the images which cannot be altered. Behind all divine pleas and

---

[1]   See Jeremiah 2.13.

reproaches there stand the images which give them their sense and bearing: the image of the God who is as man and not as man: the image of the divine word, a spell which makes and mars all human things: the image of the covenant made on such strange terms between God and Israel under Mount Sinai: the image of divine indwelling in the hill of Zion, which is yet only a shadow of a heavenly enthronement: these and so many other images besides. Apart from them the divine pleading and threatening which flowed in sublime poetry through the prophet's brain would have no meaning at all. In the prophets, as in the apostles, we must distinguish between the master-images for which there are no equivalents, and the subordinate images by which the master-images are set forth or brought to bear.

Is this a sufficient clarification of our difficulty? Not quite. We must certainly allow for the unalterable figures, the axiomatic images of faith, which stand behind all the prophet's particular oracles. But they stand behind, that is precisely the difference. Whereas in the apostles the great images of faith are being freshly minted and reborn through Christ's incarnation, in the prophets they undergo no such transformation.[2] It is not the images, nor anything about the substance of the images, that is being revealed in the prophets: the images are taken for granted, and something else is revealed on the basis of them: the particular warnings and pleadings of God.

It is impossible for any Christian, I should even say, for any historian, to deny altogether the validity of such a distinction. The prophets were not publishing a new religion, the apostles were. The appearance of a new religion, and the transformation of basic images, are not simply connected things: they are one and the same thing. There was a crisis of images in the experience of the witnesses to the incarnation which cannot in any case be paralleled in the experience of the prophets. The results are visible in the two sets of writings: the apostles know that they are transforming the images by referring them to Christ, or rather, that Christ has transformed them, by clothing himself with them and dying in the armour. The prophets are not aware of any such transformation: so far as the fundamental images of their faith are concerned, they see themselves for the most part as pure traditionalists, appealing over the head of a degenerate and paganized monarchy back to Moses and David.

Nevertheless we cannot say that the revelation through prophets was not a revelation of fundamental images, but merely of something else erected on the basis of them. It is absurd to say that the great images are 'taken for granted', or that they are buried presuppositions. It is the images themselves that thunder and lighten in the prophetic oracles. It is the covenant, the word, the divine kingship, the session on the mercy-seat, that burst forth with threatening, persuasion and hope, by way of reaction to the abominations of Israelite apostasy and the movements of Chaldaean conquest. The images of faith do not only reveal themselves freshly when they are undergoing alteration: they reveal themselves continually by always

---

[2]   This idea of the images being 'reborn through Christ's incarnation' is further explored in Farrer's next book, *A Rebirth of Images: The Making of St John's Apocalypse* (Westminster: Dacre Press, 1949).

being alive. We may compare our own experience: divine mercy is always the same, we are receiving no new revelation about it. Yet in being always the same it is always new; try as we may we cannot take it for granted. Every reconciliation to which Mercy brings our foolish will is a new miracle: it is as familiar and as unexpected as the greenness of each succeeding spring.

Thus the divine pleadings in the prophets reveal the images of faith for what they are, and have always been. Yet this is not the whole truth. For the fundamental images do not simply remain what they have always been in the prophets: in being expressed and applied, they change their nature very gradually, and as it were invisibly. For the religion of Israel, considered as a total phenomenon, was always in suspense between idolatry and incarnation: and the breath of inspiration in it blew always towards incarnation and away from idolatry. For this reason the fundamental images are being continually and imperceptibly reinterpreted in the direction of a supernatural sense, even though the prophets themselves do not know it. The presence and act of deity so fill the images that all past or contemporary embodiments of them are rejected: God must make a *new* covenant, he must circumcise the *heart*, he must raise up a *new* David, the earthly vessel of heavenly grace must be made worthy of it; not by itself, but by grace. The prophets do not know that the images are changing their natures – they do not know that the true temple will have to be no temple, but the flesh of the Virgin's Child. But they are so purifying and exalting the image that nothing merely natural will ever be able to embody it. In this sense the great images themselves are undergoing change in the prophets: and the act of soul by which this happens in them is a supernatural act, it is the process of the incarnation of God preparing its own way and casting its shadow before.

It is not, then, that a slight change of basic images was revealed in the prophets, and a different and greater change in the apostles. There is only one change: in the prophets the images are prepared for this change by being detached from their earthly moorings and drawn back into the hands of God; in the apostles we see the images already refashioned by the fingers of the divine potter. In the prophets the image of the kingdom is driven towards the clouds: in the gospel the clouds are parted, and the kingdom comes down in the Son of Man.

We see, then, that there are both in the prophets and apostles master-images and subordinate images. The master-images are undergoing change in both prophets and apostles, but not in the same manner or degree. Neither prophets nor apostles are inspired to devise simply new master-images. That is an impossibility. It is only through images already implanted that revelation grows. But the images, in growing, are transformed, they throw out fresh branches, they fertilise neighbouring and as yet purely natural imaginations.

Let us now leave the special problem we propounded concerning the prophets and the apostles. Whatever differences have to be acknowledged, they do not bear on the point we are just now most concerned to make: prophets and apostles alike are inspired by a quasi-poetical movement of images. I wish now to illustrate the quasi-poetical character to be found in the New Testament writings: I wish to show that the sort of criticism of most use for getting to the bottom of the New Testament is often more like the criticism we apply to poetry than we might incline to expect.[3]

I will take one of the most famous and the most discussed of critical problems, the ending of St Mark.[4] We all know that the last twelve verses of this gospel, as they are printed in our bibles, have no defensible claim to be genuine. They were added by a competent scribe to round the story off and bring it into parallel with the conclusions of the other gospels. We know that the other evangelists read St Mark before they wrote their own books, and the evidence strongly suggests that they had no more of St Mark before them than we have: their Mark ended where our genuine Mark ends, with the flight of the women from the empty sepulchre.[5] So we ask ourselves whether St Mark in fact ever wrote, or meant to write, any more. There is, of course, no difficulty in supposing that just as St Mark reached the words 'for they were afraid', a heavy hand descended on his shoulder, and a heavy official voice pronounced the fateful words: 'Here, what's all this? You'd better come along with me to the pretorium', and so the saint's literary career came to an abrupt conclusion. Alternatively we may suppose that he finished the book, but his housekeeper used the last page of it to light the fire, and he always told his friends that he would rewrite it one day, but he never did. Suppositions of this kind are easily made, but those who have played the game of history longest and hardest will probably agree that the fewer of them we have to make, the better it will be. So far as our evidence goes, St Mark decided to end his gospel at verse eight of chapter 16.

But could he have done so? That is what learned men have asked themselves. I am not so much concerned with the proper answer to this question, as with the meaning of the question itself. If you say '*Could* he have taken his pen off

---

[3]    As Farrer indicates, his application of the techniques of literary analysis to the New Testament was – at this point – highly unusual. Farrer was thus a pioneer in this important development, which has since become more common but which still remains somewhat controversial in biblical scholarship.

[4]    Farrer later discussed this 'critical problem' in *A Study in St Mark* (Westminster: Dacre Press, 1951), 172–81, and *St Matthew and St Mark*, Second Edition (Westminster: Dacre Press, 1966 – first edition published in 1954), 144–59. In *A Study in St Mark*, Farrer defends in a more academic manner the position presented in the remainder of this chapter, namely that Mark 16.8 can be reasonably regarded as the original ending of the Gospel, based on purely 'literary' arguments. However, it is important to bear in mind that in *St Matthew and St Mark* Farrer later revised his position and argued for the plausibility of an additional, lost final phrase that was removed when the 'new ending' of Mark 16.9–19 was added. Commentators such as Helen Gardner and Frank Kermode seem more interested in engaging with Farrer's earlier arguments: see David Jasper's chapter in Part II for further detail.

[5]    In the Authorised Version (1611): 'And they went out quickly, and fled from the sepulcher; for they trembled and were amazed: neither said they any thing to any *man*; for they were afraid.'

the paper there?' what do you mean by 'could'? Some sort of a psychological difficulty, no doubt, is intended. *Could* he have felt that this was the proper place to stop? Well, why not? You cannot obviously mean 'He could not stop here, because things still went on happening after the women fled from the tomb'. Of course they did. History does not stop. St Matthew, whose conclusion nobody cavils at, stopped short of the Ascension and Pentecost, though they are integral parts of the saving mystery. Nor can you mean 'He cannot stop yet, or he will have left us in ignorance of the principal thing, the Resurrection Christ', for those to whom he writes know about that in any case. Before their baptism they were taught the formula 'He rose again from the dead according to the Scriptures, and appeared first to Cephas, then to the Twelve'.[6] Nor can you really mean (as is sometimes suggested) that he cannot stop yet, because his previous story contains hints of things still to be described, for example, St Peter's restoration to grace. For this consideration proves too much: the gospel story contains hints of all sorts of future things which cannot in any case form part of its concluding narrative – the descent of the Spirit, the mission to the Gentiles, and the fall of Jerusalem. Nor is it a question of logic. If St Mark is writing the history of Christ's earthly life, it is reasonable enough for him to end with his burial – an attempt was made to dispose of his body in the usual way, but when they came back to complete the funeral rites, it was no longer to be found – faith knows why. So ends the story of Christ's earthly life: what would follow would be the story of the Risen Christ and of the Church.

When we object that St Mark could not end so, we mean none of these things. We mean that the conclusion lacks poetical inevitability, just that. In spite of our conventional sniffs at St Mark for not writing grammarian's Greek, like Lucian of Samosata, we pay him an unconscious literary compliment; his supposedly artless story holds us as Lucian's artfulness never could (even if Lucian had ever had anything to say). St Mark has built up in our mind strong poetic expectations: we feel them to be disappointed by his conclusion, and we cannot believe that such a writer could have written so ill.

The debate, then, is a literary debate: and if we try to defend the abrupt ending, we must do it by literary arguments. We must try to persuade ourselves that we have been missing the true poetic pattern of the book: either, like some of Mr Eliot, it defeats us at first sight through our failure to pick up the crucial literary allusions; or we have been reading it through a haze of memories from St Matthew and St Luke, and not in its own clear light. The purpose of our arguments must be to show that the last line is inevitable in its finality – we must show that, so far from its being impossible for St Mark to stop here, it would be impossible for him to go on.

I am not so foolish as to think that I can here and now make a decisive contribution to the controversy. But I shall say a little more about it by way of

---

[6]   First Corinthians 15.5 – citing creedal material that Paul says he had 'received' in turn from earlier Christians. 'Cephas' is Peter.

illustration; I do not want you to be convinced that my argument is conclusive, I want to persuade you that it is the proper sort of argument for the purpose, and that it belongs to the *genre* of literary criticism.

What we desire to show is that the conclusion has poetical inevitability. The best way to suggest what this poetical inevitability would be, is to compose a short copy of verses which would give expression to it. Suppose we say something like this:

> 'Now walks Barabbas free, and Christ is bound.
> The sun is up: our hope is underground.
> Come, Mary Magdalen, Salome, come,
> With funeral odours grace the guarded tomb'.
> Seeking immortal Act among the dead,
> They heard his angel, trembled, turned, and fled.

Now if you say to me 'Go on: give us another pair of rhymes to tell us what happened after that' I shall break all the strings of my lyre, and hang myself upon a willow tree.[7]

My verses end where they do because, I hope, they have said what they set out to say. The act of God always over-throws human expectation: the Cross defeats our hope: the Resurrection terrifies our despair. Is this what St Mark, also, wanted to say? It would not be surprising if it were. A theme which stands out as clearly as any other in his passion narrative is that no man knows what to do with the divine when it falls into his hands: we are reminded of the Philistines in uneasy possession of the Ark of the Covenant.[8] A woman tries to anoint the Lord for glory, only to learn that she has fore-anointed him for burial. The apostles attempt heroics in defence of Christ, but when it comes to it they forsake him and flee, that he may remain and die for them. The priests condemn him to preserve their priesthood, but in condemning him they tear up their priesthood and overthrow their temple. Pilate crucifies him, falsely accused of claiming the earthly shadow of an eternal kingdom which is actually his. The Arimathaean carefully buries him whom no sepulchre can hold, and the women, not understanding why his fore-anointing for burial with that festal nard had been providential, bring funeral myrrh to embalm the already risen God. The mere rustling of the hem of his risen glory, the voice of the boy in the white robe, turns them to headlong flight: 'and they said not a word to anyone, for they were afraid'. Do we stop there or do we go on? I think we stop.[9]

---

[7]    An allusion to Psalm 137.2 – except in the psalm the *instruments* are hung upon the trees, not the musicians!

[8]    See First Samuel 4–6.

[9]    But see note 4 above for Farrer's later change of mind. 'The Arimathaean' is Joseph of Aramathea, in whose name Farrer finds significance, as discussed below.

This is to decide the question simply on the grounds of theme. Such a treatment cannot, of itself, be sufficient. We must judge it equally on the grounds of phrase.

'And issuing forth they fled from the sepulchre, for trembling and panic possessed them: and nothing did they say to any man, for they were afraid.' Has that the ring of finality? But in whose ear? Not in the ear of the student of Attic oratory, perhaps, or even the student of biblical Greek in general. But in the ear of the reader of St Mark? St Mark builds up his own rhythms, which gradually work themselves into our heads as we read his gospel through from the beginning. The element of rhythmic repetition is so obvious in this gospel that guileless critics have been led to see in it nothing but a string of spoken anecdotes, one reflecting the pattern of another with childish iteration. But the formal recurrences are St Mark's poetical magic: one paragraph subtly echoes another, emphasising persistent themes and throwing variations into relief.

Is it natural, upon this background, that the flight of disciples should provide a termination? Let us consider the parallel between two sections, one describing the last experiences of Jesus in the body at the hands of his disciples, the other describing the body of Jesus in the hands of his disciples after his death. The first section, which is much the longer, provides the following sequence: When Jesus was at supper, a woman brought a jar of nard and anointed him: a good work, he said, for they would not have him always – she had fore-anointed his body for burial. Presently Jesus is seen at supper again: he gives his disciples his sacramental body, and says to them: after I am risen again I will go before you into Galilee. In the garden he admonishes them – especially three of them – to watch, but they are taken unprepared by the catastrophe: all forsake him and flee, among them a youth in a linen cloth, who left it in his pursuer's hands to make good his escape.[10]

The second sequence is this: Joseph obtains the body of Jesus from Pilate, and buries it, wrapping it in a linen cloth: three women bring perfumes to embalm it. Entering, they see a youth in a white stole. He bids them tell the disciples that Jesus goes before them into Galilee, as he had said to them (at the Supper). The women flee, saying nothing to anyone.[11]

We may list the common features of the two sections. A woman in the one case, women in the other, come to perfume the body of Jesus: Jesus himself says that the first perfuming is what the second was intended to have been, a funeral anointing. In the first section Jesus prophesies that he will precede his disciples into Galilee: in the second the prophecy is explicitly recalled. In the first Jesus gives his disciples his sacramental body, which it really concerns them to have: in the second, disciples obtain and vainly wall up his physical body, which they are unable to keep. In both a symbolical part is played by a linen cloth – the youth in the garden is stripped of one, the sacred body is wrapped in one. The word 'linen cloth' is rare – St Mark does not use it elsewhere. In both 'a lad' (again the word is confined to this pair of texts) 'clad in' some named garment

---

[10]   See Mark 14.1–52.
[11]   See Mark 15.41–16.8.

plays a prominent part. In both a sudden catastrophe falls on disciples – the women at the sepulchre, the three special watchers in Gethsemane with their companions: and in both they react in the same way – by flight.

Of these points of comparison, the symbolism of the two linen cloths and of the two 'lads clad in' this or that attire may be completely opaque to us, but if we allow ourselves to neglect them for the present, we cannot be in any great doubt as to the sense attaching to the rest of the parallel. Jesus had said that the anointing at Bethany was – by anticipation – his burial-anointing: yet the women come and try to anoint him on the third day. Jesus had given his disciples his crucified body after a heavenly manner at the Supper, likewise by anticipation: yet they attempt to secure and reverence his crucified body after an earthly manner in the tomb. Jesus had promised them that he would be before them in Galilee; but here they are looking for his body outside the walls of Jerusalem. Jesus had many times forewarned them of the passion: he had as often promised them the Resurrection. The first breath of the approaching disaster caught them unprepared in the garden: the first sign of the dawning joy caught them unprepared at the tomb. The enemy's envoys grabbed a lad's shirt in the garden, and met in him and in the rest with no reception but headlong flight. The Saviour's envoy appeared as a lad in a robe at the tomb, and met with no reception from the women but headlong flight.

We see, then, that the firm ending to the Gethsemane episode prepares us to find a firm ending in the last words of the sepulchre episode. But we have not yet completed our task. 'Flight' is the last word in Gethsemane, and that seems a firm ending. But at the sepulchre 'they said not a word to anyone, for they were afraid' is the last word, an addition which may appear a weak ending. It may, so long as we confine our attention to the parallel we have so far drawn out. But the episode of the tomb, being the last in St Mark's Gospel, may be expected to awaken echoes from many of the preceding pages, as well as from the narrative of Gethsemane. The narrative of the tomb is the last and greatest of the miracle-stories, and so it challenges comparison with the preceding stories, especially those of healing: for in his own resurrection Christ finally displays the principle of power by which he raised up the sick and the dead. We remember, then, how the healings of the ministry were again and again followed by popular proclamation, even though Christ enjoined silence. 'See that thou say nothing to any man', said he to the leper: but the leper went forth and began to publish it much.[12] Now at last the day for publication has come, and the women are tongue-tied. The angel said, 'Tell his disciples and Peter', but they went forth and said nothing to any man, such was their fear.

The phrase about silence is therefore no weak addition or apologetic device: it keeps up the theme of human perversity to the last, and gives it its final expression. St Mark is writing 'the Good Tidings of Jesus Christ, the Son of God', as his title declares.[13] The Good Tidings are summed up in the Resurrection of the Son of God;

---

[12]   Mark 1.40–45.
[13]   Mark 1.1.

now Christ is risen, and the gospel is laid upon the women's lips by his angel. But they 'said nothing to any man, for they were afraid'. St Mark offers small comfort or support to believers in natural wisdom or virtue. Nothing earthly, not even Jesus in the flesh, not the healing touch of those blessed hands, or the divine persuasions of his tongue, not the spectacle of his passion or the angelic tidings of his resurrection, nothing but the Godhead of Jesus apparent in his risen being could lift men up to take hold of the life of God. Not until Peter and the rest were apprehended by the Lord of Glory in Galilee would they be made to stand, for Godhead itself would have come upon them, from which we can no more run than we can from the dawn. Then they would be made wise, and filled with the preaching. The message of an angel was not enough: the women ran from him, and were dumb.

In conclusion to this matter, we ought perhaps to say something of the linen winding sheet, the boy in linen, and the boy in a white robe. There is surely some symbolic motif here, if we could only hit upon it. It is not that there is anything inexplicable about the facts. In the scuffle at Gethsemane one disciple hit out with a sword before he ran: another left his coat in his pursuers' hands. Yet why does St Mark trouble to mention it, and why (still more) does he trouble to tell us that it was 'fine linen'? Again, the Arimathean, burying Jesus' body, would of course wrap it: but why does St Mark tell us so, and why does he specify the stuff as 'fine linen'? Again, all tradition knows that the women were met by an angelic vision, but where else in scripture is an angel described as 'a lad in a white robe'? Is not St Mark turning his three phrases for the sake of allusion to one another? But if so, what is the point?

The confusion and flight of the disciples in Gethsemane is revealed as the natural effect of their failure to watch: they had fallen asleep, they could not watch one hour, so they fell into temptation. Now the priestly watchers in the temple who were caught sleeping on duty were beaten and had their robes taken from them; to which St John makes allusion in his Revelation, when he is inspired to say in the name of Christ: 'Behold I come as a thief: blessed is he that watcheth and keepeth his garments, lest he walk naked and men see his shame'.[14] Thus, the young man's loss of his linen coat is a dramatic symbol of the idea, 'Caught asleep on duty'. The sleeping guard, whose robe was snatched from him, was stripped of honour, and must slink naked away. The naked body of the crucified is wrapped in fine linen, to bestow honour upon it, and that its nakedness may not appear. It is part of the pathos of human burial that we bestow honour in vain on what must decay: it is part of the irony of the burial of Christ's body that men seek to wrap in the decency of funeral respect the flesh which God will immediately clothe with the radiance of glory, that mortality may be swallowed up in life. When the women come to anoint him whom Joseph had shrouded, he already wears the white stole of immortal being: his angel wears it when he gives the women his message. Those who fled from Gethsemane lost their honour; Joseph vainly sought to spread human honour upon the crucified; the angel in the tomb revealed the unspotted honour of heaven.

---

[14]  Revelation 16.15.

The three texts about the boy in the garden, Joseph's shrouding of Jesus, and the boy in the tomb, are held together by verbal echoes: they are also held together by the name of Joseph. The name of the Arimathean is remembered among so many names of minor persons forgotten, because it is significant. Joseph the Arimathean was indeed a Joseph, for as he had begged Pilate's permission to bury Jesus, so Joseph the patriarch had begged Pharaoh's permission to bury Israel, which cost him a troublesome journey.[15] Now just as a Jew could not hear the story of a Joseph who fulfils the pious duty of burial under difficulties, without thinking of Joseph the patriarch, so he could not hear of a boy who leaves his coat in his captors' hands and escapes without thinking of the same patriarch; the story of Joseph and Potiphar's wife being a favourite moral tale for the instruction of the young.[16] Thus, of our three allusions, two are Joseph-themes: but what of the third? Joseph was stripped, first by his eleven false brethren, then by Potiphar's wife: he was buried in prison and believed by the eleven to be dead.[17] But in due course he appeared to them as though alive from the grave, clothed in a robe of glory as the man of the king's right hand: he said to them, 'I am Joseph'. But his brethren could not answer him, *for they were confounded.*[18] Compare the women, confronted not, indeed, with the new Joseph in person, but with one who wears his livery, and unable to speak, *for they were afraid.*[19] A glance at the Greek Old Testament will show the exactness of the verbal parallel.[20] Joseph proceeded to overcome the shame and terror of the eleven who had sold him, and St Mark's readers will know that Jesus is going, in Galilee, to overcome the shame and fear of the eleven who had deserted him: but to include that encounter within his gospel is a thing he cannot do: every sentence in the gospel points a finger towards it, but the poem ends with finality at the words 'for they are afraid'. The rest cannot be written.

We have discussed the ending of St Mark, not to prove a thesis, but to show what sort of argument is appropriate. Such argument belongs plainly enough to the

---

[15]    Genesis 50.1–14.
[16]    Genesis 39.1–18.
[17]    Genesis 37.1–24; 39.19–23.
[18]    Genesis 45.1–3.
[19]    Mark 16.8.
[20]    For a critical discussion of Farrer's argument here, see Robert Titley, *A Poetic Discontent: Austin Farrer and the Gospel of Mark* (London and New York: T&T Clark International, 2010), 64–5. Titley says that the verbal parallel is not as 'exact' as Farrer indicates, and even calls his claim 'misleading'. The Greek of Mark 16.8 is ἐφοβοῦντο γάρ (ephobounto gar), and the Greek of the Septuagint of Genesis 45.3 is ἐταράχθησαν γάρ (etarachthēsan gar). But a more sympathetic reader might place the emphasis less on 'exact(ness)' and more on 'parallel': for there is clearly a striking similarity of phrase, event and response in Jesus' revelation of himself to the women and Joseph's revelation of himself to his brothers. The parallel with the boy leaving his linen cloth in the hands of his pursuers (Mark 14.51–2) and Joseph leaving his coat in the hands of Potiphar's wife (Genesis 39.11–12) is also suggestive. Titley grants this much, but then asks whether it sufficiently establishes what Farrer thought it did (see also 50–3).

criticism of poetry, that is its *genre*. The further we go into the question, the more clearly we see that St Mark's words are shaped by a play of images and allusions of the subtle and elusive kind which belongs to imagination rather than to rational construction. It may be, after all, that St Mark's ending is not good poetry; that there is a clumsiness about it, in spite of all we have said in favour of it. But if it is imperfect poetry, it is still poetry, and our dissatisfaction with it (if we still feel dissatisfaction) is a poetical discontent.

The patterns of theme, phrase and symbol which we have been examining in St Mark do not put before us the sense and substance of revealed truth. No one's salvation depends on the comparison between Joseph with his eleven false brethren and Jesus with his eleven cowardly disciples: or on the antique symbolism of the robe of honour; or on the inverted parallels which give opposite expression to the theme of human perversity. Do not let us suppose that these things are the substance of saving truth. The substance of the truth is in the great images which lie behind, in the figure of the Son of Man, in the ceremony of the sacramental body, in the bloody sacrifice of the Lamb, in the enthronement of the Lord's Anointed. What we have been looking at is a play of secondary images and ideas under the pressure of the great images. Because the great images are alive and moving in the inspired mind, the rhythm of secondary images is set in motion to be their development and application. Through the secondary images the force of the primary images is felt. The passion of Christ will be more powerfully experienced through St Mark's poem than through the bare consideration of the plain idea of it. The Christ of the passion speaks to us through the very words: it is the words we must taste and meditate. If we try to go round behind the words we have nothing but theology, that is to say, nothing but dust and ashes. Theology is an indispensable rule for reading the scriptures: it is not the substance of the word of God.

Conclusions are not of much profit, or much interest – by the time one comes to conclude one has said what is going to be said; to conclude is only to say it again. In a course of lectures such as this there is no sensational discovery saved up for the last page – no last lightning flash of theological detection. But it may still be of use to correct the desultory movement of the exposition by drawing together certain of the themes into an ordered summary.

How does divine truth make itself apprehended by the human mind? Through what is highest, most central, most characteristic in the human mind, the understanding. Supernatural revelation extends the natural power of this faculty, it does not distort or supplant it. The understanding is wit and reason, no more the one than the other. Wit divines its object and begets a representation of it: reason disciplines the product of wit and works out its inspirations to a systematic construction. To know God by revelation man needs both reason and wit; without reason he could not make sense of revelation, without wit he could not receive it. It is the reception, not the interpretation of the revealed truth, which is the mystery: and so we have talked more of wit than of reason.

In what we call the ordinary operations of the mind the working of wit is mysterious enough, but it does not perplex us because we are accustomed to it. It is mysterious enough how wit proceeds when from signs of personal behaviour it divines and pictures another man's mind, or imagines upon indirect evidence the thought of a character in history. But we accept such inspirations without amazement, content with being able to identify the stimulus to which our wit has responded. Never mind how wit has worked, that is her own secret: but anyhow she was working upon the sense-perceptions we had of our neighbour's behaviour, or upon the written words which have descended to us from ancient authors. We are more consciously perplexed when we cannot see to what it is that wit has responded, as often happens in the case of the poet. His wit is creative invention, and yet it is not mere invention: it responds to what we vaguely call the character of human life. Somehow or other the symbol on which his mind fixes awakens unconscious echoes of memory in many levels of his mind, and through these the reality which first imprinted the memories controls the development of the poetic symbol, and makes it deeply and widely expressive.

In the case of divine inspiration the mystery is profounder still: the inspired mind projects images, but to what is it that the formation of the images responds? Not to any diffused sense of human life, but to the supernatural action of God. Christ, perhaps, we can conceive as simply the poet of his own active being, which he as directly knows as any poet knows the movement of his own natural mind. But to others, say to the apostles, the mystery of Christ is communicated by the overflow of Christ's Spirit upon them: what it communicates to them is nothing that they are, but a transcendent mystery which they no more than touch in the fine point of their own supernaturalised act.

Poetry and divine inspiration have this in common, that both are projected in images which cannot be decoded, but must be allowed to signify what they signify of the reality beyond them. In this respect inspiration joins hands with poetry, certainly, on the one side: but with metaphysical thinking on the other. Inspiration stands midway between the free irresponsibility of poetical images, and the sober and criticised analogies of metaphysical discourse. For metaphysics can express its objects in no other way than by images, but it pulls its images to pieces and strips them down in the exact endeavour to conform to the realities. Inspiration does not merely stand at a midway point between poetry and metaphysics; it actively communicates with both. The subjective process of inspiration is essentially poetical, the content it communicates is metaphysical. For inspiration teaches us about God, and God's existence is one of the mysteries which metaphysical discourse describes. Certainly, supernatural inspiration reveals about God what no natural metaphysicising could ever apprehend. But what inspiration reveals, it reveals about God, so that the thought of the sheer deity of God is embedded in the revelation. To think this thought out is to enter on a metaphysical enquiry. Even if we do not think it out, the thought of sheer deity is still the raw material of metaphysics, that is to say, it belongs to the natural knowledge of God. Without it no supernatural revelation can be either received or understood.

If we take something from supernatural revelation and attribute it to natural reason we take nothing from God, for God is all. If we think we take anything from him we must suppose that we give it to another; but that other will also be he. Of all actions and effects he is the first originative cause. He has wonderfully ordained our natural state, and more wonderfully has redeemed it. Nature and divinising grace are his alike, in both he is glorified, and more particularly in the compassion whereby he has grafted grace on our degenerated nature. But all is his. From the Father issues the Eternal Son, to be inbreathed with his co-equal Spirit, and from the threefold fount of deity proceed all creatures, the manifold reflections of immortal love. *Therefore to the One God in Three Persons, Father, Son and Holy Ghost, be ascribed as is most justly due all might, dominion, majesty and power, henceforth and for ever.*

# PART II
## Commentary

Chapter 1

# Metaphysical Philosophy, Scriptural Revelation and Poetry [1985]†

David Jasper

> The lectures which follow are no more than a modest attempt to state what I do, in fact, think about the relation borne to one another by three things – the sense of metaphysical philosophy, the sense of scriptural revelation, and the sense of poetry. These three things rubbing against one another in my mind, seem to kindle one another, and so I am moved to ask how this happens.[1]

These opening words of Austin Farrer's Bampton Lectures for 1948, *The Glass of Vision*, immediately link it with the themes of the present study of Coleridge. There were two major critical attacks on *The Glass of Vision* in the 1950s, one theological by H.D. Lewis in his book *Our Experience of God* (1959), one literary by Dame Helen Gardner in her Riddell Memorial Lectures, *The Limits of Literary Criticism* (1956). Farrer defended himself against both his critics in his paper 'Inspiration: Poetical and Divine' (1963). But the debate has not ended there, for

---

† When David Jasper wrote this chapter he was Chaplain and Fellow of Hatfield College, University of Durham. It consists of a section that formed most of the final chapter of his study, *Coleridge as Poet and Religious Thinker: Inspiration and Revelation* (London and Basingstoke: Macmillan, 1985). Although primarily focused on Coleridge, the book itself begins with an epigraph from Charles C. Hefling, Jr, *Jacob's Ladder: Theology and Spirituality in the Thought of Austin Farrer* (Cambridge, MA: Cowley Publications, 1979): 'Revealed truth does not lie in propositions or sentences or concepts, but in images that are related, compared, and interwoven by inspired imagination' (49). Jasper introduces this section on Farrer as follows: 'Austin Farrer's work in our century may be regarded as the practical working out, in a deeply literary theologian, of Coleridge's notion of Polar Logic. There is little direct evidence of Coleridge's influence on Farrer, and he is chosen, in part, to illustrate the universality of Coleridge's concerns. Farrer was fascinated by the analogy between divine self-disclosure and human self-disclosure, and by the processes of reflection upon the self as made in God's image. He recognised the similarity in the processes of poetry and divine inspiration and the importance of perceiving that while they are ultimately necessarily different, they also require and suppose each other. Farrer was a theologian who read the Bible as a work of literature and whose faith and theology was profoundly affected as a result. Coleridge, in his own day, was a poet who discovered in the literature and poetry of the Bible an enlightening mystery which uniquely illuminated the religious matter of the relationship between man and God, the finite and the infinite' (144–5).

[1] GV ix / 12 [original pagination / this volume].

it has been renewed in the recent exchanges between Professor Frank Kermode, whose book *The Genesis of Secrecy* (1979) rests heavily on Farrer's work on St Mark's Gospel, and again Helen Gardner, in her latest book *In Defence of the Imagination* (1982). This argument involves now a conservative defending herself against a structuralist criticism – and it is the structuralist who looks back to Farrer.[2]

But first the earlier debate should be considered in outline. Professor Lewis first turns his attention to Farrer's statements about the authority of certain images whose terms 'are taken from our finite experience but which have a reference beyond that experience'.[3] Farrer's point in *The Glass of Vision* had been quite clear: 'The choice, use and combination of images made by Christ and the Spirit must be simply a supernatural work ... The images are supernaturally formed, and supernaturally made intelligible to faith'.[4] Lewis respects Farrer's development of his position, that a religious image may be capable of accretions of meaning in new contexts and almost a life of its own. But his questionings begin with what he regards as Farrer's inability to distinguish between these regulative religious images and other images. Lewis's criticism can readily be illustrated from *The Glass of Vision*. Does it help to make the required distinction, for example, when Farrer asserts that 'within the field of revealed truth, the principal images provide a canon to the lesser images'?[5] Or again, that natural theology may provide a rule of 'a highly general kind', affording analogies for supernaturally formed images and 'a rule by which to regulate our intuition of what they mean'?[6]

Lewis does, however, admit the role which natural theology must play. Presumably he would not quibble with Farrer's suggestion that:

> The apostles were not, indeed, philosophers: but the philosophy of natural knowledge presupposes the knowledge it analyses and refines, and that natural knowledge, in abundant measure, the apostles had. What God bestowed on them through Christ was revelation of God's particular action. They had not known before that God would send his Son for us men and our salvation, but they had known that God was God; and what they now learnt was not that some superhuman Father had sent his Son, but that God had done so. Natural theology, then, provides a canon of interpretation which stands outside the particular matter of revealed truth.[7]

---

2    [As its name implies, structuralism is a literary theory that focuses on what it regards as the underlying conventional 'structures' (i.e., fixed forms and symbols) of the text rather than authorial intent or historical context.]

3    H.D. Lewis, *Our Experience of God* (London: George Allen and Unwin Ltd/New York: The Macmillan Company, 1959), 132.

4    GV 109 and 110 / 92.

5    GV 111 / 94.

6    GV 110 / 93.

7    GV 110–11 / 93.

This reflects almost exactly Coleridge's position in the 'Confessio Fidei' (1810).[8] Lewis follows Farrer thus far, but as soon as he moves into the realm of particularity he begins to ask questions. Lewis points out that if the course of God's particular action can simply be educed out of the idea or knowledge of his *being*, then revelation is barely necessary. The question must be asked again, what principle of selection is to be applied to distinguish between the 'principal' and the 'lesser' images?

Lewis criticises the ambiguity of Farrer's account of religion as the 'supernaturalizing of events in the existing world',[9] since Farrer appears to want it both ways – that an event be supernaturalised and also retain the fullness of its independent natural character. It is at this point that he begins to write in terms of 'a double personal agency in our one activity',[10] that is of seeing happenings in the world as acts both of God and of man. This concept of double agency rests upon something very like Coleridge's Polar Logic, 'opposite, not contrary powers', and seeing the universal in the particular and the particular necessarily requiring the universal.[11] Farrer, in his way, was a poet – and Professor Lewis does not seem to respond readily to what is poetic.

Farrer lays the primacy firmly upon the images, and revelation presents 'the extreme example of irreducible imagery'.[12] Lewis seems to assume that, if this is the case, such images must necessarily be self-authenticating. But for Farrer, as for Coleridge of biblical revelation, this need not be so.[13] For Farrer certainly does not subscribe to what naturally follows from this, that we take the substance of the Bible and biblical imagery, *ab initio*, as ultimate and beyond question. Images, rather, are to be tested by experience and must answer to the deepest demands of man's spirit. Lewis himself believes that God works primarily in the world through 'the very substance of living' rather than 'given images'.[14] Images, therefore, are generated in the context of human activity. Farrer – content again to live with paradox – suggests that particular 'given images', when tested in universal experience, will be discovered to characterise man as he properly is, made in God's image. Revelation must be found in both image and experience, and not simply experience untreated by a necessary and 'irreducible imagery'.

Lewis's final criticism of *The Glass of Vision* is in the context of his discussion of art and religion. He refers particularly to Farrer's distinction between poetry and prophecy, and, once again, he has a one-sided view. For Lewis, poetry and

---

[8]     [For further discussion, see Jasper, *Coleridge as Poet and Religious Thinker* (consult the volume's index for specific references).]

[9]     GV 12 / 23.

[10]     GV 33 / 36.

[11]     [Coleridge's 'Polar Logic' is discussed extensively in Jasper, *Coleridge as Poet and Religious Thinker* (consult the index for specific references).]

[12]     GV 62 / 58.

[13]     See Huw Parry Owen, 'The Theology of Coleridge', *Critical Quarterly* 4 (1962), 60–61.

[14]     Lewis, *Our Experience of God*, 138.

prophecy are ultimately one and the same, so that poetry and religion will, in the end, merge into one another.[15] But he fails to perceive the delicacy of Farrer's distinction. The prophet, certainly, is not necessarily the poet, and of the prophet Farrer writes that

> What he has got to say is determinate and particular, it is what the Lord God declares and requires on the day which he speaks. It is designed to evoke not an exquisite and contemplative realization of human existence, but particular practical responses to God.[16]

Nevertheless, Farrer continues, 'the poetical character of the prophetic utterance' is not immaterial, since 'poetry, for the prophet, is a technique of divination, in the poetic process he gets his message'.[17] Thus, what the prophet and poet share is the technique of inspiration. Both, writes Farrer, 'move an incantation of images under a control'.[18] But all poetry is not therefore prophetic or religious. Literature and its insights may indeed irrigate the religious imagination, at the heart of which remains the irreducible mystery. Farrer might even go so far as to suggest that as the controlling images are tested in experience, so divine illumination is not so much a vision, but, as Coleridge expressed it, a 'state of consciousness' or an 'inward experience'.[19] Yet it has a particularity perceived in the common experience – again the Polar Logic: poetry and religion, necessarily different while supposing and requiring each other.

In *The Limits of Literary Criticism*, subtitled *Reflections on the Interpretation of Poetry and Scripture*, Helen Gardner criticised *The Glass of Vision* in her role as literary critic. She concentrated upon one point only, Farrer's discussion of the ending of St Mark's Gospel, and writes:

> He approaches the literary criticism of the New Testament with a mind steeped in secular literature both ancient and modern, and he shows himself fully aware of the parallels between what he is doing and what is being done by modern critics of poetry. How whole-heartedly he had adopted the methods of modern literary criticism can be seen from his handling in *The Glass of Vision* ... of a classic problem in the New Testament.[20]

---

[15]   See Lewis, *Our Experience of God*, Chapter XIII, 'Art and Religion', 198–210, esp. 204–10.

[16]   GV 127–8 / 104.

[17]   GV 128 / 105.

[18]   GV 129 / 105.

[19]   Samuel Taylor Coleridge, *Aids to Reflection* [1825, 1831] (London: G. Bell and Sons, 1913), 3.

[20]   See Helen Gardner, *The Business of Criticism* – incorporating two series of lectures, *The Profession of a Critic* [1953] and *The Limits of Literary Criticism* [1956] – (Oxford: Clarendon Press, 1959). The lecture dealing with Farrer, 'The poetry of St Mark', is on pages 101–26 of this volume, and this citation is from page 108.

Farrer treats the abrupt ending of St Mark, the words 'ἐφοβοῦντο γάρ', as a literary question, examining parallels and structures, or what he calls the 'formal recurrences [of] St Mark's poetical magic'.[21] The Gospel then demands that we see it as an overall pattern, 'all cohering in a structure of meaning'.[22] Farrer parallels the Marcan narrative with the Old Testament story of Joseph, the last words of the Gospel echoing the Septuagint version of the reaction of Joseph's brothers when his true identity in Egypt is revealed – 'ἐφοβοῦντο γάρ' – 'for they were afraid'.[23]

Gardner's criticism is primarily historical. In all these literary parallels and structures, what we see, she says, is not the 'mind and imagination of St Mark', but the 'lively and fertile mind and ... profoundly poetic and Christian imagination of Dr Farrer'.[24] True, she admits that Farrer does say that 'the principal importance of St Mark's Gospel lies in its historical content', yet nevertheless his 'method is often oblivious of, and impatient with, the historical'.[25] Coleridge similarly has been criticised inasmuch as 'he failed to conceive of [Jesus Christ] as being a *particular* man with his own peculiar characteristics'.[26] Gardner, however, concludes with some curious remarks:

> It is surely an odd phrase to speak of St Mark's imagination being 'controlled' by facts. If we believe that what he is recording *are* facts – and that is the crux of the matter between Christian and non-Christian – then it is surely filled by the wonder of those facts, and not merely respectful to them. It is curious that the study of images, which began from a high theory of the imagination's power to apprehend the truth and value of experience, and to express its apprehension of the world, has led only too often in practice to an ignoring of the primary imagination, which degrades the secondary, or creative, imagination into an instrument for perceiving analogies and making connexions.[27]

It is strange that her criticism of Farrer should conclude by calling up Coleridge on the primary and secondary Imagination, since Farrer in many ways might have been schooled by Coleridge. For Gardner, history is composed of irrefutable facts, and Christianity must stick to them. But she does not seem to be aware of the problem and paradox of the incarnation as the ahistorical and atemporal breaking into history. The particularity of Christianity is always a problem for the poet, and Helen Gardner,

---

[21]   See GV 136–45 / 110–17, citation from 140 / 113.

[22]   Gardner, *The Business of Criticism*, 113.

[23]   [But now see Robert Titley's comments on the not-quite-exactness of the verbal parallel: *A Poetic Discontent: Austin Farrer and the Gospel of Mark* (London and New York: T&T Clark International, 2010), 64–5.]

[24]   Gardner, *The Business of Criticism*, 121.

[25]   Ibid., 122.

[26]   David Pym, *The Religious Thought of Samuel Taylor Coleridge* (Gerrards Cross: Colin Smythe, 1978), 70.

[27]   Gardner, *The Business of Criticism*, 122–3.

like Professor Lewis, fails to see that image and imagination play upon the historical, seeing the eternal through the temporal and the universal through the particular.

Farrer replied to Lewis and Gardner in his paper 'Inspiration: Poetical and Divine'.[28] He was unrepentent and vigorous in his defence of *The Glass of Vision*. Once again, he draws close parallels between the *processes* of 'religious seers and secular poets'. But, he continues:

> it is most necessary to emphasize the limitations attaching to the parallel. Religious seers and secular poets may be led to seek inspiration in these similar ways; but the fact casts no light whatsoever on the fundamental mystery of divine inspiration. Shelley uses certain methods to set his imagination acting; and this gives his imagination scope to act. St John uses similar methods; and this gives the Holy Ghost scope to move his imagination ... Belief in inspiration is a metaphysical belief; it is the belief that the Creator everywhere underlies the creature, with the added faith that at certain points he acts in, as, and through the creature's mind. We have argued that if this really happens a part will be played by the imagination. Imagination, in such an employment, will be suppled and made responsive or creative; there will surely be an analogy here to the workings of the poetic mind. But that which obtains expression in the two sorts of case will be widely different; and so will be the significance of the product.[29]

This is both disturbing and yet, somehow, right and adequate. No doubt Lewis and Gardner will continue to say that he wants to have it both ways, and, in the end, how can we tell the difference between the religious seer and the secular poet? Certainly a common criticism levelled against Coleridge, despite his many writings on the Bible, is that Scripture, Nature and almost all literary and artistic products of the imagination are equally sources of 'revelation'.[30] Is 'The Rime of the Ancient Mariner' a religious poem, or not? Coleridge's answer is no less unsatisfactory and no less true than Farrer's; try it, and see! In literature, the Bible, he claimed, 'finds me at a greater depth of my being ... [than] all other books put together'.[31] The difference, however, is one of degree. Where the principal images work with the Spirit within the poetic imagination they will work in a unique and unmistakable way upon man's spiritual constitution and needs.

---

[28] 'Inspiration: Poetical and Divine', in Austin Farrer, *Interpretation and Belief*, edited by Charles C. Conti (London: SPCK, 1976), 39–53 – originally published in F.F. Bruce (ed.), *Promise and Fulfilment* (Edinburgh: T&T Clark, 1963). [See also Farrer's response specifically to Gardner, 'On Looking Below the Surface', originally published in *Proceedings of The Oxford Society of Historical Theology* (1959–60), now in *Interpretation and Belief*, 54–65.]

[29] Farrer, 'Inspiration: Poetical and Divine', 53.

[30] See, for example, M. Jadwiga Swiatecka, *The Idea of the Symbol: Some Nineteenth Century Comparisons with Coleridge* (Cambridge: Cambridge University Press, 1980), 65.

[31] Samuel Taylor Coleridge, *Confessions of an Inquiring Spirit* [1840], edited by Henry Nelson Coleridge (Menston: Scholar Press, 1970), 13.

But all this needs disinfecting with a strong dose of hard-headed criticism. It is supplied in the renewed debate in which Helen Gardner is engaged, on almost exactly the same ground, with Professor Frank Kermode. In 1969, Kermode published a paper entitled 'The Structure of Fiction'.[32] He begins thus:

> The question is whether there is a chance that some mode of structural analysis can satisfy the requirements of criticism, if we take those to be: first, that there should be available for any work we take to worthy of preservation and of public interest some fairly systematic account which is itself acceptable to an informed public; and secondly that this account should try to tell the truth and know how much the truth it can tell.

Kermode takes his criticisms into the world of structuralism[33] and uses as one of his examples of the determination of structure and meaning Farrer on St Mark's Gospel in *The Glass of Vision* and *A Study of St Mark* (1951).[34] His concern is with typological structure and pattern, precisely those things which were regarded with such suspicion by Gardner. Certainly he is very well aware of her fears that the study of the Gospel by structural analysis (and Kermode groups Farrer with Levi-Strauss and Roland Barthes as a 'structuralist') disastrously reduces the historical actuality and immediacy which most Christians seek in it. However, Kermode's contention is that the Gospel writer is dealing with a story in which nothing is merely *historisch*, all is *geschichtlich*.[35] The universal importance of the literal truth of the story is evoked by a deliberate and sometimes, indeed, artificial patterning and structuring which establishes necessarily (and not randomly, as in purely fictional narrative) the authority of the 'principal images', those peculiar to divine revelation. Thus the Gospel rests upon, and yet moves beyond, the plain facts, for, says Kermode: 'If Farrer is to be believed, a narrative which we should regard as of the highest historical importance merely as a plain account of what happened, is yet at the same time very elaborately structured'.[36] It is precisely in this deep structure that the irreducible mystery which always eludes description is said to lie.[37]

Here Gardner returns to the lists, and her complaints against Kermode in her latest book, *In Defence of the Imagination*, the Charles Eliot Norton Lectures at Harvard 1979–80, are an almost exact repetition of her complaints against *The*

---

[32]   Frank Kermode, 'The Structure of Fiction', *Modern Language Notes* 84 (1969), 891–915.

[33]   For a comment on Coleridge and structuralism, see Jasper, *Coleridge as Poet and Religious Thinker*, 96.

[34]   Austin Farrer, *A Study of St Mark* (Westminster: Dacre Press, 1951).

[35]   Kermode, 'The Structures of Fiction', 904. [A conventional German distinction between history as empirical fact (Historie), and history as having significance and meaning (Geschichte).]

[36]   Ibid., 905.

[37]   Ibid., 915.

*Glass of Vision* in 1956: that the author of St Mark's Gospel is reduced to 'a mere exemplar of timeless laws governing the development of narrative of all and every kind'.[38] Kermode had elaborated his defence of Farrer earlier in the same Harvard lecture series, published in 1979 as *The Genesis of Secrecy*. The issues remain the same. 'As to Farrer', Kermode sadly remarks,

> his work was rejected by the establishment, and eventually by himself, largely because it was so literary. The institution knew intuitively that such literary elaboration, such emphasis on elements that must be called fictive, was unacceptable because damaging to what remained of the idea that the gospel narratives were still, in some measure, transparent upon history ... [Farrer] assumes that there is an enigmatic narrative concealed in the manifest one.[39]

According to Gardner, Farrer and Kermode offer a Jesus who is simply a mirror image of our contemporary selves, and the Gospel is merely a set of puzzles or diagrams, there to be decoded.

Indeed, for Kermode it would be true to say that the narrative possesses significance, not meaning, and that criticism must attend only to how what is said is written and not to what it is written about. It is in the intense thematic opposition of one puzzle after another that we are drawn back, inevitably, to those irreducible, primary images which so troubled Professor Lewis. For this opposition – Polar Logic again – keeps its meaning 'secret' by producing what is, precisely, irreducible – secrecy which is to be perpetually reinterpreted.

Gardner, on the other hand, demands of criticism the elucidation of meaning rather than significance, and wishes to safeguard as normative the 'main' or 'literal' sense. A narrative, for her, is not a source of inexhaustible meanings, although she admits that great books may be almost inexhaustibly fertile. The debate can almost be defined in terms of the biblical fundamentalist who holds to the primacy of the literal sense of scripture against the structuralist, bred upon the structured typology of Farrer's analysis of St Mark. John Coulson, in his review of Gardner's book concludes that

> The underlying question is how we gain meaning when the form in which it is contained is the highly ambiguous one of metaphor, symbol or story. If the symbol [or image] gives rise to thought, who verifies that thought, and by what authority?[40]

---

[38]  Helen Gardner, *In Defence of the Imagination* (Cambridge, MA: Harvard University Press, 1982), 114.

[39]  Frank Kermode, *The Genesis of Secrecy: On the Interpretation of Narrative* (Cambridge, MA: Harvard University Press, 1979), 63 and 64. The lecture dealing with Farrer is titled, 'The Man in the Macintosh, the Boy in the Shirt' (49–73).

[40]  John Coulson, Review of Helen Gardner, *In Defence of the Imagination*, in *Theology* 86 (1983), 71.

Here is a return to the old question. Kermode, now the secular critic, side-steps the issue and refers, elusively, to 'control by an institution', whatever that means. Farrer and Gardner, therefore, are left facing each other once again. For Farrer the problem must be: by what authority are these particular images confirmed if the literal sense of scripture is continually disturbed by a shifting pattern of parallels and types? At base, the problem is one of faith, or rather, the nature of the connection between what we hold in the language of faith and what we explain in the derived and second-order language of belief. The simple structuralist denies the connection; the biblical fundamentalist denies the distinction. Farrer lies somewhere between these extremes, the mystery threatened by reductionism on either side, to pattern or single meaning. 'Pattern and meaning', writes Coulson, 'are dependent upon each other and are separable only for purposes of comprehension'. Once again it is Polar Logic, 'both ... and', not 'either ... or'.

Literature certainly can never be merely a pattern, but yet a pattern demanding perpetual reinterpretation is necessary to preserve narrative from the trap of a simple literalism or the fetters of normative meaning. Imagination given play over certain images which are rooted in a 'given' set of historical circumstances, obtains a release from a simple adhesion to fact, which is rediscovered afresh in an eternity of new circumstances. The mystery is recognised anew, not in propositional faith or an assent to metaphysical assertions elicited from the primary, literal meaning of scripture, but in the perpetual demand of the structure for re-examination in the light of experience. Terence Hawkes sums up structuralist thinking in this way:

> At its simplest, it claims that the nature of every element in any given situation has no significance by itself, and in fact is determined by its relationship to all the other elements involved in that situation. In short, the full significance of any entity or experience cannot be perceived unless and until it is integrated into the *structure* of which it forms a part.[41]

Again, it is significance, not meaning, which is sought for; the significance of what is going on between God and man in revelation through the processes of inspiration and poetry. Farrer concludes *The Glass of Vision* on precisely this point:

> Poetry and divine inspiration have this in common; that both are projected in images which cannot be decoded, but must be allowed to signify what they signify of the reality beyond them. Inspiration does not merely stand at a midway point between poetry and metaphysics; it actively communicates with both. The subjective process of inspiration is essentially poetical, the content it communicates is metaphysical. But what inspiration reveals, it reveals about God, so that the thought of the sheer deity of God is embedded in the revelation. To think this thought out is to enter on a metaphysical enquiry. Even if we do not

---

[41]     Terence Hawkes, *Structuralism and Semiotics* (London: Methuen, 1977), 18.

think it out, the thought of sheer deity is still the raw material of metaphysics, that is to say, it belongs to the natural knowledge of God. Without it no supernatural revelation can be either received or understood.[42]

Coleridge would have approved of this. For God, and man made in God's image as a living and creative soul, as opposites, the one generated from the other, have a tendency to reunion, as 'all polar forces, i.e. *opposite*, not *contrary*, powers, are necessarily *unius generis*, homogeneous'.[43]

---

[42]    GV 148–9 / 118.
[43]    Thomas Carlyle, *The Life of John Sterling* [1851], Part I, Chapter 8, in Alan Shelston (ed.), *Thomas Carlyle: Selected Writings* (Harmondsworth: Penguin, 1971), 317.

# Chapter 2
# God and Symbolic Action [1990]†

## David Brown

Traditional accounts of revelation, particularly of biblical revelation, have typically assumed what has often been labelled an interventionist view of divine action, that is, that God over and above his general ordering and sustaining of the world performs certain specific actions. Though I think this model requires considerable modification to account for the extent of fallibility in the scriptures, none the less it seems to me to be essentially along the right lines. We may think of revelation as a divine dialogue[1] in which God acts to speak to a community of faith and further its understanding, but always in such a way that the freedom of individual response is respected. This will explain why failures of moral insight sometimes occur, even for

---

† When David Brown wrote this chapter he was University Lecturer in Ethics and Philosophical Theology at the University of Oxford, and Chaplain and Fellow of Oriel College; by the time it was published, he was Van Mildert Canon Professor of Divinity at Durham. It was delivered at a conference held at Louisiana State University in 1986, the proceedings of which were published as Brian Hebblethwaite and Edward Henderson (eds), *Divine Action: Studies Inspired by the Philosophical Theology of Austin Farrer* (Edinburgh: T&T Clark, 1990). About a decade later Brown published *Tradition and Imagination: Revelation and Change* (1999) and *Discipleship and Imagination: Christian Tradition and Truth* (2000, both volumes from Oxford University Press). In a paper delivered at the Farrer centenary conference held in Oxford in 2004, Brown wrote that 'although Farrer is not mentioned' in these two volumes, Brown had nevertheless 'taken seriously his stress on the power of images and their capacity to generate new meanings. Where I differ is first in insisting that the process did not stop with the closure of the canon, and second in stressing the key role of factors extraneous to the texts themselves': 'The Role of Images in Theological Reflection', in Douglas Hedley and Brian Hebblethwaite (eds), *The Human Person in God's World: Studies to Commemorate the Austin Farrer Centenary* (London: SCM Press, 2006), 92. Brown also notes that although Farrer indeed speaks of 'images' the 'images he has in mind are essentially verbal rather than visual' (86), and that 'extending [his] insight to visual as well as verbal imagery could only strengthen Farrer's point' (88). Brown's own work has thus creatively developed Farrer's image-based approach to divine revelation. This earlier chapter, 'God and Symbolic Action', likewise argues for a further development of Farrer's seminal ideas in *The Glass of Vision*, particularly in regard to giving a greater role to both 'natural symbols' and the un- or sub-conscious than Farrer was willing to do, at least in 1948.

[1] This dialogue model of revelation I defend in detail in chapter 2 of my *The Divine Trinity* (London: Duckworth/La Salle, Illinois: Open Court, 1985). This article is intended to supplement, rather than repeat, what I say there.

example in the prophets or psalms. It is because God values something more, that the individual comes to appreciate for himself what the truth is.

The first part of my paper therefore is concerned to defend just such a model against some of the more obvious philosophical objections. This will then provide a natural transition to the second half, in which I shall focus more narrowly on one particular mode for such a dialogue, that it be sometimes mediated through symbols. This was a proposal made by Austin Farrer, and I want to explore how that suggestion might be further developed.

## Revelation as Divine Dialogue

To speak of an unembodied agent like God 'acting' does not seem to me to present any insuperable difficulties. Not only do phenomena like telepathy and telekinesis give ready intelligibility to the idea of acting without a physical medium, even in the ordinary human case where such a medium seems essential, this apparent essentiality surely stems merely from the contingent fact of constant concurrence and not because the action would be unintelligible without it. Further confirmation of this emerges from the realisation that what makes something an action is its intentionality, and we can know our intentions without first checking our bodily behaviour. In other words, because what is indispensable to the concept of action is intentionality and not a particular medium, there can be no logical incoherence in the notion of action, including divine action, that involves no such medium.

But why place such action within an interventionist framework? 'Interventionist' is perhaps not entirely a happy term. It has two principal defects. First, it suggests that God is uninvolved with the world except where he is specifically intervening. Secondly, intervention can very easily suggest manipulation or authoritarian interference. My stress in this model of divine dialogue on a free human response demonstrates clearly that the latter idea of manipulation is very far from my mind. 'Interactionist' might be a better description. But there is some truth in the first charge. For, while I wish to insist on God's creative role as sustainer and orderer of the universe, I do find it hard to locate sufficient involvement in the non-interventionist cases, such that the accusation can then be resisted that the term 'action' is here not merely being used in an attenuated sense. Thus it is only action in the same way as troops winning a battle can be described as the action of the general leading them, or the bursting of a dam as the incompetent action of the engineer who built it. Clearly in these two situations the size of possible contribution from the general and engineer can range from the merely permissive, for example a doddery, senile general giving a command to brave troops, to the absolutely decisive, the engineer building a dam unable to restrain even ordinary levels of water. So, in answer to what Owen Thomas in *God's Activity in the World* has called the 'fundamental' question, 'Does God act in all events or only in some?',[2] it is clear that we must say that there are degrees of appropriateness in speaking of divine action, but that these culminate in what I, for better or worse, have labelled the interventionist cases.

There seems to me at least two good reasons why the term 'divine action' must find its most natural application in this context. Both are linked in the sense that they are drawing out implications of the fact that 'action' belongs to the category of the 'personal'. For, as we have seen, integral to the notion are intentions and only persons can have intentions.

First, in ascribing intervention to God we are only in effect according to him the same kind of personal freedom of interaction that we would wish to ascribe to ourselves. For many, Christians and non-Christians alike, would agree that we have a contra-causal freedom that can be subsumed under no laws, whether psychological, physiological or otherwise, and that it is precisely in the exercise of that freedom that we most show ourselves to be persons and not automata. Why then should divine activity be brought under any such laws? The failure of theologians to take with sufficient seriousness this analogy with our human situation is well illustrated by F.B. Dilley's article, 'Does the "God who acts" really act?'.[3] He ends by presenting us with a stark choice between miracles and uniform natural laws, with the former discounted because of the difficulty of believing in them in the modern age. Thomas rightly points out that this is not as difficult as is often supposed,[4] but, more importantly for our purposes here, it needs to be observed that Dilley has totally ignored a third alternative. For, just as our interaction with each other can be subsumed under no natural law, so also with God's gracious interaction upon us. In short, so far from intervention necessarily involving the miraculous, it seems indispensable if we are to allow God the same power and dignity of action as we are prepared to ascribe to ourselves.

Secondly, in insisting that not all divine action is of the same kind we are doing something also to preserve our own personal freedom and dignity, as it has been given to us by God. For were we to say that it is all of the same sustaining kind subsumable under natural laws, at once both the divine distance and the divine closeness would be swallowed up in one, except perhaps subjectively, whereas both are in fact integral if human action and its relation to the divine are properly to be described as personal. Thus one needs divine distance in order to preserve room for independent human decision-making, and a non-ubiquitous divine closeness or activity if the relation is to be regarded as personal, that is, with intentions shaped

---

[2]   O.C. Thomas (ed.), *God's Activity in the World: The Contemporary Problem* (Chico, CA: Scholars Press, 1983), 237.

[3]   In Thomas (ed.), *God's Activity in the World*, 45–60; reprinted from *Anglican Theological Review* 47 (1965), 66–80.

[4]   Ibid., 6. He refers us to A.M. Greeley's *Religion in the Year 2000* (New York: Sheed & Ward, 1969).

in response to the free actions of the other. It is precisely because of uncertainty whether Farrer's theory of 'double agency'[5] meets this criterion that I find it so unsatisfactory, or at any rate the version of it which I am about to mention. For it has recently been revived and defended by Vernon White in *The Fall of the Sparrow*.[6] He develops the idea with an impressive consistency and clarity, but that in turn makes it all the more easy to see what is wrong with the idea, at least as he presents it. What White is most concerned to defend is the divine sovereignty, that nothing can be allowed to frustrate the divine intention. So significantly Barth is quoted to the effect that God 'would not be God ... if there were a *single* point where he was ... only *partly* active or restricted in his action'[7] (my italics), and accordingly natural events and human actions are both equally brought under the rubric that 'whatever happens is caught up to serve God's intention'.[8] But it seems to me that to insist that in any situation God is always an agent, always more than just a permitting cause, even when due qualification is made for the problem of evil, cannot but be to call into question human freedom. If we are truly in the divine image and thus truly persons, this cannot but mean an ability to frustrate the divine purpose, and frustrate it ultimately. For to suggest otherwise must inevitably mean envisaging God interfering in human freedom to ensure that his purposes are always realised.

That is of course to place a high value on freedom, but apart from the intrinsic merits of the position such a course seems to me the only plausible course open to someone willing to admit the extent of fallibility in the scriptures but at the same time concerned to defend the notion of an interactionist or interventionist God. God valued something more highly than his will and purposes for mankind always being perfectly understood, namely a free human response. As I have put it elsewhere, 'revelation is a process whereby God progressively unveils the truth about himself and his purposes to a community of believers, but always in such a way that their freedom of response is respected'.[9] Let me offer two analogies which may help to clarify the sort of process I have in mind.

First, if it does not suggest too narrow a perspective, the Oxford tutorial system may be used by way of illustration, especially where one-to-one tutorials are involved. Dialogue suggests interaction between the two parties involved, with

---

[5]    Austin Farrer, *Faith and Speculation: An Essay in Philosophical Theology* (London: A&C Black/New York: New York University Press, 1967). [Double agency is the idea that two agents, in this case divine and human, can be in some sense the agents of the same act. Farrer defends one version of this Aquinas-inspired idea in *Faith and Speculation*, and it is the focus of many of the chapters in the volume *Divine Action*, cited above, in which Brown's 'God and Symbolic Action' was first published.]

[6]    Vernon White, *The Fall of a Sparrow: A Concept of Special Divine Action* (Exeter: Paternoster Press, 1985), esp. chapters 4 and 5.

[7]    Ibid., 115; cf. also 113. The quotation is from Karl Barth, *Church Dogmatics* 3.3 (Edinburgh: T&T Clark, 1957), 167.

[8]    Ibid., 133.

[9]    Brown, *The Divine Trinity*, 70.

the dialogue moving at the pace of one's dialogue partner rather than the pace of one's own knowledge, with the concern that he really understand rather than simply absorb a number of facts. Clearly there are numerous things one could say to a first-year philosophy student which, though true, would not be properly understood by him. But clearly also, if the student is to know not only that certain things are true but how they are true, the teaching system is not just a matter of telling him simpler facts first but inducting him into a particular way of thinking, that has as its cost allowing him to make mistakes of assessment as he goes along, exaggerating the force of a consideration here, underestimating there, with these defects of understanding being only gradually overcome. For example, in the philosophy of religion one will only really manage to assess Plantinga's anti-foundationalism or Swinburne's probability approach if first one has understood properly the more traditional deductive approach and in turn is in a position to weigh the status of anti-foundationalism or the use of probability arguments outside the philosophy of religion.[10] But inevitably before the undergraduate gets there, he may well have made several somersaults in his position, even perhaps to the extent of denying the role of reason in religion at all.

Some may think the teaching analogy over-intellectualist, with revelation seen as essentially the communication of facts. But, if that objection is raised, my response would be that it is rather the objector who demonstrates his misunderstanding of the point of teaching. For in philosophy one is surely primarily concerned to teach a method, a way of thinking to which facts and rules are of course relevant but not the whole story. Similarly then with revelation as dialogue. The objective is teaching a method, a way of life, to which none the less certain rules of thinking and certain facts are indispensable if maximum effectiveness is to be achieved.

But the tutorial analogy is perhaps less effective at bringing out the personal character of the relationship than another possible analogy, that of getting to know someone as a friend. Seldom, if ever, do we begin to know someone in isolation. In fact, almost invariably we come to any relationship with certain presuppositions that shape the way in which that relation then proceeds and develops. Thus, the reader of this paper will already have begun to perceive me in a certain way even before he has met me, even if the facts he knows about me are absolutely minimal. Suppose that he knows just two – that I am an Oxford philosopher and that I am a priest of the Church of England. Already, that will have predisposed him to interpret anything I

---

[10]   For Plantinga, see Alvin Plantinga and Nicholas Wolterstorff (eds) *Faith and Rationality* (Notre Dame, IN: University of Notre Dame Press, 1983), esp. 16–93. For Swinburne, Richard Swinburne, *The Existence of God* (Oxford: Clarendon Press, 1979; 2nd ed., 2004). For a recent, interesting discussion of the question of foundationalism without reference to religion, cf. R.J. Bernstein, *Beyond Objectivism and Relativism: Science, Hermeneutics, and Praxis* (Oxford: Basil Blackwell, 1983). For the use of probability arguments not only within the context of religion, but also in regard to science, history and literary interpretation, see Basil Mitchell, *The Justification of Religious Belief* (London: Macmillan, 1973), esp. chapters 3 and 5.

say in a particular light, depending on his experience of other specimens of the same two breeds. Thus perhaps the former leads him to expect this paper to be clinical and dry, the latter woolly and compromising. Nor is it true that such prejudices are easily overcome. If what he reads turns out in his view to be imaginative, then this may be explained, not in terms of this requiring some modification of his understanding of what is meant by Oxford philosophy, but instead it being said that on this occasion the author was really writing as a theologian, and so on. Again, on the latter stereotype, any chaplain of a college knows that it may well take years of very patient work to turn some atheist colleagues's stereotype of the clergy into a different shape. So often, no matter what one does, it is read in a predetermined way. In other words, for better or worse, our perceptions are already heavily conditioned by the society about us and by our previous experience, and so whether we take the teaching analogy or the more intimate personal relationship, there is just no escaping the distortions and gradualism that must inevitably accompany any dialogue that truly respects human freedom.

But, it will be objected, to describe revelation as a dialogue in this way is hopelessly misleading for at least three reasons. All of them, though accepting the fact of revelation, call into question whether what is taking place could ever be appropriately described as dialogue. The first, of which I intend to say the least, would come from those who insist on the authoritative, peremptory challenge of revelation. That it is often so experienced, as with Jeremiah, I do not for a moment deny. But even Jeremiah can at other times describe his experience in terms of just such a dialogue.[11] In fact even commands can involve complex dialogue and misunderstanding, as anyone who has had to exercise authority knows to his cost. It is the other two reasons for doubt about the model which I find more interesting, since they require its more detailed development, if it is to retain plausibility. They both concern the fact that at most what we seem to have is an inferred dialogue, since we have no independent access to what one of the interlocutors, that is God, said, only access to the resultant blend of God's and his own thoughts in the recipient's mind. Thus, except in auditions which are scarcely the norm, there is no clear parallel to speech in the divine case, and so there appears to be lacking the most obvious and essential feature in any dialogue. Coupled with that is the related fact that in human dialogue its time and place as well as an independently verifiable description of one's interlocutor seem invariably available, whereas normally all these features are problematic in a claim to be the recipient of a divine address. However, Austin Farrer in *The Glass of Vision* threw out some hints which can, I think, be used to restore the model's plausibility. It is, therefore, to consideration of the role of symbols in revelation that I next turn.

---

[11]    Contrast Jeremiah 20.9, where he obviously cannot restrain the word within him despite his wish to do so, with the more obviously dialogue form of the opening chapter.

**The Role of Symbols**

These Bampton Lectures were certainly intended as a defence of what I have called an interventionist view of revelation, and indeed we find Farrer himself occasionally using that very word. They were delivered in 1948, but 15 years later in 'Inspiration: Poetical and Divine' we already find him admitting that his case has been 'demolished', though significantly still then going on to say something in defence of it![12] There are a number of reasons why Farrer's understanding of revelation in terms of the communication of images failed to achieve any wide acceptance. Two in particular stand out, both connected with the inchoate nature of his suggestion. Firstly, he seems simply to have transferred the problem, from words to images, leaving us puzzled as to why definitive significance should be attached to one if not the other, especially as no explanation is given to account for the former's peculiar liability to error. Secondly, he offered no account of the mechanics involved, except to suggest that it was both like poetic inspiration and different from it. We are told that 'the poet is a maker, the prophet is a mouthpiece',[13] but as I have already argued, we need a more complex story than that. There is a short, intriguing passage in which Farrer summarily dismisses the idea that the matter has anything to do with images in our unconscious.[14] Inspiration, he insists, belongs to the top and not the bottom of our mind, and elsewhere too we find him exhibiting the same hostile attitude to a creative role for the sub-conscious.[15] However, it is precisely with that thought that I wish to engage, and through exploring the role of images and symbols in our sub-conscious and unconscious to argue that something like what Farrer suggested might after all be right.

First, it should be noted that this can provide us with a clear analogue for communication, for dialogue, that has no explicit verbalisation in at least one, sometimes both the partners in the dialogue. Such dialogue on the human level can be both intra-personal and inter-personal. Modern French literature provides some impressive examples of the former. One thinks of Marie Cardinal's *The Words To Say It* or some of Nathalie Sarraute's novels.[16] Thus the former describes the way in which Cardinal became mentally ill through the threatening 'It' which she discovered emerging from her unconscious, and the novel describes her fight back to sanity. Certainly she describes that fight in terms of an internal dialogue

---

[12] 'Inspiration: Poetical and Divine' [1963], in Austin Farrer, *Interpretation and Belief*, edited by Charles C. Conti (London: SPCK, 1976), 39.

[13] GV 129 / 105 [original pagination / this volume].

[14] GV 26–7 / 32.

[15] 'Poetic Truth' [c. 1943], in Austin Farrer, *Reflective Faith: Essays in Philosophical Theology*, edited by Charles C. Conti (London: SPCK, 1972), 24–37, esp. 25 and 33.

[16] Marie Cardinal, *The Words To Say It* (London: Picador, 1984); Nathalie Sarraute, for example, for her reflections on the interaction between the world of her characters and the 'real world', cf. *Between Life and Death* (London: Calder & Bayers, 1970).

with herself, with the It expressing itself not, however, in words but in symbols, as for example in the unrestrained flow of menstrual blood.

Perhaps, however, it is with the inter-personal dialogue that we are more familiar, especially if one thinks of standard Freudian theory. The child inter-relates with its parents in non-verbal discourse, where symbols take the place of words, but where none the less we do have a dialogue, perhaps continuing into adulthood, with the child unconsciously modifying and adapting its symbols in the light of its developing relations with the parent. Thus significantly one of Freud's most recent distinguished followers, Jacques Lacan, has expressed the Freudian system in precisely these terms of symbolic discourse.[17] Significant, too, is the positive assessment he gives to the initial repression. For he argues that it is only through the child's symbolic representation of the father as the other that the child's total indentification with its mother is overcome and the child achieves a sense of its own personal identity.

Thus there seems no difficulty whatsoever in envisaging a dialogue in which one or other of the partners communicates symbolically rather than directly through words. Intriguingly in the examples quoted above, in the Cardinal case it is the sender of the signals which expresses itself symbolically, whereas in the latter case it is the recipient who relates to what he believes has been communicated by expressing it in symbolic terms. So clearly we can envisage either or both sides of the equation being expressed symbolically. It should also be noted that equally the above examples can be used to illustrate the way in which even in the human case it does not count decisively against the occurrence of symbolic dialogue that there was no recognition at the original time and place of encounter that this was in fact what was taking place.

But what then of the divine case? The idea of progressive revelation which I have been developing must I think carry with it the notion of God communicating in the context of an existing canon of assumptions, as it were – which the community of faith believes itself to have reached in relation to God and which in consequence conditions what the believer is led to understand by whatever God says to him. But that must inevitably raise the question of how one can best conceive this dialogue as beginning, of what mechanics might be employed in the initial stages before there really was any prior revelatory canon of assumptions.

Now I certainly do not want to deny that many a purely intellectualist or rational thought might be the result of divine promptings at the sub-conscious level, as at times when we marvel at some particular notion that has just come into our heads and can think of no obvious source for it. Nor do I wish to challenge the revelatory status of the particular images upon which Farrer concentrates, the Kingdom of God and the Son of Man, without which Farrer insists that Jesus' teaching 'would not be supernatural revelation'.[18] But these, it seems to me, are already very refined symbols, and thus the story of man's symbolic dialogue with

---

[17]    Pursued in lectures and talks, published under the title *Écrits* (Paris: Éditions de Seuil, 1971).

[18]    GV 42 / 42.

God can only be properly told if we try to penetrate further back into the more basic elements in our consciousness which God might use to communicate with us. In other words, we need to investigate the possibility of natural symbols.

Farrer in a memorable phrase informs us that 'people are everywhere wrestling with the mystery of the shadow of the infinite', but significantly the example he gives of extrapolation to the infinite is an intellectualist one, pure will.[19] However, there is no shortage of those prepared to argue that there are such things as natural symbols. A good case in point is Mary Douglas in her book of the same name. Though admitting that different social matrices will produce different symbols, at the same time she does argue for recurring patterns within the same general social form. So, for example, she contrasts societies with restricted and non-restricted codes of social rules and suggests that the latter will lead to a lack of symbols of solidarity and hierarchy, or again she notes that different conditions apply for the emergence of ritualism and effervescence but that both will have their corresponding symbols.[20] However, her concern is primarily with the transcendent as it reflects itself in social relations and this means that she loses sight of an even more basic shared naturalism in symbols.

Here Mircea Eliade has been more successful in his *The Sacred and the Profane*. He argues that primitive religion treats the world as a 'replica of the paradigmatic universe' of the gods, and that this leads to notions of sacred time and place which mean that 'nature is never only "natural"'.[21] The result is that nature is seen as constantly manifesting or symbolising the divine. As he puts it, 'for religious man, the world always presents a supernatural valence ... every cosmic fragment is transparent'.[22] Now of course much of this will go as soon as man ceases to perceive his universe in this reflected way. But that does not mean that all natural symbols of the transcendent therefore collapse. For instance, Eliade mentions an awareness of transcendence coming through at the 'height' of the sky,[23] and it is hard not to see that as an image which will survive, whatever the social context.

Among other examples which might be given of essentially natural symbols are two basic elements in the Christian sacraments, water and blood. F.W. Dillistone in *Christianity and Symbolism* mentions a wealth of associations for water,[24] but again it is hard to envisage the perception of water totally detached from the notion of cleansing and purification. In the case of blood he suggests that the root idea may be 'because being blood it can more easily be imagined as reaching in some

---

[19] GV 92 / 79 and 89 / 78

[20] Mary Douglas, *Natural Symbols: Explorations in Cosmology* (London: Penguin, 2nd ed., 1973). For the former contrast, 44ff., esp. 55; for the latter, 103–4.

[21] Mircea Eliade, *The Sacred and the Profane: The Nature of Religion* (San Diego: Harvest/HBJ, 1959), 34 and 116.

[22] Ibid., 138.

[23] Ibid., 118.

[24] F.W. Dillistone, *Christianity and Symbolism* (London: Collins, 1955), 183ff.

way the divine mouth'.[25] But this is surely quite wrong. Blood as the life-force seems pre-eminently a natural symbol. Even today schoolboy gangs sometimes think a small surface cut and the mixing of each other's blood as the most effective sign of gang identity. Their lives are thus united, and in sacrifice what could be more natural than to offer the symbol of life back to its owner or creator?

In a discussion of *Le Mythe et le Symbole* at the Institut Catholique in Paris, J.-R. Marello, while identifying at least four natural symbols, fire, water, sexuality and light, has warned us of the human capacity to resist any reading, however natural.[26] That is true, but we must also beware of treating as natural what can in fact bear an excluding alternative symbolic meaning. Light may be used by way of illustration. For both Cassirer and Eliade point out that darkness only becomes a symbol for evil once sun and darkness are no longer seen as part of a single cosmic unity.[27] None the less, even with all these qualifications made, we can I think endorse the view that there are such things as natural symbols, and that Jung, who has perhaps insisted more strongly than anyone else on their existence in our unconscious, was in fact on the right lines.

In *Man and his Symbols* he does not hesitate to declare that it is primarily through the unconscious and its symbols that God speaks to man: 'We are so captivated and entangled in our subjective consciousness that we have forgotten the age-old fact that God speaks chiefly through dreams and visions'.[28] I am reluctant to quantify, but that symbols exercise a crucial role in God's dialogue with man must, I think, be right. Let me therefore give three reasons for insisting on this, before going on to indicate how, starting from natural symbols, revelation might be seen as a dialogue that develops in terms of their elaboration and refinement.

A first reason for thinking that symbols might play a crucial role in God's dialogue with man is because, as we have seen, there are such things as natural as well as socially created symbols. For an implication of this is that God does not first have to create a common language of communication. This emerges naturally – the everlastingness of the hills, the purifying powers of water, blood as the essence of life and so forth.

Secondly, precisely because such language is symbolic, with one thing standing for another, it is already admirably suited to be the language of religion. For the language of religion has to be analogical, since it involves the transfer of language used in ordinary empirical contexts into a transcendent context. But, it cannot be too strongly emphasised, this is exactly what symbolic discourse is doing all the time. Hence Lacan's fondness for word-play in his *Écrits*. For

---

[25]    Ibid., 226, though he does also offer as an alternative the rather vague possibility of its 'mysterious potency'.

[26]    J.-R. Marello, 'Symbole et réalité – Réflexion sur une distinction ambigue' in Institut Catholique de Paris, Philosophie 2, *Le Mythe et le Symbole* (Paris: Editions Beauchesne, 1977), 155ff., esp. 162.

[27]    Ernst Cassirer, *Language and Myth* (New York: Dover Publications, 1953), 13–14; Eliade, *The Sacred and the Profane*, 157–8.

[28]    Carl Jung, *Man and his Symbols* (London: Picador, 1978), 92.

symbolic perception refuses to be bound by accepted categories, but instead insists on identifying comparable features outside the accepted classifications acknowledged by analytic discourse. Indeed, this perhaps gives one possible explanation of why the verbal content of religious experience is characteristically so non-logical and unargumentative. One thinks, for example, of the prophets and the strange connections of thought which they sometimes made. It is not just that they are reaching out to realities which are in any case difficult to describe, but that such crossing of categories is in any case symptomatic of the symbolic way of thinking which is at work in our unconscious.

Finally, since, for whatever reason, this seems to be the primary language of our sub-conscious, God interacting with it offers a model for dialogue with the divine that no more requires the partner in the dialogue to be always recognised and acknowledged than does the creation and modification of symbols through other unconscious interaction, for example with one's father, if the Freudian theory is true. This is important because it makes it a medium through which God can act upon us, without destroying our freedom in the process. For in speaking thus he speaks without us being fully or even at all aware of who it is at work, addressing us. The crucial decision thus becomes clearly ours and not God's, in the sense that what finally matters in determining whether the dialogue continues to develop is whether we choose to bring these images to conscious awareness so that they can be creatively used and communicated to others.

To all this it may be objected that it is far from obvious that the unconscious is really under our own control. Let me therefore give a personal example to illustrate the strong sense in which I believe it to be in fact just so. It was with something almost bordering on shock that I read a philosopher like Stephen Clark speaking in praise of glossolalia in his recent Gifford Lectures, *From Athens to Jerusalem*.[29] To me the loss of reason and self-control seems almost terrifyingly disconcerting. Now such fears may in their turn be irrational. But my point here is simply, to generalise, the enormous resistance one's conscious self can put up to any stirrings of one's unconscious, and so effectively the great power it has over the unconscious in continuing to maintain one's freedom.

Paul Ricoeur is another thinker who seems to accept the existence of natural symbols. Thus he writes: 'An essential characteristic of the symbol is the fact that it is never completely arbitrary ... there always remains the trace of a natural relationship between the signifier and the signified',[30] and this he thinks pre-eminently true of what he calls 'primary' or 'archetypal' symbols. Not only that, he also attempts to bring out the creative role of the symbol, depending on whether the individual responds to the forward movement of the Spirit and produces a

---

[29]   S.R.L. Clark, *From Athens to Jerusalem: The Love of Wisdom and the Love of God* (Oxford: Clarendon Press, 1984), esp. 76.

[30]   Paul Ricoeur, *The Conflict of Interpretations: Essays in Hermeneutics* (Evanston, IL: Northwestern University Press, 1974), 319.

'recollection of the sacred' or makes a Freudian retreat to childhood in the 'return of the repressed'. As he puts it:

> The two symbolisms are intermingled. There is always some trace of archaic myth which is grafted to and operates within the most prophetic meanings of the sacred. The progressive order of symbols is not exterior to the regressive order of fantasies; the plunge into the archaic mythologies of the unconscious brings to the surface new signs of the sacred. The eschatology of consciousness is always a creative repetition of its own archaeology.[31]

In this connection he informs us that 'an archaic symbol survives only through the revolutions of experience and language which submerge it ... a symbol is first of all a destroyer of a prior symbol'.[32] Whether destruction is the right term to use, when something of a family resemblance survives, is questionable, but more important for our purposes here is the fact that in *The Conflict of Interpretations* Ricoeur offers us two essays in which he analyses the way in which specific symbols can undergo just such a creative transformation.[33]

One symbol he takes is that of original sin. In its case he is careful to point out that Genesis already represents a creative modification of earlier Babylonian traditions, and to draw our attention to the way in which through Israel's experience the symbol is modified from external stain to internal guilt.[34] At the same time he suggests that Augustine must take the blame for turning an originally potent symbol into a doctrine, and that for us it is necessary to 'deconstruct' Augustine to get back to the original powerful symbol. That way we escape the supposition that the story explains anything, and instead latch on to the fact that 'it has an extraordinary symbolic power because it condenses in an archetype of man everything which the believer experiences in a fugitive fashion and confesses in an allusive way'.[35]

Again, in his essay on fatherhood as a symbol he notes the universality of the image in all religions as a description of God,[36] and its modification in Hebrew religion through the way in which a non-sexual word is used of creation or again the way in which Jeremiah combines it with the image of spouse, further

---

[31]   Ibid., 333–4. Both his articles on 'The Hermeneutics of Symbols' are particularly valuable in this connection. Cf. ibid., 287–334.

[32]   Ibid., 291.

[33]   '"Original Sin": A Study in Meaning', ibid., 269–86; 'Fatherhood: From Phantasm to Symbol', ibid., 468–97. However, in the former case it should be noted that the earlier part of the story of its development is in fact told in a subsequent essay, 'The Hermeneutics of Symbols I', 287ff.

[34]   Ibid., 294 and 289–90.

[35]   Ibid., 283. His 'deconstruct' comment occurs on 281.

[36]   Ibid., 483.

undermining its sexual content.[37] Then of the New Testament he remarks that not only does Jesus give it a fresh dimension with his use of *Abba*, the basic Freudian pattern is overthrown with the father's compassionate 'dying with' symbolically taking the place of being 'killed' by the child.[38]

Whether Ricoeur has chosen the best examples of such creative transformation need not concern us here. There are, of course, numerous other instances that could equally well have been taken, from a very basic symbol like blood and the way in which it is transformed from a life-force owned by God into a life-force given by God to man, to much more culture-specific images like that of shepherd and its alteration from an image of authority in past tradition to one of sacrificial care in John, or the new kingdom whose recognition Luke perceives on and through the Cross.[39] But this is not the place to pursue such questions in detail. All I have been concerned to establish is the conceivability of revelation operating in this way through the creative transformation of symbols present in our unconscious, and that I think I have shown.

But, it may be objected, I have done my task too well. For in trying to make conceivable a revelatory divine dialogue through symbols it looks as though I may have removed the necessity for any talk of divine intervention or interaction. Can it not all be explained simply in terms of one initial divine act, his creation being such that it naturally produces certain symbols, and thereafter man's reflection on those symbols can be allowed to take over? Of course, it is possible to read the story like that, and give an intelligible account. But it strikes me as the poorer story, the one less attuned to the facts. Elsewhere I have suggested four tests for what is to be classed as revelatory experience – the character of the recipient, the unexpectedness of its challenge to our existing perspectives, its congruity with other such experiences and 'the extent to which interpreting it in anything other than revelatory terms would be to denigrate it'.[40] Let me here concentrate exclusively on the last, as I think it highlights the way in which one must cease to have the same symbols, the same story, unless one tells it in an interventionist way.

Farrer informs us that 'the recipients of revelation see themselves to be addressed by God ... And this is nothing like poetical experience, anyhow on the face of it; it is like personal encounter'.[41] But it is not just the note of personal encounter which is lost if interaction ceases to be part of the story, it is, I think,

---

[37]   Ibid., 486 and 489.

[38]   Ibid., 492.

[39]   For the transformation of the symbol of blood, contrast the absolute prohibition on drinking blood in, for example, Leviticus 17.10–14 with the injunction of John 6.53–6. Passages like Jeremiah 2.8 or Ezekiel 34.2ff. demonstrate that the original primary significance of the image of 'shepherd' was one of authority, and so are in stark contrast to John 10.11. Likewise, the words of the penitent thief (Luke 23.42) transmute all normal understandings of kingship.

[40]   Brown, *The Divine Trinity*, 79–84, esp. 82.

[41]   Farrer, 'Inspiration: Poetical and Divine', 44.

the symbols themselves. For I would wish to argue that it is integral to acceptance of a symbol (or myth for that matter since this is surely just a symbol in story form) that one accept that it conveys the reality it is supposed to represent. Roland Barthes may be mentioned as an example of a non-religious thinker who accepts this very point.[42] In an impressive discussion of myth he claims that not only is there a condensation or concentration in any myth that defies any easy analytic unpacking, it is integral to the acceptance of the myth that it be seen as non-reducible.[43] Intriguingly, Ricoeur has taken Bultmann to task on this very point, in insisting that the symbolic or mythical is irreducible, that to demythologise is already to change the meaning and in any case to pursue an impossible goal. Farrer too, in his well-known essay, 'Can Myth be Fact?' insists that on a true understanding of myth it 'was a guarantee that man's beliefs were not mere ideals or aspirations but the very laws of being', and that in consequence even the myth of Adam but still more so the Incarnation 'cannot be allegorised or evaporated into general statements without losing its force'.[44]

These are, I think, points too easily forgotten. As Ricoeur puts it, 'the symbol gives: I do not posit the meaning, the symbol gives it'.[45] In other words, it ceases to be the same encounter, the same conveying of reality, unless one believes that there is something interacting with us to produce those modifications of the image in us. Hence Barthes's insistence that to demythologise, to deny correspondence between the symbol and objective reality, is already to rob the symbol of its power. To take examples we considered earlier, just think of the contrast between Cardinal's 'It' and the Freudian father figure. For Cardinal, to discover that the It was only her other self was already to undermine its power; for us to understand the possible sources of our relationship with our father makes that power now explicitly acknowledged, but need do nothing to undermine its reality, unless of course it involves coming to see envy of our father as groundless. In other words, just as we need to see interaction with our father throughout our lives modifying that unconscious image and there being a father whose interactions help to produce these modifications, if there is to be any continuing significance in the symbol, so I suggest the same must hold in our relation to God.

It is not that this demands any miracles. I have already argued in the first part of this paper that in suggesting such interaction all we need be seen as doing is according to God the same freedom of action which we do not hesitate to accord to ourselves. Nor is appeal to the more supernatural elements of religious experience like visions integral to my argument. No doubt on many an occasion (though not

---

[42]    For a discussion of Barthes on myth, cf. my *Continental Philosophy and Modern Theology: An Engagement* (Oxford: Basil Blackwell, 1987), chapter 2. For another treatment of symbol, chapter 5.

[43]    Roland Barthes, *Mythologies* (London: Granada, 1973), for example 123.

[44]    'Can Myth be Fact?' [1945], in Austin Farrer, *Interpretation and Belief*, 165–175, citing 166 and 170.

[45]    Ricoeur, *The Conflict of Interpretations*, 288.

I think on all) these are simply the projection of the individual's unconscious, as for example with Jung's vision of Christ.[46] No, what is indispensable, irrespective of whether they appear before the waking or the unconscious eye, is that their creative density can only be acknowledged satisfactorily if we see them as vehicles of encounter and interaction. For only thus are we effectively acknowledging that they could and do have a power that is irreducible and not of themselves.

Let me end with an illustration suitably drawn from the nation to which I belong. It is precisely because the symbol of the monarchy interacts with the British nation, reflecting, reinforcing and to some extent creating the nation's values that it has its power, and it is clearly this that has made it of such interest of late to semiologists.[47] Were the monarchy to cease to express these values, were it to cease to find an answering chord in the British heart, were it to cease to interact with the nation's sub-conscious, then it would also die as a symbol. For then reality and symbol would cease to coincide. So also then with God and the symbols through which he chooses to interrelate with us.

---

[46]  C.G. Jung, *Memories, Dreams, Reflections* (London: Fontana, 1983), 236–7.

[47]  See, for example, D. Dayan and E. Katz on the Royal Wedding in M. Blonsky (ed.), *On Signs* (Oxford: Blackwell, 1985), 16–32.

Chapter 3

# The Stuff of Revelation: Austin Farrer's Doctrine of Inspired Images [1992]†

Ingolf Dalferth

Austin Farrer was a philosophical theologian who took revelation seriously. He did not hold God's creation and government of nature to be truths received by way of revelation and otherwise uncertified. But he was convinced that we cannot progress very far in our attempts to understand these rational truths about God if we ignore the truth which 'God himself has revealed'.[1] All our knowledge of divine truth, as he was well aware, depends on God's prior self-manifestation: there is no knowledge of God unless he reveals and we reason. But, he insisted, merely to 'distinguish between God's action and ours' is not enough: we must go on to distinguish between 'two phases of God's action': his revelation by way of nature and his supernatural self-revelation in particular actions in history. There are

---

† When Ingolf Dalferth wrote this chapter he was Professor of Systematic Theology and Philosophy of Religion at the University of Frankfurt, and Hulsean Lecturer at the University of Cambridge. Although a German Lutheran, he developed a specific ecumenical and intellectual interest in Anglicanism. This manifested itself in an earlier teaching position at the University of Durham in England, and two substantial articles on Farrer. The first compared Farrer and Luther on a contested point of doctrine: '"Esse Est Operari": The Anti-Scholastic Theologies of Farrer and Luther', *Modern Theology* 1 (1985), 183–210. According to Dalferth, 'Both thinkers have their intellectual roots in the voluntarist rejection of the scholastic synthesis of Aristotelian metaphysics and the Christian faith … [But] whereas for Farrer the analogical imagination takes precedence over the dialectical vision of reality, for Luther it is the other way round' (184 and 185). The second article, included here, was delivered at a conference at Durham in 1989 and originally published in Ann Loades and Michael McLain (eds), *Hermeneutics, the Bible and Literary Criticism* (London: Macmillan/New York: St Martin's Press, 1992). Although Dalferth subjects Farrer's 'doctrine of inspired images' to a searching critical analysis, he clearly appreciates what he sees as Farrer's unapologetically theological and even specifically Trinitarian biblical hermeneutics, as well as his distinctively Anglican emphasis on the 'mystical Christ'. Nevertheless, Dalferth concludes that Farrer's 'idea of revealed theology as the grammar of Christian image-thinking is underdeveloped … He did not work out the implications of his fruitful insight into revealed theology as image-thinking'. Dalferth thus suggests a way of repairing what he sees as Farrer's dichotomy of 'rational theology' and 'literary criticism' through a more *integrated* theological hermeneutic of biblical revelation: 'Christian doctrine … is more than the combination of the principles of rational theology, poetical imagination and literary criticism'.

[1]  GV 1–3 / 15–16 [original pagination / this volume].

divine mysteries such as the Trinity or the incarnation which are 'inaccessible to natural reason, reflection, intuition or wit', and 'Christians suppose such mysteries' to have been revealed in Christ and 'to be communicated to them through the scriptures'.[2]

But then we cannot bypass Scripture in our attempts to understand the divine truth as most contemporary philosophers of religion have thought: understanding Scripture is necessary for understanding God's revelation, which in turn is necessary for fully understanding the divine truth. Bishops who 'wished that Farrer would leave the Bible alone and return to philosophy where he was a redoubtable defender of the faith', understood neither Farrer nor philosophy.[3] For Farrer, scriptural hermeneutics was an intrinsic part of philosophical theology itself, not an arbitrary addition to it or a whimsical pastime of an otherwise serious thinker. Scripture is the key to revelation and to a full understanding of the divine truth. Hence no serious student of the Christian faith can avoid probing into the working of revelation and scriptural inspiration.

Farrer himself set out to do this in a series of highly provocative works beginning with his Bampton Lectures of 1948, *The Glass of Vision*. There he outlines his view of revelation and inspiration and the basic hermeneutical principles of his scriptural studies, namely 'that images are the stuff of revelation, and that they must be interpreted according to their own laws'.[4] These principles rather than their actual application in his studies of Mark's Gospel and Revelation which so infuriated the bishops are what I want to discuss in this essay. These studies have proved to be puzzling, controversial and provocative not merely because of their extravagant methods and unorthodox results but precisely because of the interpretative principles that governed them.

There are a number of features of Farrer's biblical work which have often been noted: his change from author-intention to text-meaning, from form criticism to an unashamedly literary approach to the gospels[5] and from solid historical exegesis to speculative numerology and arithmological juggling with numbers.[6] But the decisive point of his hermeneutics is, I suggest, that he approached Scripture neither as a historical critic nor as a literary critic but as a *theologian*: he was unashamedly *theological* in his approach – that is, he read Scripture in the light of hermeneutical

---

[2]    GV 35 / 37.

[3]    Michael Goulder, 'Farrer the Biblical Scholar', in Philip Curtis, *A Hawk Among Sparrows: A Biography of Austin Farrer* (London: SPCK, 1985), 193.

[4]    GV 51 / 49.

[5]    John Blakeley, 'Pictures in the Fire? Austin Farrer's Biblical Criticism and John's Gospel – a Comment', *Literature and Theology* 1 (1987), 184–90.

[6]    See Philip Curtis, 'The Biblical Work of Dr Farrer', *Theology* LXXIII (1970), 292–301; and Frank Kermode, *The Genesis of Secrecy: On the Interpretation of Narrative* (Cambridge, MA: Harvard University Press, 1979. [Now see also Robert Titley, *A Poetic Discontent: Austin Farrer and the Gospel of Mark* (London and New York: T&T Clark International, 2010).]

principles grounded in trinitarian and incarnational reflections. Hence the basic principle of interpreting Farrer is that we must always read him as a *theologian* interpreting Scripture, even where he uses methods of literary criticism.

His theological approach explains why Farrer does not fit common hermeneutical classifications. True, he turned away from the traditional kind of historical criticism and the intentionalist paradigm of post-Enlightenment hermeneutics that goes with it. But he was not simply an early exponent of modern structuralism, symbolical formalism or canonical criticism. He indeed concentrated on the meaning of the biblical texts and the intertextuality of Old and New Testament writings rather than the intention of their authors. But he developed his complicated numerological and typological theories precisely because he wanted to discover the way in which the mind of the biblical writers worked. This is not to say, as Margarita Stocker has suggested, that he committed the 'intentional fallacy' of confusing the intention of the biblical authors with the meaning-pattern and senses of the biblical texts.[7] Nor did he believe, as Frank Kermode thinks he did, that John, Matthew or Mark 'must have intended these senses' which he thought he had detected in their writings:[8] he was interested in the working of their imagination, not in their intentions, because he believed their imagination to be the locus of divine inspiration and revelation; and for the same reason he was interested in the literary pattern of the biblical texts because he believed them to be the sole guide to their writers' imagination and hence to God's revelation.

What I want to suggest, therefore, is that, contrary to what Helen Gardner, Frank Kermode and many others have thought, the principles which govern Farrer's biblical work are not principles of a 'new symbolical or typological' kind of literary criticism applied to the Scriptures;[9] and, if Farrer himself gave reason to think so, so much the worse. His literary constructions follow hermeneutical principles whose point is *theological* rather than exegetical, historical or literary. They are not principles of literary but of *theological hermeneutics*. They aim at elucidating divine actions, not human texts, the way God works in revelation and inspiration, not the intention of the biblical writers or the meaning-pattern of the biblical texts as such. They are not hermeneutical principles which stand on their own but are intrinsically bound up with Farrer's views about God's activity in nature and history.

Thus to understand Farrer's hermeneutics we must concentrate on his account of revelation. This I want to do in this essay, by asking the following questions:

1. What is wrong with our common accounts of revelation?
2. What, therefore, are we to understand by 'revelation'?
3. How does revelation work?

---

[7] Margarita Stocker, 'God in Theory: Milton, Literature and Theodicy', *Literature and Theology* 1 (1987), 70–88.

[8] Kermode, *The Genesis of Secrecy*, 62.

[9] Helen Gardner, *The Business of Criticism* (Oxford: Clarendon Press, 1959), 126.

Let us look at Farrer's answers to each of these questions in turn.


## I

Any theologically viable account of revelation, according to Farrer, must keep clear of two common misunderstandings. The first is the 'cardinal false assumption' of pre-modern thought 'that revelation was given in the form of propositions' dictated to the apostles by the Divine Spirit and inerrantly put on paper by them.[10] The other is the modern theory – explicitly held by many of our contemporaries – that scriptural propositions express the response of human witnesses to the events of 'Christ, his life, words, passion, resurrection' and that these events themselves rather than the scriptural record of them by human witnesses are the revelation of God. John Hick, for example, writes that 'revelation is not a divine promulgation of propositions ... The theological propositions formulated on the basis of revelation have a secondary status. They do not constitute the content of God's self-revelation but are human and therefore fallible verbalizations'.[11]

This is a widely held view today. But, as Farrer points out, 'the theory of revelation by divine events alone' is at least as unsatisfactory as 'the theory of dictated propositions'.[12] The latter understands the New Testament to be 'uniquely inspired' by turning it into a catalogue of inerrant propositions, which it manifestly is not. The former understands the New Testament to be 'uniquely informative': it informs us in the best way available about the revelatory events of Christ's life and death by presenting us with the reactions of the primary witnesses to them. But to know how the New Testament writers felt about Christ is not to know God's self-revelation in Christ: historical or biographical reports about (reactions to) revelation are not revelation. The traditional view underrated revelation and overrated Scripture by identifying it with (the content of) revelation. The modern view mystifies revelation and underrates Scripture by turning it into a mere historical record of (the event of) revelation. But, just as revelation cannot be identified with scriptural propositions, so it cannot come in events by themselves without interpretation: bare historical events are not revelation but neither is revelation a mere interpretation of events. Rather, Farrer argues, it is the interplay between a particular event and a particular interpretation: namely, Jesus' life and death and the apostolic interpretation of these events. Hence to deny authority to the apostolic interpretation is not merely to reject their interpretation of revelation but to lose sight of revelation itself. In short, an adequate account of the authority of Scripture must be based on an adequate theory of revelation which avoids both the pitfalls of the propositional account of revelation and of the event account. That is, we must argue from revelation to scriptural inspiration, not vice versa.

---

[10]    GV 36–7 / 38.

[11]    John Hick, *Faith and Knowledge*, 2nd ed. (Ithaca, NY: Cornell University Press; London: Macmillan, 1966), 29.

[12]    GV 38 / 39.

**II**

This is what Farrer's own account of revelation tries to do. Any event which is to count as revelation must, he argues as late as *Faith and Speculation*, meet two conditions, which we may call the *soteriology condition* and the *intelligibility condition*. It must

(1) be 'involved in an activity of God for the eternal salvation of his rational creatures'; and

(2) be such 'that men effectively know and intelligibly proclaim what God does in them or before their eyes'.[13]

These two conditions of a saving action of God which becomes effectively known by us are met above all by Jesus Christ himself. And already in *The Glass of Vision* Farrer states as his basic principle that 'the primary revelation is Jesus Christ himself'.[14] This sounds deceptively simple. But the principle is more complex than it appears to be. Four aspects in particular must be noted to grasp its full import for Farrer's position.

1. It rejects a too narrow or abstract view of revelation: if Jesus Christ himself is the primary revelation, God's revelation to us does not consist merely in the historical teaching of Jesus or only in his historical actions and sufferings. Jesus reveals God by word *and* deed, in the totality of his life to us – not simply in the quantitative sense that his actions and teaching must be taken together, but in the qualitative sense that his actions interpret his teaching, and vice versa, and thereby reveal God to be saving love: Jesus' whole life is revelatory by being a process of complete mutual interpretation of word and deed.

2. But even in this sense *the whole of Jesus' life* is not the same as *Jesus Christ himself*: not even the totality of Jesus' words and deeds mutually interpreting each other is all there is to revelation. The actions of his will, the expressions of his mind, 'these, certainly, are the precious seeds of revelation, but they are not the full-grown plant'.[15] They are a necessary part but not the whole of God's self-revelation. As William Temple wrote, 'there is event and appreciation; and in the coincidence of these the revelation consists'.[16] That is to say, the inspired apostolic comment on Jesus' life and death is as much part of revelation as are Jesus' own words and deeds: the latter reveal God's saving love, the former that this

---

[13] Austin Farrer, *Faith and Speculation: An Essay in Philosophical Theology* (London: A&C Black, 1967), 102f.

[14] GV 39 / 39.

[15] GV 40 / 40.

[16] William Temple, *Nature, Man and God* (London: Macmillan, 1934), 314.

revelation is true, and only Jesus' revelation of God's love together with the Spirit's revelation of the truth of what Jesus has revealed constitute the self-revelation of God.

Thus God's self-revelation, for Farrer, comprises two equally important components: what Jesus revealed in and through his life (the presence of God's saving love in him), and 'what the Spirit revealed to the Apostles' about Jesus' life (the truth of his revelation).[17] Each of the two components is a complex interpretative process or relationship between certain events (the *interpretandum*) and their interpretations (the *interpretans*); and the two components are related in such a way that the first interpretative process constitutes the *interpretandum* of the second. Thus Jesus 'both performed the primary action and gave the primary interpretation' by proclaiming the presence of God's saving love in everything he said and did; and 'the Apostles, supernaturalised by the Spirit of Pentecost, worked out both the saving action and the revealing interpretation' of Jesus as Christ by recognising that his proclamation is true and that his life *is* the presence of God's saving love for all of us. That is, God's self-revelation comprises both Jesus' self-interpretation and the apostolic interpretation of Jesus' self-interpretation summarised in the confession 'Jesus is the Christ'.

3.  But, then, only Jesus' self-interpreting life as a whole together with the apostolic interpretation of Jesus as Christ constitutes the locus of God's self-revelation: for Farrer the phrase 'Jesus Christ himself' in the principle we are discussing denotes not simply the historical person Jesus of Nazareth nor merely the kerygmatic Christ of the apostles but also 'the mystical Christ',[18] that is the incarnate second person of the Trinity who was present as a man in the life of the historical Jesus, who is now present as Lord in the life of the Church, and whose Spirit testifies to his different but in each case personal presence both in Jesus and in the Church. That is to say, Farrer's account of revelation is thoroughly trinitarian and – in the Anglican tradition of J.B. Mozley, O.C. Quick and Leonard Hodgson – incarnational. There is an absolute difference between incarnation and inspiration, the first being the human presence of the Son, the second of the Spirit; and, while the incarnate Son was, like the apostles, inspired by the Spirit, he alone was incarnate and his incarnation was not constituted by the Spirit. But God's self-revelation takes place only in incarnation *together* with inspiration, not in one of them just by itself; and, while this revelation could have taken place in Jesus' life as such, in so far as the incarnate Son, like the apostles, was inspired by the Spirit, it in fact took place – as we know from the difference between Easter and Pentecost – also in the life of the apostles who interpreted the life of Jesus, including Jesus' own self-interpretation by word and deed, as God's definitive self-revelation to us as creative and redeeming love in the gospel.

---

[17]    GV 41 / 40.

[18]    GV 41 / 41.

That is to say, God's revelation necessarily involves both the Son and the Spirit, whose roles as persons of the Trinity are different in incarnation and inspiration; but it contingently occurs only in that the Son and the Spirit act in different ways both in Jesus and in the Church. Thus, by constantly referring away from himself to the Father who sent him, Jesus revealed himself as the eternal Son and thereby God as saving love; but the truth of what he revealed came to be known only through the Spirit who revealed it to Jesus and to others alike; and this was made explicit to us through the apostles. For, just as the Father indwells the Son by his Spirit, opens his eyes to his salvific presence and inspires his complete conformity to his divine love, so the Spirit of the Son indwells the Church as the body of the living Christ, opens our eyes to the truth of the gospel and inspires our conformity to Christ in faith. In short, God's self-revelation as love takes place through both the historical self-interpretation of Jesus by word and deed and the apostolic interpretation of Jesus' self-interpretation in the gospel; the first is the inspired self-interpretation of the incarnation, the second the inspired interpretation of that incarnational self-interpretation as true; and both interpretations are performed through the same Spirit, who is active both in incarnation and in inspiration.

4.  It is this trinitarian and incarnational approach which takes Farrer's account of revelation and inspiration decisively beyond both the barren alternative of propositional or event accounts of revelation and merely subjectivist views of interpretation. Revelation is the *coincidence of divine incarnation and apostolic inspiration*, that is, God's inspiration of the apostles to explicate the truth implicit in incarnation. The interpretative work of the apostles is thus not just their private view of the life of Jesus. It 'must be understood as participation in the mind of Christ, through the Holy Ghost'.[19] That is to say, the apostolic comment on Jesus' life and death is not just an external interpretation of these events which we may or may not accept but an internal continuation of them: it is part and parcel of revelation itself, not an arbitrary addition which can be discarded without much loss. God's revelation is not a bare historical event but neither is it a strange human interpretation of such an event. Rather it is the divine self-interpretation of the triune God which he performed under the conditions of our human existence through both inspired incarnation and apostolic inspiration, that is, through Jesus' self-interpretation and the apostles' interpretation of his self-interpretation.[20]

---

[19]  GV 42 / 42.

[20]  [An excursus on interpretation, comparing and contrasting the views of John Hick and Ludwig Wittgenstein, has been cut from the original version of this chapter: this material may be found on pages 78–81 of the original.]

**III**

This brings us to the last question mentioned: 'How does revelation work?' That is, what are the 'media of revelation'?[21] Farrer's answer embraces both the incarnational and the inspirational component of revelation: by *inspired images*. He puts the stress on '*inspired*', not on 'images', whereas most students of Farrer have been more interested in what he says about images and the role of imagination. But if Farrer must be read as a theologian, as I think he must, it is primarily his doctrine of inspiration which needs elucidating if we want to understand his hermeneutics of images. So how does he describe inspiration? The short answer is: as the *rebirth of images* in a two-stage process – Jesus' self-interpretation and the apostolic interpretation of it.

Thus Jesus' self-interpretation, I have said, consisted in the complete interplay between his word and deed. Now, his thought and teaching 'was expressed in certain dominant images' such as the Kingdom of God, the Son of Man, the family of Israel, the redemptive sacrifice, the Suffering Servant and the paternal love of God. Without these images his teaching would have been 'instruction in piety and morals', not 'supernatural revelation'. He did not invent these images but took them from the stock of the prophetic, cultic and apocalyptic traditions of Israel in which he was reared and in which he lived. Yet he did not simply use these images but creatively changed, that is enhanced and intensified, their meaning by a twofold operation: he implicitly applied them to himself by interpreting them through his own actions and sufferings, and he thus opened the way for forging them into fresh unities that attracted and assimilated further image material. That is, the images he used interpreted the events of his ministry, and the events interpreted the images; and the interplay of the two revealed God's saving love in a way which enabled others to know it.[22] In short, Jesus not only taught in parables but also became himself a parable: the self-enacted parable of God's saving love.[23]

The same interplay of image and event continued in the apostolic interpretation of Jesus' self-interpretation. The apostles drew on the same stock of images as Jesus had used; they explicitly applied them to Jesus' life and death, that is to his implicit reinterpretation of them in his words and deeds; they thus explicitly brought out the continuity and contrast between their old or archetypal and their new Christologically-conditioned meaning; and they thus proved the unceasing creative force of these images which in their minds and use combined to form new unities and a growing web of images organised and structured by their common reference to Jesus Christ. Thus incarnation and inspiration are a continuing story: the rebirth of images which began in Jesus' own life was continued by his Spirit in the minds of the apostles.

---

[21]    Farrer, *Faith and Speculation*, 103.

[22]    GV 42–3 / 42.

[23]    See Austin Farrer, 'Revelation', in Basil Mitchell (ed.), *Faith and Logic: Oxford Essays in Philosophical Theology* (London: George Allen and Unwin, 1957), 99.

To assess this account, let us consider an example which is not Farrer's. In Matthew 12 we find images from the Jewish tradition (temple, son of David, Solomon, a prophet like Jonah) used to explain who Jesus is. However, in order to convey the incomparable status of Jesus, they are qualified by statements that Jesus is 'more' or 'greater' than the temple, Solomon, Jonah and so on. The same hermeneutical dialectics of comparability (continuity) and incomparability (contrast) is characteristic of the titles applied to Jesus. Thus Mark 8 shows that Christians could apply the title 'Messiah' or 'Christ' to Jesus only after it had been purged of its misleading political overtones and redefined in the light of his suffering, cross and resurrection. More generally, it was the story of Jesus' self-interpretative life which modified or redefined, and thereby enhanced and intensified, the meaning of the images, titles, predicates and so on, used to elucidate and communicate the mystery of his life. Many of these images, titles and so on were originally unrelated and brought into a semantic relationship only by their common reference or application to Jesus. Gradually, however, through liturgical practice and theological reflection, they were brought into a closer semantic relationship and integrated into a common field of meaning. While at the beginning the image material was primarily taken from the Old Testament and Jewish background, soon ideas and images from Hellenistic and other religious traditions also came to be used. And, so that the process of semantic integration would not transform and distort the mystery of revelation which these images were used to express, theological reflection was soon required in order to formulate explicit rules (dogmas) about how the various images were to be used and understood, and which of them should play the role of master images.

Now, clearly Farrer would not have wholly agreed with this story. For him there was a decisive difference between the God-given images used by Jesus and the apostles and all others. He did not think that the images themselves are 'what is principally revealed: they are no more than instruments by which [revealed] realities are to be known'.[24] Yet he was quite explicit that the 'choice, use and combination of images made by Christ and the Spirit must be simply a supernatural work: otherwise Christianity is an illusion'.[25] Christians cannot claim that Jesus Christ is God's self-revelation and deny that the images used by Jesus and the apostles are inspired: the two stand or fall together.

It follows that for Farrer, Jesus' self-interpretation and the apostles' interpretation of Jesus' self-interpretation are different in kind from all later interpretations: the former are God's self-revelation through incarnation and inspiration, the latter our interpretations of God's self-revelation. Similarly, the images used by Jesus and the apostles are God-given or inspired because they are used as media of revelation. Our images, concepts and doctrines, on the other hand, are not inspired, but only more or less useful instruments of our creative intentions to understand and appropriate God's self-revelation through understanding the images by which it is mediated to us.

---

[24]   GV 57 / 55.
[25]   GV 109 / 92.

In short, Farrer's central claim is that, unless the choice and combination of images in the New Testament is inspired, there is no revelation. For revelation is the process of divine incarnation and apostolic inspiration; inspiration is the becoming explicit of what is implicit in incarnation; and this inspirational explication of the incarnation takes place through inspired images in both Jesus and the apostles. But this view of revelation and inspiration results in a *fundamental epistemological circle at the centre of Farrer's hermeneutics.* If we want to interpret the New Testament writings adequately we must identify the inspired images used and trace their combinations and interconnections to bring out how they communicate God's revelation to us. But how do we know that the images used in the New Testament are inspired? They must be inspired if there is to be a revelation. How do we know that there is a revelation? Because Scripture tells us. How do we know that what Scripture tells us is true? Because it tells us through inspired images. That is to say, we know God's revelation because Scripture discloses it to us; we know that it does so because it uses inspired images; we know that these images are inspired because if they were not there would be no revelation; but there is revelation, as we know because Scripture discloses it to us – and so on.

How did Farrer get into this circle, and how can we get out of it again? He does not, I suggest, find himself in this situation because of his view of inspiration but because of his theory of revelation. He draws a distinction in kind between the *constitution* and the *communication* of revelation: revelation is constituted through incarnation and apostolic inspiration, and it is communicated through the use and combination of inspired images – images used by Jesus in his life and by the apostles in their interpretation of Jesus' life in the gospel. But in which sense do they, or we, communicate God's self-revelation when we communicate the gospel? All we have are claims by Jesus and the apostles that what they proclaim is God's revelation. Without divine corroboration these are human claims, not divine revelation. Jesus' life became God's self-revelation only when corroborated by God in the resurrection, and the same is true of the apostolic witness to this: unless it is corroborated by the Spirit it does not, and certainly not by inspired images, communicate it. The proclamation of the gospel gives occasion for God's self-revelation to occur but it does not, not by inspired images, communicate it.

But then we cannot distinguish between the constitution and communication of revelation in the way Farrer does: *vis-à-vis* revelation, the apostles are not in a different position from us. They could not understand that Jesus is the Christ without the Spirit, and neither can we. It is the same Spirit who indwells and inspires the apostles and all Christians alike. In either case revelation about the truth of the incarnation occurs only through the Spirit. Hence, if the apostles were inspired, so is every believer. The difference is not that they were inspired while we are not, but that they, inspired by the Spirit, arrived at faith by discerning the truth of Jesus' life while we, inspired by the same Spirit, arrive at faith by discerning the truth of the gospel.

Where Farrer goes wrong, I suggest, is not in his account of inspiration and the role of images as the stuff of revelation, but in restricting God's self-revelation, that is, the revelation of the truth of the incarnation, to God's inspirational activity in the apostolic imagination alone. He rightly sees that to know the apostolic gospel is a necessary condition for us to arrive at the God-given insight of its truth. But he wrongly concludes that the apostolic witness to Jesus as Christ is part of God's revelation while our believing what they propose is not.[26] This view of revelation is misleadingly historical: while it is true that God's incarnation occurred once and for all in the life, death and resurrection of Jesus Christ, God's self-revelation occurs wherever the Spirit inspires persons to accept the truth of the incarnation. It is an eschatological, not a historical event. And it can take place at any time and place in history where the gospel of Jesus Christ is proclaimed.

In short, Farrer's account of revelation and inspiration is much too historical. This is a very different kind of criticism from the common complaint that Farrer's method was 'often oblivious of, and impatient with, the historical'[27] and that his hermeneutics are a matter of weird subjectivity which lead him to discover nothing but 'pictures in the fire'.[28] So what are we to make of his views in the light of these criticisms?

Contrary to what critics such as Helen Gardner have suggested, Farrer takes history extremely seriously. It is given a status which could hardly be more prominent. Just because he concentrates on revelation, not only the particular events of the history of Israel, Jesus and the Church, but also the specific image material used by the prophets, Jesus and the apostles, become irreplaceably important for him. He takes the particularity, contingency and historicity both of the incarnation and of revelation through incarnation and inspiration so seriously that he is prepared to stake the validity or invalidity of the Christian faith not only on the events of Jesus Christ's life and death as such but even on the specific images used to communicate their saving significance in the New Testament.

Similarly, Farrer concentrates on the New Testament texts rather than on their historical settings and authors not because he is more interested in meaning-patterns than in historical fact but precisely because he is serious about history: God's revelation took place through incarnation and apostolic inspiration in a particular stretch of history; it is accessible to us only in the historically contingent form of the apostolic writings; hence for Farrer *understanding revelation depends on understanding Scripture.*

Now, this I do not want to dispute. But the problem is, what does it mean to understand Scripture? And how does it help us to understand revelation? Two principles of theological hermeneutics are important here. First, *understanding Scripture is not the same as understanding revelation.* Second, *Scripture must be understood as the key to revelation.* That is to say, understanding Scripture is necessary, not sufficient, for understanding revelation. The New Testament writings communicate the gospel to us; they do not as such show it to be true.

---

26    Farrer, 'Revelation', 105.
27    Gardner, *The Business of Criticism*, 122.
28    Goulder, 'Farrer the Biblical Scholar', 193.

They convey what their authors believed to be revealed, but not that it *is* revealed or that what they communicate is true. Farrer's talk of the 'revealed' or 'divine truth' conveyed by Scripture blurs this important difference.

On the other hand, if understanding Scripture is necessary for understanding revelation, then understanding Scripture is the key to revelation. But in which way? For Luther the use of Scripture in preaching and proclamation presented the *verbum externum* of the gospel which we must know and understand before it can be corroborated as true in the *verbum internum* of the Spirit: only in this way can we come to see the truth of the incarnation, that is, understand God's revelation. Farrer, on the other hand, understands the principle of the hermeneutical priority of Scripture quite differently. He takes it to refer not to a particular use of Scripture but to its textual structure: the choice and combination of images in the New Testament constitute patterns of meaning which disclose the working of God's inspiration through the imagination of the apostles. Hence what we should try to find out when reading the biblical texts as the key to revelation is not primarily what their authors wanted to convey by the images they use, nor what the images convey by the way they are combined in the texts, but what God makes them convey by making the authors use and combine the images in the way they did.

Now, I fully agree that we must study Scripture not primarily as historians or literary critics but as theologians who want to understand God's self-revelation through incarnation and inspiration. But this means that we must concentrate on the ecclesial *use* of Scripture rather than on its textual structure. This is not to deny that the apostles are exemplary in creatively explicating, by inspiration, what is implicit in the incarnation. But there is no reason to restrict God's inspirational activity to the apostolic mind and ministry only. If the 'interpretative work of the Apostles must be understood as participation in the mind of Christ, through the Holy Ghost',[29] the same must hold of our attempts to speak from faith and proclaim the truth of the incarnation: to speak from faith is to speak by inspiration; we cannot speak from faith without using images; and our images are inspired if God, by making us use the images we do, uses them to reveal the truth of his incarnation to us and others in such a way that we respond to it in faith.

What I propose, therefore, is to free Farrer's account of revelation from its misleading historical restrictions: revelation is the *coincidence of divine incarnation and inspired faith in the truth of incarnation* – not only in the apostles but in all believers. This is not to deny the special role of the apostles, whose articulation of faith in Christ is the norm and standard by which we judge the adequacy and appropriateness of our articulations of faith. This does not mean, however, that the Apostles were inspired while we are not. The New Testament is neither 'uniquely inspired' nor 'uniquely informative' but *uniquely normative* for the Christian community – not because of a specific quality of its texts but because their use in the Christian Church continuously gives occasion for the Spirit to inspire persons to have faith in Christ, that is, to accept the truth of the gospel.

---

[29]   GV 42 / 42.

It follows that Farrer's account of inspired images must be corrected not by denying inspiration to the apostles but by claiming it for all Christians. All human talk uses images, and all Christian talk from faith is inspired. Farrer underlines the first, but not the second. 'The human imagination', he writes in *A Rebirth of Images*, 'has always been controlled by certain basic images, in which man's own nature, his relation to his fellows, and his dependence upon the divine power find expression'.[30] Some of these images can be found wherever there are human persons; others are more closely restricted to particular contexts and historical environments; and some of these have been chosen by God to become vehicles of his revelation to us. But again Farrer understands this in a specifically historical rather than eschatological way. Thus the 'birth of Christianity', according to Farrer, was 'essentially a transformation of images', a 'visible rebirth of images' already in use in Israel and put to an enhanced use in the thought and action of Jesus Christ and the apostles.[31] Taken as such, these 'archetypes', as Farrer calls them in *The Glass of Vision*,[32] are not revelatory. But they became media of revelation by being used and fused in Jesus Christ's very existence; and this 'advance under the leading of God from archetypes to incarnation'[33] and, under the guidance of the Spirit, to inspiration constituted the particular historical process through which God disclosed himself.

Two comments are necessary here. First, Farrer restricts what he says to the birth of *Christianity*, that is, the beginning of the faith of the Christian community. But there is a similar story to be told about the birth of each *Christian*, that is, the beginning of the faith of the individual believer. We cannot talk about the 'birth of Christianity' in the sense of a particular historical movement (as Farrer does) without raising questions about the birth of faith in the particular life-stories of Christians. The two questions involve different historical, psychological and sociological issues. But theologically, that is with respect to the activity of the triune God, the birth of faith in the first sense cannot be different in principle from the birth of faith in the second. If we share the same faith as the apostles, we acquire it by the same divine inspiration as opens our eyes to the truth of the incarnation – whether known directly in the form of Jesus' life as such or indirectly in the form of the apostolic interpretation of this life in the gospel.

Second, if this is true, Farrer's doctrine of inspired images can hold for the apostolic writings only if it also holds for Christian thinking and speaking in general. Images, whether used by apostles or by other Christians, are inspired or God-given only in so far as they have actually been used in the process of coming to see the truth of the incarnation. The 'title of "inspired" is conferred upon [them] ... retrospectively'.[34] It signifies not a specific quality of the images

---

[30]   Austin Farrer, *A Rebirth of Images: The Making of St John's Apocalypse* (Westminster: Dacre Press, 1949), 13.

[31]   Ibid., 14f.

[32]   GV 103 / 88.

[33]   GV 108 / 91.

[34]   Farrer, 'Revelation', 107.

as such but a fact about their actual use, that is, their role in the process of God's faith-constituting revelation – whether at the beginning of Christianity or at the beginning of individual Christian lives.

Now, Farrer does not deny that inspiration is the touch of the divine presence in Christ, prophet, apostle and believer. But for him there is a difference of degree: Christ was supremely inspired and prophets and apostles more so than ordinary believers because they enlarged the revealed truth which believers believe.[35] But, surely, what is at stake here is the salvific presence of God, not the quantity of revealed truth; and, while God was fully present in Christ, he was not more present to the apostles than he is to every Christian: how he used them was different from how he uses most of us, but this is another matter.

Again Farrer's approach to revelation is too historical to appreciate this. He unduly restricts his analysis of inspired images to the case of prophets and apostles who created the images through which we participate in the mind of Christ. For Farrer it is a historical fact beyond further justification that the images of Israel provided the matrix of the media of God's revelation at the historical beginnings of Christianity: Jesus and the apostles inherited their vocabulary of images from Israel's long tradition; they combined, rearranged, compared, contrasted and mutually modified these images by focusing them on Jesus Christ; and the New Testament writings manifest in their various ways the manifold syntax of these combinations and rearrangements of images.

This is fine as far as it goes. But it does not follow, as Farrer thinks it does, that only the New Testament images are inspired, or that they are more inspired than others. To assume this is to confuse the issues of *scriptural authority* and *inspiration*. The authority of Scripture is not derived from the exceptional inspirational quality of its texts or their authors but, on the one hand, from God's activity in incarnation and inspiration to which it testifies, and, on the other, from its use in the Church: it reliably presents the gospel, which is the necessary though not sufficient condition for the Spirit to inspire the hearers to accept the truth of the gospel. Scripture plays a normative role in the life of the Christian community not because it alone is inspired but because by inspiration it alone is accepted as reliable source of the gospel: its continual use in the Church safeguards the continuity of the *verbum externum* of the Christian gospel message and thus continually provides the occasion for the Spirit to communicate the *verbum internum* to us by opening our hearts and minds to the truth of that message.

Finally, what follows from all this for theology? Theologians, according to Farrer, must elucidate the grammar of the image-discourse of Scripture to enable us to read and understand it appropriately. They do so, first, by identifying its image-vocabulary, that is, 'the elements of its imaginative language':[36] this is where the Old Testament plays an irreplaceable role in Christian theology; and they do so,

---

[35]    Ibid., 104f.

[36]    Charles C. Hefling, Jr, *Jacob's Ladder: Theology and Spirituality in the Thought of Austin Farrer* (Cambridge, MA: Cowley Publications, 1979), 102.

second, by spelling out the syntax or set of rules by which they are combined especially in the New Testament texts. Thus Farrer agrees with Wittgenstein that theology is grammar, but he differs from him by conceiving it as 'a rule by which to understand ... the revelation of God in Jesus Christ'[37] and not merely as the grammar of a particular religious form of life. Similarly, he agrees with Luther that theology's grammar of revelation must be based on the biblical writings. But – and this is decisive – he differs from him by concentrating on their poetical rather than theological structures: Luther read Scripture in the light of the soteriological dialectics of law and gospel which he derived not from the texts as such but from their (ecclesial) use in proclaiming and provoking faith in Jesus Christ. Farrer, on the other hand, studies Scripture in the light of the cosmological paradox of double agency by probing into the working of poetical imagination as the analogical key to the working of divine inspiration. This allows him to appreciate the image-thinking of biblical discourse. But his interpretations are criticised as 'too fanciful, too speculative, too elaborate'[38] precisely because he fails to provide theological criteria by which the validity, viability and appropriateness of the image patterns he discovers could be assessed. All he does is to apply the internal standards of literary criticism and the external standards of rational theology. But he fails to offer any standards specific to revealed theology as articulated in Scripture.

Yet how do we know that the images, or patterns of images, which we find in the New Testament writings are adequate to convey God's revelation? Farrer offers a number of criteria ranging from efficacy through orthodoxy and rationality to applicability of fact. But he is well aware that they are compelling neither individually nor taken together: 'there is no intrinsic guarantee of validity'.[39] All he proposes is the internal standard of literary criticism that 'the principal images provide a canon to the lesser images', and the external standard of rational theology that 'the conception of God supplied to us by natural theology' is the 'canon to interpret revelation'.[40]

That is to say, rational theology fixes the reference of 'God' and thereby the reference range of the imaginative language of Scripture: what cannot be true of the 'supreme being' of rational theology cannot be an adequate image of divine truth. This amounts to saying that, contrary to traditional understanding, the Book of Nature provides the key to the Book of Scripture, not vice versa. Farrer is quite explicit: unless we know God by rational analogies as the infinite correlate of finite activity and will, we are unable to appreciate what we know from Scripture as revelation.

On the other hand, we 'cannot criticise the revealed images from [our] acquaintance with their object: [we] can only confront them with one another'.[41]

---

[37] Austin Farrer, *Saving Belief: A Discussion of Essentials* (London: Hodder and Stoughton, 1964), 107. [Now also on page 132 of Ann Loades and Robert MacSwain (eds), *The Truth-Seeking Heart: Austin Farrer and His Writings* (Norwich: Canterbury Press, 2006).]

[38] Hefling, *Jacob's Ladder*, 80.

[39] Farrer, 'Revelation', 106.

[40] GV 110–11 / 94 and 93.

[41] GV 76 / 67.

We can critically compare the images we find in Scripture, distinguish between principal and lesser images and correct the images by one another. But there is no further justification for taking them to be inspired and appropriate than the fact that they are used there: the only reason to believe that they are inspired, that only they are inspired and that they are appropriate to communicate the divine truth is the fact that they are actually used in Scripture. We 'cannot by-pass the images to seize an imageless truth',[42] as Farrer stresses. The truth of revelation is accessible to us only through the scriptural images chosen by God himself as media of his revelation. If we believe this, then it is not because it is obvious but because it has been made obvious to us by God's Spirit. And this, for Farrer, is only another way of saying that the determination of the appropriateness of the images of Scripture lies, in the last resort, not with us but with God himself.

However, to know the images and their combinations in Scripture is not to know that they convey God's revelation, that they are inspired, that they are chosen by God who made the apostles choose and use them or that their patterning discloses the working of divine inspiration in the apostolic imagination. All this is assumed prior to analysing the imaginative language of Scripture. And Farrer offers little more by way of justifying this assumption than the assurance that this is what Christians expect to find in Scripture.

So in the final analysis Farrer's approach to Scripture does not really move beyond the dichotomy of rational theology and literary criticism: his account of revealed theology as the grammar of God's revelation in and through the inspired images of Scripture remains within the limits of rational theology alone and fails to work out proper doctrinal principles of revealed theology for reading Scripture. He remains a rational theologian even where he studies Scripture; and he so closely assimilates the task of a theological reading of Scripture to that of a literary critique of the biblical texts that they become virtually indistinguishable. This is not to deny the importance of his insights into the imaginative language of Scripture. But his idea of revealed theology as the grammar of Christian image-thinking is underdeveloped, to say the least. He did not work out the implications of his fruitful insight into revealed theology as image-thinking. So let me end this essay by suggesting the direction in which this could be done.

## IV

John McIntyre has pointed out that 'Image-thinking, like parabolic thinking is ... particular and specific', not generalising and abstract.[43] Farrer made a similar point by contrasting images and concepts. 'Behind the symbolism of God as king is not an idea of royalty but something more concrete – the actual human king at

---

[42]    GV 110 / 93.

[43]    John McIntyre, *Faith, Theology and Imagination* (Edinburgh: The Handsel Press, 1987), 102.

Jerusalem'.[44] That is, concepts present general ideas which can be applied to a variety of things; images, on the other hand, represent individual facts. They are, as Sartre saw it, 'the way objects that are absent have of being present'.[45] Thus, whereas concepts are descriptive devices to characterise something, as a particular of a certain sort (lines on a paper as a cross), images are cognitive devices to represent the particular as something unique. The former are generated by our mind's capacity to analyse and abstract particular aspects of things and generalise them; the latter result from the capacity of our imagination to contemplate the concrete and use symbolic media and patterns to make present the (spatially and temporally) absent.

It is clear even from this crude distinction that we must not try to treat images as if they were concepts. Farrer was well aware of this. If we begin to use images such as paternal love or Kingdom of God like concepts, confusion is bound to result. On the other hand, he thinks that all concepts in theology are analogical, and that analogies are sober and critically refined images, though no closer to the truth than the images they refine. That is, we cannot generalise images or replace them by a set of neatly defined concepts without emptying them of content. But neither can we simply cut them off from concepts without severing the link between images and truth. Wittgenstein and Hegel exemplify this in their different ways. According to Wittgenstein we must not confuse images and concepts if we want to grasp their truth; according to Hegel we must concentrate on their conceptual content if we want to bring out their truth. Thus Wittgenstein insists that images or pictures are not concepts and that theology has to do with the technique of using the pictures of a given religion rather than with transforming its imaginative language into a pseudo-scientific conceptual language. Hegel, on the other hand, presents an elaborate theory of the relationship between imagination (*Vorstellung*) and concept which seeks to show that images must be transformed into concepts by distinguishing between their imaginative form and conceptual content and by generalising the latter in such a way that the truth content of images can be preserved in the more adequate form of concepts. So Wittgenstein rejects the conceptualisation of images in the name of truth, while Hegel champions it for the same reason. What both fail to see, or to see clearly enough, is the difference between *generalisation* and *universalisation*: while images do not generalise in the sense of presenting general aspects or features of things, they universalise. Images, as John McIntyre put it, have a universalising function: they universalise 'an experience or event which had a subjective character or one which was very much bounded by its original historical origins'.[46] Whereas concepts generalise features common to many things, images universalise what is unique. Hence if theology is *image*-thinking rather than conceptual-thinking, it must concentrate on the unique and singular rather than on the common and general – this is what

---

44    Hefling, *Jacob's Ladder*, 52.
45    McIntyre, *Faith, Theology and Imagination*, 90.
46    Ibid., 172.

distinguishes theology from all forms of scientific and metaphysical theory. On the other hand, since it is image-*thinking*, it does not simply use, quote and rearrange the images of the discourse of faith but develops them into doctrinal *models* which preserve the uniqueness and singularity of the underlying image but have a wider, even universal application. Christological, soteriological, trinitarian or pneumatological doctrines are all cases in point: they are based on biblical images, or sets of images, which they elaborate and universalise into models in terms of which not only Scripture but the whole of our experience is interpreted. That is to say, there is a constructive or doctrinal aspect of (revealed) theology which necessarily goes beyond the hermeneutical task of reconstructing the image patterns of the biblical texts as Farrer practised it. And Christian doctrine – as Farrer clearly knew from the way he employed trinitarian and incarnational thought, although he did not help us to see how it should be creatively developed – is more than the combination of the principles of rational theology, poetical imagination and literary criticism.

Chapter 4

# Making it Plain: Austin Farrer and the Inspiration of Scripture [1992]†

Gerard Loughlin

'God is his own interpreter, and he will make it plain.' I take this couplet of William Cowper's to lie at the heart of Austin Farrer's reading of scripture, the essence of his biblical hermeneutics.[1] In this essay I want to suggest that it provides a key to

† When Gerard Loughlin wrote this chapter he was teaching Religious Studies at St Dominic's Sixth Form College, Harrow, and by the time it was published he was Lecturer in Religious Studies at the University of Newcastle upon Tyne. It was originally delivered at a conference at Durham in 1989 and published in Ann Loades and Michael McLain (eds), *Hermeneutics, the Bible and Literary Criticism* (London: Macmillan/New York: St Martin's Press, 1992). However, four years later its substance was incorporated into a chapter, 'Making it plain', in Loughlin's *Telling God's Story: Bible, Church and Narrative Theology* (Cambridge: Cambridge University Press, 1996; corrected paperback edition, 1999), 107–38. In a footnote in the volume's preface, Loughlin writes: 'The present book is really no more than scribbling between the lines of [Hans] Frei's essays, which are themselves written upon the pages of [Karl] Barth's tomes' (x, note 4). This mention of Frei is suggestive, as Frei's essays are sprinkled with appreciative references to Farrer, in particular to *The Glass of Vision* and Farrer's essay 'Revelation' in Basil Mitchell (ed.), *Faith and Logic: Oxford Essays in Philosophical Theology* (London: George Allen and Unwin, 1957), 84–107. Aside from its intrinsic merit as an interpretation of Farrer's thought or as an original argument in its own right, Loughlin's engagement with Farrer is thus significant in both pointing toward Farrer's influence on Frei and narrative theology, and in bringing Farrer back into conversation with an important movement in contemporary theology. Loughlin uses Farrer's work to (i) develop a viable doctrine of scriptural inspiration while simultaneously (ii) questioning the hegemony of historical-critical approaches to the biblical text and (iii) advancing a more inter-textual and communal understanding instead. The Christian Church, he argues, is itself, at least in part, a 'socio-textual reality'. Loughlin thus proposes an account of inspiration that 'locates inspiration in the community that both writes and reads Scripture, and one moreover that … locates the writing of Scripture as a moment within its reading. For then it is the reading or interpretation of Scripture that is inspired, and such an interpretation, precisely as God's interpretation, is contingent upon human fallibility'

1 [From Cowper's familiar poem and hymn, 'God Moves in a Mysterious Way', the last verse of which runs: 'Blind unbelief is sure to err,/And scan his work in vain;/God is his own interpreter/and he will make it plain'. Farrer invokes this verse in 'The Inspiration of the Bible' [1952], in Austin Farrer, *Interpretation and Belief*, edited by Charles C. Conti (London: SPCK, 1976), 11. This text is also now available in Ann Loades and Robert MacSwain

a contemporary understanding of the doctrine of biblical inspiration. My purpose is not, as it was for Farrer in the third of his Bampton Lectures, 'to construct some account of scriptural inspiration from first principles',[2] but to sketch an account of biblical inspiration that draws upon Farrer's subtle and penetrating investigations in *The Glass of Vision* and the essays collected in the volume *Interpretation and Belief.* I trust that the subject of biblical inspiration will not, as Farrer feared it might, 'seem to many people a topic so old and so wearisome that it can be no longer endured'![3] As Farrer rightly noted, in the question of biblical inspiration, 'interests more vital than those of curiosity are at stake'.[4]

'God is his own interpreter.' My statement of this axiom requires a few initial clarifications before I embark upon its detailed explication. First, my use, after Farrer and the larger part of the Christian tradition, of masculine pronouns to designate divinity is a matter of grammar and custom and not of semantics. God is her own interpreter also. Secondly, by using the word 'interpretation' I intend only to draw attention to the inevitable and irreducible contextuality of reading, both of the object that is read and of the subject who reads it. Thus interpretation is simply a thematisation of reading. So to put the matter serves as a reminder that 'interpretation' is not something that follows after 'reading', as if it were a sort of 'second reading'. Reading is always interpretative, and interpretation is always a matter of reading. The distinction between 'exegesis' and 'eisegesis' is one not of hermeneutics but of ethics; between readings approved and disapproved. God, then, is her own reader; both of what she has done and of what she has written.

It is all too difficult for us as Western thinkers not to read the scriptures of the Christian Church, the Bible – which I take, whatever the vagaries of its circumscription, to be a recognisable corpus – other than in the context of modern historicism. We are all schooled in seeking to discern the historical constraints on the production, transmission and interpretation of the biblical texts, and moreover on their own interpretation or reading of the events they are held to record, the mighty acts of God in history and above all in the life of Jesus of Nazareth. As heirs to well over 200 years of Enlightenment endeavour it is all too easy for us to succumb to the allure of the historian's scientific vision. However, it is precisely this allure and seduction that we must resist if a contemporary or post-modern rendering of biblical inspiration is to be achieved.

It is thus a necessary task, preliminary to articulating the axiom that 'God is his own interpreter', to place historical criticism in its proper place, namely in the tool-box. In saying this I am conscious of needing to avoid the sort of 'facile' condemnation of historical criticism noted by Frank Kermode; the sort

---

(eds), *The Truth-Seeking Heart: Austin Farrer and His Writings* (Norwich: Canterbury Press, 2006), 14–19, citation on 16.]

[2]    GV 39 / 39 [original pagination / this volume].

[3]    GV 35–6 / 37.

[4]    GV 36 / 37.

of condemnation advanced, as James Barr alleges, by 'persons unqualified'.[5] Nevertheless it is, I think, necessary to condemn a misuse of historical criticism that is blind to its own prejudices and ambiguities and overconfident of the insights it attains. It is necessary to criticise a practice that cajoles the Church into treating its Scriptures as if they were any other sort of text. It is both necessary to recognise the limitations of historical criticism and the status of Scripture as inspired within the Church.

The need to demarcate the scope of historical criticism and the limitation of its methods were acutely recognised by Farrer. Historical criticism, he wrote,

> is a net with its own sort of meshes let down into the ocean of total fact and gathering whatever harvest of fishes that sort of net will catch. No net will catch all the living matter in the water and no historical method will fish up the whole of live historical reality, unless we give to 'historical reality' the tautological sense of 'what our historical method fishes up'.[6]

In many ways Farrer's image is too generous, for it allows that the net of historical criticism fetches up at least something of historical reality if not the whole of it. But often even this should be in doubt. To change the metaphor, the critical historian is often no other than a prospector who finds 'fool's gold' at the bottom of the pan.

One example of such gold is the 'discovery' of Q, the source document of the early Church, long since lost, that provided the writers of Matthew and Luke with the material common to them both. Farrer of course was a notable writer 'On Dispensing with Q',[7] arguing that it was more sensible to suppose that Luke read Matthew than that both read Q. The scholarly world, having invested so much imaginative force in the reality of Q, is loathe to countenance, let alone accept, the sort of argument advanced by Farrer. However, the judgment of Michael Goulder seems correct, even if the supposition of Q is yet to be falsified: 'Farrer's achievement is the not inconsiderable one of reducing Q from a fact to a hypothesis'.[8] But it is the very power of the historico-critical consensus to turn fancy into fact, base metal into gold, that constitutes its disturbing power. It is a power to persuade with little evidence, while all the time pretending to a scientific rigour, the originary location of which is increasingly in doubt. It is the same sort of power exercised upon us by such ubiquitous dogmas as those of Darwin, Freud and Einstein. It is a power which, as Wittgenstein noted, has the appeal of letting

---

[5] See Frank Kermode, 'The Argument about Canons', in F. McConnell (ed.), *The Bible and the Narrative Tradition* (Oxford: Oxford University Press, 1986), 84–5.

[6] 'Very God and Very Man' [c. 1952], in Farrer, *Interpretation and Belief*, 127.

[7] Austin Farrer, 'On Dispensing with Q', in D.E. Nineham (ed.), *Studies in the Gospels: Essays in Memory of R.H. Lightfoot* (Oxford: Basil Blackwell, 1955), 55–88.

[8] Michael Goulder, 'Farrer the Biblical Scholar', in Philip Curtis, *A Hawk Among Sparrows: A Biography of Austin Farrer* (London: SPCK, 1985), 198.

us in on the secret of things, a revelation of hidden mechanisms. No doubt it is a power made attractive and forceful by our desire.

The biblical scholar can take Scripture apart in order to show us how it was so craftily put together. But once we know how it works there is no need, let alone any room, for ideas of inspiration, divine or otherwise. We have before us a wholly human work, a text like any other.

The doctrine of biblical inspiration does not deny that Scripture is a wholly human work, it simply adds that it is also a wholly divine one. To see how this may be so, in the face of a historical inquiry that would have Scripture a merely cultural product, we must, I want to suggest, take seriously the axiom with which I began this paper.

'God is his own interpreter.' If one takes this seriously with regard to the relation between Scripture as testimony and that to which it testifies, one must construe the relation as more intimate than that of event and record, let alone of event and second-hand report. One then cannot suppose, as Farrer puts it facetiously, that Scripture 'is just the record of the witnesses', or their successors', reaction to the events. It is what St Luke couldn't help fancying someone's having said he thought he remembered St Peter's having told him: or it is the way St Paul felt about what Christ meant to him'.[9] Such a view leaves little if any room for a notion of inspiration, and calls into question the role of Scripture as both source and criterion of the Christian life. Consequently it calls into question the very self-understanding of the Christian Church as the divinely constituted and enabled community of the forgiven in whose existence the sacramental presence of the incarnation is realised and continued.

If God is his own interpreter, then Scripture, as imaginative testimony to God's revelation, is itself part of that revelation, part of God's intimate self-disclosure, part of God's incarnation. As Farrer puts it, 'God speaks without and within; he reveals himself both through the situation with which he presents the recipients of revelation, and through the imagination, in terms of which he leads them to see and hear the voices and the sights surrounding them'.[10] It is, I take it, this aspect of the Christian faith that the doctrine of biblical inspiration is intended to delimit, but this aspect that is precisely difficult of such delimitation.

One must suppose Scripture to be in part constitutive of the events it discloses, as they are of it; one must suppose the relation of event and text to be inter-constitutive. It is a part of the mystery of the incarnation that it is disclosed or mediated to us in the reading and appropriation of four canonical gospels, whose agreements and disagreements are irreducibly part of the event they re-present.

In describing the events of revelation and their appearing in the testimony of the Church as inter-constitutive I want to draw attention to the fact that the Christian Church is at least in part a socio-textual reality. It exists as a society or community of people who are in part constituted by the sacred texts that they have

---

[9]   GV 37 / 38.
[10]   Farrer, 'Inspiration: Poetical and Divine' [1963], *Interpretation and Belief*, 44.

inherited and those that they have written, texts that they read both when they are gathered together in liturgical celebration and when they are apart in private prayer and meditation.

The Scriptures constitute the Church that has already constituted the Scriptures. The letter of the text is a dead thing until and insofar as it is taken up and performed in the Church. It is thus that the Scriptures, when read together as the canonical story of God, open up a 'world' in which the reader can live, construing his or her own life, past, present and future, as a continuing part of the biblical story. But to enter the world of the Bible, to become a part of its story, is to enter the community that reads Scripture as that which delineates the world of the community; it is to become a part of the community's own story. There is thus a dynamic of communal reading, the precise delineation of which is above all difficult, for it is not simply sequential but always inter-animative, socio-textual.

Thus it has always been. There never was, at the first, a non-textual event of which the text is but a record or to which it is but a response. For all events within the life of the people of God, which is always a traditioned and traditioning life, forming the future as it is formed by the past, are themselves traditioned events. They are, if one likes, always already interpreted, always already a reading of what has gone before, in part constituted by a preceding textual reality. In this sense all origins are belated.[11]

Jesus of Nazareth, whose life, death and resurrection are the historical origin of Christian faith, comes after the words of God given in the Hebrew Scriptures, both as their continuation and as their fulfilment. Precisely as the figure who meets us in the New Testament, Jesus the Christ is already prefigured in the Old. Jesus himself is in part a textually-constituted reality. As Farrer reminds us, the advent of John the Baptist is written out of the text of Isaiah, 'but it is an imperceptive reader ... who supposes that the Christ of the blessed message springs out of Scripture any less evidently than his messenger does'.[12] Christ, for Farrer, self-consciously constituted himself in his reading of the Hebrew Scriptures, a constitution continued by the Church. 'Christ', Farrer writes, 'both performed the primary action and gave the primary interpretation: the Apostles, supernaturalised by the Spirit of Pentecost, worked out both the saving action and the revealing interpretation of Christ'.[13] Christ clothed himself in scriptural 'images', and, in the clothing, constituted the character and identity of God's Messiah. The inter-constitution of man and image – an existential-textual reality and event – was and is the self-disclosure of God. For Farrer, 'The great images interpreted the events of Christ's ministry, death and resurrection, and the events interpreted the images; the interplay of the two is revelation'.[14]

---

[11] See D. Foster, 'John Come Lately: The Belated Evangelist', in McConnell, *The Bible and the Narrative Tradition*, 113–31.

[12] Farrer, 'On Looking Below the Surface' [1959], *Interpretation and Belief*, 64.

[13] GV 41 / 41.

[14] GV 43 / 42.

If, then, Christ and the community he inaugurates and enables through the power of the Spirit are socio-textual realities, irreducibly bound in their identities to the word of God, and if Christ is the self-disclosure and revelation of God, God as he is in himself in the world, then Scripture is inevitably a part of God's revelation. Person and text are inter-constitutive, the Word and words of God. The one is necessary for the meaning of the other. Christ and the life of the Church are only properly understood in the light of Scripture, and Scripture is only properly understood in the light of Christ and the life of the Church.

Nevertheless, it remains the case, as Farrer notes, that the 'primary revelation is Jesus Christ himself' and not Scripture.[15] Hence it is proper to say that the inspired Scripture is not itself revelation but inter-constitutive of revelation and thus, and only thus, properly said to be inspired. Scripture, precisely in itself, extracted from the life of the community in which it lives, is not, and cannot be, inspired. It is then but a dead letter, an ancient text, a curiosity. To speak of Scripture as inspired is to speak of it enjoying that life in which it is taken up and used as inter-constitutive of the user. To be inspired is to be filled with the Spirit, and that is to be part of the community to which the Spirit is given, sent from the Father by the Son. The location of biblical inspiration is not the text itself, but the community in which the text is located. To speak of biblical inspiration is to speak of a Church charism, a gift of God's grace to the Church. It is people not things that are inspired, for to be inspired is to be made alive.

Taking biblical inspiration as a charism of the Spirit, a gift given to the Church, and thus a practice within the Church, a Church usage, one can present an account of biblical inspiration thematised on the writing and the reading of Scripture.

In the first place, the writers of Scripture were inspired. This does not mean that the biblical writers were, as Farrer puts it, 'out of their ordinary senses when they composed ... God [did not suspend] their normal consciousness and [wag] their tongues and hands for them as a showman does his puppets'.[16] When they were inspired they were not any less themselves; they were just themselves. But they were themselves as people writing for their fellow Christians, writing accounts of the life, death and resurrection of Jesus, writing about living the kind of life wrought by that death and resurrection, attending to the mystery of that life. Their inspiration was different from that of others in the Church only in that they were doing something different from others in the Church, then and now. 'We', as Farrer reminds us, 'may be inspired to embrace what St Paul revealed: he was inspired to reveal it. We may be inspired to expound what he taught: but he was inspired to teach it'.[17]

The problem with articulating the inspiration of the biblical writers is that, in wanting to establish their writing in relation to the action of God as self-revealing,

[15]   GV 39 / 39.

[16]   Farrer, 'The Inspiration of the Bible', *Interpretation and Belief*, 10 / *The Truth-Seeking Heart*, 15.

[17]   Ibid., 10 / *The Truth-Seeking Heart*, 16.

the particular thematisation of their creatureliness as dependent upon and open to the one action of God's self-disclosure in the event of Christ crucified, buried and risen, one is all too likely to forget that their own action in writing for their communities was precisely that, their own action. To speak of God inspiring is not to speak of someone behind the scenes pulling strings. It is rather to speak of the relation that existed between those writers and the eternal reality of God; more concretely, it is to speak of their context in the life of the Church. But in order to make evident the force of the latter claim it is necessary to turn to the other pole on which an account of biblical inspiration can be thematised, namely the reading of Scripture. In so doing it should be evident that these two poles cannot be held apart but must be seen as two moments within the one dynamic of the Church's life.

If God inspired St Paul to reveal further the mystery of God, to teach what he taught about Christ, about Christ's life and death, and our own in relation to Christ, then equally, as Farrer suggests, God inspires us in so far as reading St Paul's writing we discern what is to be read there of God's mystery. In what I take to be a key passage in Farrer's paper 'The Inspiration of the Bible', he writes, 'If we do not believe that the same God who moved St Paul can move us to understand what he moved St Paul to say, then ... it isn't much use our bothering about St Paul's writings'.[18]

Farrer, with his usual 'translucency' and precision, here states the crux of biblical reading, the single point that is so often either overlooked, ignored or denied by the scholar. Thus Maurice Wiles, in his essay 'Scriptural Authority and Theological Construction', looks forward to a time when Scripture will be seen as an 'indispensable resource rather than as a binding authority'. He desires an 'abandonment of the idea of the Bible as authoritative', and since, as he admits, 'the notion of authority is implicit in the notion of scripture, the abandonment of the Bible as scripture'.[19] For Wiles there is no room in the Church for biblical inspiration. This is because, as he puts it, 'critical study of the Bible has enabled us to see things about the nature of scriptural texts ... whose general truth cannot seriously be questioned'.[20] These unquestionable things include the social conditioning of the texts, the diversity of opinions within them, and the historical unreliability of their witness.[21] Where in such a determinate nexus, the contingency of Scripture's all-too-human production, could God insinuate his inspiration so as to accord Scripture some degree of veracity? Where exactly could he hide the string? Farrer poses the same problem with regard to St Paul: 'If God inspires St Paul to speak, how are we to strain out St Paul, so as to be left with the pure word of God? We do not want St Paul's national prejudices or personal limitations,

---

[18] Ibid., 11 / *The Truth-Seeking Heart*, 16.

[19] Maurice Wiles, 'Scriptural Authority and Theological Construction: The Limitations of Narrative Interpretation', in Garrett Green (ed.), *Scriptural Authority and Narrative Interpretation* (Philadelphia: Fortress Press, 1987), 50–51.

[20] Ibid., 43.

[21] Ibid., 43–4.

which, good man as he was, he could not wholly escape'. But Farrer replies that 'no one can, it is like trying to jump off one's own shadow'.[22]

As I have already suggested, an answer to these dilemmas can be approached by considering what it is for the Church's reading of Scripture to be itself inspired and not just the authors' writing of it. Farrer writes that when God inspires a good action it is the action itself that God inspires.[23] This is the matter precisely. God inspires the action, the doing, the writing of the evangelist, the reading of the believer. There are no hidden strings, no inspirational mechanisms. God's inspiration is not a further determinate or condition, in addition to all the others and in competition with them. Rather God's inspiration is the relation each event bears to the Creator in so far as the Creator is revealed in it. Wiles wants to do away with the idea of inspiration because he cannot find it; he cannot detect the mechanism by which he supposes it to work if it does work. But there is no such mechanism to be found. Inspiration is a matter, one might say, of hermeneutics.

If Wiles's problem is to have confused metaphysics with hermeneutics, there still remains the question of discernment raised by his consideration of contingency. Surely the Bible is full of errors and monstrosities, matters that we today would never have thought to write and certainly don't want to read? Can these disquieting texts, along with the more comforting, really be the word of God's revelation, the moment of his self-disclosure? In milder tone Farrer notes that 'St Paul's astronomy is (as astronomy) no good to us at all. St Luke appears to have made one or two slips in dating, and St John was often content with a very broad or general historical effect, and concentrated more on what things meant than just the way they happened'.[24]

One cannot iron out the disagreements and contradictions of Scripture, nor simply forget those parts that counter our most cherished beliefs and sentiments. Scripture everywhere displays itself to be what it is, the fallible production of an erring humanity. This problem is most difficult of resolution for an account of biblical inspiration that locates the action of the Spirit in the placing of ink on paper; that would have it as an infallible dictation. The problem is only slightly less for those accounts that speak of the action of the Spirit on the temper of the scriptural writers. The problem is, I think, easier of resolution for an account that locates inspiration in the community that both writes and reads Scripture, and one moreover that, as I shall shortly argue, locates the writing of Scripture as a moment within its reading. For then it is the reading or interpretation of Scripture that is inspired, and such an interpretation, precisely as God's interpretation, is contingent upon human fallibility.

In order to see how the problem of scriptural inconsistency and incongruity can be resolved as I have suggested, it is necessary to explore further the reading of Scripture within the Church and the way in which the writing of Scripture can be

---

[22]   Farrer, 'The Inspiration of the Bible', 10–11 / *The Truth-Seeking Heart*, 16.

[23]   Ibid., 12 / *The Truth-Seeking Heart*, 17.

[24]   Ibid.

understood as a moment within that reading. I have already indicated how Jesus Christ meets us in the New Testament as in himself an interpretation of the Old, a person who in his action and teaching constitutes a living reading of the prophets. 'And he closed the book, and gave it back to the attendant, and sat down; and the eyes of all in the synagogue were fixed on him. And he began to say to them, "Today this scripture has been fulfilled in your hearing"' (Luke 4.20–1). Jesus is God's own midrash on the Law and the Prophets; his own reading of his own writing. And the writing of the New Testament itself, in the gospels and in the letters and in Revelation, is the Church's inspired reading, and therefore God's reading, of God's own writing. Precisely because it came after, the writing of Scripture is constituted a moment in the reading of the Church; a moment in God's own reading of his own life.

It is because the Bible is in this sense God's own reading of himself and his action, God's reading of his own story, his dealings with the world, with kings and prophets, saints and fools, with Abraham, Isaac and Jacob, with Mary and the apostles, that the Bible is chaotic and incoherent, requiring discernment. This account of the matter is not so perplexing once it is remembered that the God of which it speaks is the God that became incarnate in Jesus of Nazareth. The eternal reality of God is given over, so Christian faith affirms and prays, to the contingent history of one man and the Church of which he is the head, for the sake of the world. Here one must take with full seriousness what Ronald Gregor Smith called 'the wholeness of God's condescension in Christ, his complete entering into the world through his Word'.[25] And, with equal seriousness, the whole work of Christ, which is, as Farrer writes, 'the work of the mystical Christ, who embraces both Head and members'.[26] Farrer continues, 'The interpretative work of the Apostles must be understood as participation in the mind of Christ, through the Holy Ghost: they are the members, upon whom inflows the life of the Head'.[27] But this understanding, I want to suggest, must be extended to the reading of Scripture by the whole Church. Revelation in this sense has not come to an end with the death of the last apostle, only the writing of which it is a reading.

God is his own interpreter, but his interpretation is incarnate, concrete and human. The mystery of God, as spoken in the Christian Church, however falteringly, is that, in being given over to human contingency, humanity is taken up into the mystery of the triune life of God, and that is the mystery of our salvation. To speak of biblical inspiration as I do here is to take but one perspective on this reality, but it is one that seeks to show how it is that Scripture, in being both the writing and the reading of God's own life with us, is, at one and the same time, a wholly human work. When Scripture, as writing inspired of God, is understood in the way I have tried to suggest, its all-too-obvious signs of human production should be expected rather than deplored. Just in so far as Scripture in the life of the

---

[25]  R.G. Smith, *J.G. Hamann 1730–1788: A Study in Christian Existence* (London: Collins, 1960), 20.

[26]  GV 41 / 41.

[27]  GV 42 / 42.

Church is inter-constitutive of the Church as a socio-textual reality, inspired by the love and power of the incarnate God, it cannot be treated as a text dropped from heaven, but must be read with discernment, struggling for its sense and reference. The point can be made this way: the reading of Scripture by and in the Church is the continuing incarnation of God's own self-interpretation, and, precisely as incarnate, is a wholly human work just as Jesus was a wholly human man.

This brings me to some final comments on the actual practice of reading Scripture as the word of God in and for the life of the Church. For, clearly, what I have described as the exercise of discernment in the reading of Scripture, which is equally a struggling to make sense of the text,[28] requires a certain attentiveness and a certain idea of what one is trying to do in reading the Bible in this way, in seeking to discern what God has written. This has always been a problem for the Church, an engagement of its entire history.

To begin with, a few programmatic remarks to indicate where one should and should not look for an appropriate account of biblical reading. As will already be evident, I do not think that the critical historian alone can be of much help in this matter. At best historical inquiry can, as Farrer puts it, act as a check on the Church's proclamation, as a constant reminder that what is proclaimed is the actual life and death of one man, living and dying in our human history.[29] It does this by keeping open the possible falsification of Christian claims about and for that man, that he lived a certain sort of life, taught certain sorts of thing, died in a certain sort of way and rose again on the third day. But, in the nature of the case, historical inquiry cannot verify these claims, and, above all, it cannot verify the Church's claims for the meaning and significance of the man in question.

Rather than look to the historian, we do better to return to some of the Church's earliest Scripture-readers, people such as Paul, Origen and Augustine, people not afraid as we often are of allegory and typology. Thus we have much to learn from Farrer's searching reading of biblical image and pattern. But even Farrer did not seek to overcome a common but misleading concern of the contemporary reader: the question of authorial intention. It seems to me that only when we get right about this can we embrace the literal meaning of Scripture as that which the Church seeks to discern in reading what God has written. Having thus stated my position with regard to the Church's practice in reading Scripture, I can here only briefly indicate what I mean by the struggle for the *sensus literalis*.

For many, the hermeneutical task in reading the Bible, as with any other text, is to attain the author's originary intention, to rethink the author's thought, to rehearse the authorial voice. The task is one of recognitive or logocentric hermeneutics. There is certainly nothing illegitimate about wanting to know what an author intended or meant to say; but it is entirely illegitimate to suppose that the meaning of a text is just the meaning of its author. The point can be made by

---

[28]    See C.M. Wood, 'Hermeneutics and the Authority of Scripture', in Green (ed.), *Scriptural Authority and Narrative Interpretation*, 6.

[29]    Farrer, 'Very God and Very Man', *Interpretation and Belief*, 127.

saying that a text strictly doesn't mean anything; it is people who mean things. To talk of the meaning of a text is to indulge a metaphor. It makes little difference whether one says that a text is 'full' of meaning waiting to be 'found' by the reader or that the reader 'gives' meaning to a text otherwise 'empty' of meaning. Nevertheless texts are the occasion or means of meaning, often or usually the meaning of their author but also of their readers. But there is no non-arbitrary way in which such meaning or meanings can be circumscribed. It is arbitrary to suppose that it is just the case that the author 'gives' meaning to a text which the reader then 'finds' upon reading it. The reader also can 'give' meaning to a text and the author 'find' it, for the author also can be a reader. And different readers can find or give different meanings from those of other readers, including the author. Nor are they constrained to give or find only one meaning; texts are open to a multiplicity and diversity of readings.

However it does not follow that, because the relation between text and meaning is less determinate than a strict recognitive hermeneutics would have us suppose, the relation between them is unconditioned. The meaning of a text is conditioned or constrained by the context of its reading, by the conventions of meaning that are in place at the point of its interpretation. There can be little doubt that today the Church reads its Scripture differently from how it read it in the past, especially with regard to the Old Testament. Equally, different people within the Church read Scripture differently; denominational variation in the canon of Scripture is simple evidence of this.

Thus the meaning of Scripture is equivocal, conditioned by the circumstances of its reading but not determined to a single unitary interpretation. To say this, however, is not to remove the question of its authorial meaning, which I here take to be the question of its literal sense, the sense with which it was written. This sense or meaning is, it seems to me, what most people mean by 'literal sense' when they are not using the notion of 'literality' to justify their preferred reading and when they are not being professional scholars of hermeneutics. The chief force of literality is that it constitutes a basic reading which everyone within a reading community would agree is the obvious or 'plain' sense of the text, from which other senses or meanings are at a remove. I use the notion of 'plainness' after David Kelsey, for whom it is the sense 'normally acknowledged as basic, regardless of whatever other constructions might also properly be put upon the text'.[30] Of course this meaning will be, as Kelsey argues, a consensus meaning, a communal and conventional reading. But the community that so reads its Scripture usually understands the 'plain' sense to be a literal sense, the meaning intended by the author. As Kathryn Tanner points out in her article 'Theology and the Plain Sense', Kelsey's 'plain' sense is a purely formal notion that does not 'prejudge the material character' of Scripture's sense. 'When', she continues, 'participants in a practice of appealing to texts talk about the plain sense, they need not (and perhaps usually do not) *mean* by that the

---

[30]    David Kelsey, *The Uses of Scripture in Recent Theology* (Philadelphia: Fortress Press, 1975), 43.

sense that commands general agreement. They may mean instead – for example, in the Christian community – "the sense the author intended"…"the sense that God intends"".[31] It is the sense meant by the Christian community in which I am interested, which I take to be the literal sense of Scripture.

The question of the author's intention is a vital one, but not, I would suggest, when it is taken to be about the intentions of the person who actually composed the scriptural text in question. Legitimate as such a question is, and rewarding as its answer is, it does not seem to me to be of primary theological interest. That interest is found rather in the question 'What does God, as the true writer of Scripture, mean by this text for us in our circumstances?' What is the literal meaning of this text for us now when its being divine writing constitutes its specific literality? The question has to be put in contextual terms because, insofar as God's writing is inter-constitutive, as I have already argued, of God's self-revelation, it is addressed to all times and places, but all times and places are not the same. Further, because it is God who writes, there is no supposition, as there might be with a human author, of a single or limited intention. There can be no question of finite meaning with regard to Scripture.

However, in general terms and briefly stated, I take the literal or 'plain' sense of the Bible to be the identity and character of God and of Jesus and thus, in more particular terms and with regard to specific instances of Scripture-reading in the life of the Church, either privately or in communal worship, our own identity, and thus responsibility and vocation, as followers of God's Word. For the Christian is called to be conformed to the will of God for him or her, conformed to God, to Jesus Christ, as depicted in the Bible story. But the Christ thus identified is not, as it were, waiting in the text to be found, but is constituted of text and Church in the reading of the Church which reconstitutes the historical event of Christ, itself already constituted of man and image. To put the matter otherwise, the norm by which the literal sense of Scripture is discerned is none other than Jesus Christ; he is, as it were, the reading-context within which the literal sense of God's writing is discerned, and, as such, is in part constituted by the text itself in which he is written – but only in part. For Jesus Christ, as the norm of the Church's reading, is not just the man who is mediated through the reading of Scripture by the Church, but also the risen Christ who is still walking with his Church, as with the disciples on the way to Emmaus. Christ, as the norm of Christian reading, is thus only realised in the practice of faithful reading. The Church is better able to read Scripture the better it lives in the light of its faithful reading of Scripture. The norm of Christ, by which the Church seeks to discern the sense of what God has written, the hermeneutical principle, as it were, by which the Bible is read with integrity, and which is also normative for the life of the Church, is not given simply, separate and apart from that for which it is normative, but is rather integral to it.

The Church, then, in reading Scripture seeks to read it literally, to read what God means in writing it, which writing, it must be remembered, is always a moment

---

[31]    Kathryn E. Tanner, 'Theology and the Plain Sense', in Green (ed.), *Scriptural Authority and Narrative Interpretation*, 59–78.

within the Church's reading. If the foregoing is allowed, presented as it is in very summary fashion, there arises the very serious problem of how the Church as the Church it is and has been in history, in all its diversity and self-contradiction, attains a 'plain' reading of the literal Scripture. Surely it is not so much a matter of the Church reading in agreement as of groups and individuals reading in disagreement? The Church at any one time, let alone across time, is notoriously unable to achieve agreed readings of any significant texts, and often constitutes its divisions along the lines of differing interpretations of Scripture. Scripture-reading in the Church is contested with vengeance. The problem is even more acute if one holds that the reading of Scripture by the Church is God's own reading of his own writing, as I have suggested, so that the Church's reading of Scripture is a participation within the triune life of God: the dynamic of the Spirit interpreting the Son who reveals the Father.

The first thing to be said in response to this problem, as to the earlier question of the fissures and fractures, the disquieting disagreements, within God's own writing, is that the God who thus reads, and wills the Church to read with him, the Scripture he has written with the Church, is the God who in the Son has given himself over to the finitude of his creation. This is an eternal truth worked out not just in the life of the man Jesus, but also in the continuing life of the Church. Therefore God's reading of Scripture is itself subject to the contingency and concrete circumstances of this world in the same way as the incarnate life of the second person of the Trinity was, in the Palestine of the first century.

Secondly, and here I must be extremely brief, where eternity and temporality meet we have to do with the eschatological. Only in the incarnate life of Christ was this a concrete reality, though proleptic of the consummation to which, in him, creation is to be brought. Consequently the consummation of the Church's reading of Scripture, a performance of absolute fidelity, is itself an eschatological event, proleptic, perhaps, in rare moments, but, for the most part, attendant upon a faithful struggle empowered by the grace of God. In the light of such considerations it should not seem so surprising that the Church's reading of Scripture, even if as deeply embraced in the love of God as we may hope and pray it is, should bear as it does the marks of human wilfulness, stupidity and corruption. Here I would like to quote Farrer on the exercise of ecclesiastical authority from his essay 'Infallibility and Historical Revelation':

> Through toil and tribulation, and tumult of her war – through an unending tension and debate between schools of thought within the Church – between the Church and her critics, between theological faculties and pastoral authority – it must be our faith that God guides the Church into truth, that the Catholic mind settles ever more and more firmly on essentials[.][32]

---

[32]  Austin Farrer, 'Infallibility and Historical Revelation', *Interpretation and Belief*, 163 / *The Truth-Seeking Heart*, 91. This chapter was originally published in Austin Farrer, et al., *Infallibility in the Church: An Anglican-Catholic Dialogue* (London: Darton, Longman and Todd, 1968), 9–23.

180                    *Scripture, Metaphysics, and Poetry*

Such a consideration may be supplemented by the following paraphrase of a passage from the same page of Farrer's essay, replacing the notion of 'infallibility' with that of 'God's reading': God, we may say, is a truthful reader of his own writing, and his reading takes effect in the history of the Church, through God knows what confusions and backslidings and refusals of co-operation. By holding such a faith we are led to seek God's reading with all seriousness, to respect the reading of the Church, and to do our own reading of Scripture in the humble but serious belief that it is an item in the great divine process. But God's reading is not to be spotted, pinned down, identified with an ecclesiastical organ or demanded on a given occasion. God's reading is not an oracle that one can consult.

In a sense, all that I have attempted in this chapter is to offer, in perhaps too abstruse terms drawn from theology and literary theory, a metaphorical account of what the Church may understand itself to be doing when it reads the Bible. 'Writing' and 'reading' have, of course, been my chief metaphors; yet the strong point about metaphorical usage within theology is the claim and prayer that it may be, however poorly, disclosive of the truth.

Finally, my argument, as I perceive it, has been entirely internal to the theological enterprise of Christian self-understanding, and, in so far as it has been apologetic, an entreaty to enter the circle of Christian reading. Thus I wish to conclude with a quotation from the last part of Farrer's Hulsean Sermon preached in Great St Mary's at Cambridge on 14 November 1948, a sermon which is, as his biographer Philip Curtis puts it, 'a most masterly exposition of his way of viewing the Gospels'.[33] Its relevance to my argument will, I trust, be apparent:

> Only God can understand God, even when God is incarnate. But God is in us by the Holy Ghost, and therefore we can know incarnate God. This is as true of us in our historical study, as it is of us at our prayers. We cannot know Christ in the history about him except by the Holy Ghost. The historical understanding of Christ began in St Peter and the other recipients of the Pentecostal Gift ... Later generations have received the historical testimony from the Church, the Church using the written scriptures as her norm of teaching; they have also received through the Church the Holy Ghost ... We either accept, or do not accept, the witness of the Holy Ghost. We understand the Christ who proclaimed himself the Son of God, because we understand, though but partly, what it is for Christ to be the Son of God. And we understand what it is for Christ to be the Son of God, because we perceive ourselves to be, in him, partakers of divinity.[34]

---

[33]    Curtis, *A Hawk Among Sparrows*, 133.
[34]    This sermon is published in ibid., Appendix I, 232–9, these citations from 238–9.

Chapter 5

# The Sin of Reading: Austin Farrer, Helen Gardner and Frank Kermode on the Poetry of St Mark [1992]†

Hans Hauge

## I. The Beginning of a Debate

Austin Farrer's Bampton Lectures for 1948 set in motion a debate, which is still going on, about the relation between what he called 'the sense of poetry' and 'the sense of scriptural revelation'.[1] Eight years later Helen Gardner, in her Riddell Memorial Lectures for 1956,[2] intervened in the debate with an attack upon Farrer, and Farrer defended himself in 1959 in a Presidential Address to the Oxford Society

---

†  When Hans Hauge wrote this chapter he was Senior Lecturer in English at Aarhus University and Research Fellow at the University's Centre for Cultural Research. Although all of the scholars included in Part II are interdisciplinary in scope, Hauge is the one whose primary disciplinary location and research focus is not theology or philosophy, but literature. The chapter was originally delivered at a conference in Durham in 1989 and published in Ann Loades and Michael McLain (eds), *Hermeneutics, the Bible and Literary Criticism* (London: Macmillan/New York: St Martin's Press, 1992). This chapter takes us back to Jasper's earlier discussion of the debate between Farrer and Helen Gardner, and between Gardner and Frank Kermode, on the value of Farrer's approach to biblical interpretation. Hauge summaries the state of play at that point, but then dissents from Jasper's defence of Kermode, and sides with Gardner instead. The debate, which Hauge said in 1989 was 'still going on', continues still with David Brown opting for something like Hauge's view – see his 'The Role of Images in Theological Reflection', in Douglas Hedley and Brian Hebblethwaite (eds), *The Human Person in God's World: Studies to Commemorate the Austin Farrer Centenary* (London: SCM Press, 2006), 90–92 – and Robert Titley arguing for something closer to Kermode – see his *A Poetic Discontent: Austin Farrer and the Gospel of Mark* (London and New York: T&T Clark International, 2010), 62–82. In a review of *Hermeneutics, the Bible and Literary Criticism*, Brian Horne says that Hauge's chapter is 'a delightful essay, playful in tone but serious in purpose' – although he is not entirely convinced by his argument: see *The Heythrop Journal* 35 (1994), 203–4. Twenty years after its initial publication, Hauge admits that accusing Farrer of the 'sin' of reading may have mislead or confused some readers as to what precisely this crime consisted of – but negotiating such ambiguity is also part of the ongoing work of interpretation.

[1]  GV ix / 12 [original pagination / this volume].

[2]  Helen Gardner, *The Business of Criticism* (Oxford: Clarendon Press, 1959).

of Historical Theology.[3] In his Charles Eliot Norton Lectures, 1977–78,[4] Frank Kermode wrote favourably about Austin Farrer without mentioning Gardner; and when Gardner followed Kermode as the Charles Eliot Norton Lecturer for 1979–80 she made her final contribution.[5] Yet the debate did not end there. David Jasper renewed it in his *Coleridge as Poet and Religious Thinker* and came to the conclusion that in her final intervention Gardner delivered a 'conservative' defence 'against a structuralist criticism – and it is the structuralist who looks back to Farrer'.[6] It is true that Helen Gardner was highly critical of structuralist activities, and we shall see why. It is not so certain, however, that this attitude is necessarily conservative.

As I intend to show, Gardner could be said to defend a *hermeneutic* position. She did not use the word and would probably have felt ill at ease about being classified as a hermeneutic critic. Be that as it may, my point is that the debate is between a certain structuralism – so broadly conceived that it may include Farrer – and a certain form of hermeneutics. Modern structuralism and modern hermeneutics both have some of their roots in early Romanticism. There is a clear similarity in terms of intention between Coleridge's ideas of 'removing the film of familiarity' and of 'making it new' and structuralist ideas of defamiliarisation and 'making it strange'.[7] Modern hermeneutics began with Schleiermacher and has developed in various ways, exemplified by the work of Hans-Georg Gadamer and Manfred Frank. I am interested in the debate between Farrer and Gardner not for historical reasons but in order to ask how it may affect reading of the Bible and how it relates itself to the differences between structuralism (and post-structuralism) and hermeneutics.

Farrer, Gardner and Kermode seem to agree on one point: the Bible can be read as a piece of literature. This constitutes the minimal consensus amongst them, but it doesn't amount to admitting that the Bible *is* literature, whatever that means. It only means that literary-critical theories or methods can be, or perhaps even should be, applied to biblical texts. Once this is admitted, however, one has opened Pandora's box. For one inevitably begins to ask what critical approaches are appropriate to the Bible, and what precisely is meant by calling the Bible 'literature'. In short, the question is the same as the title of a novel by David Lodge: *How Far Can You Go?*

---

   [3]   Austin Farrer, 'On Looking Below the Surface', originally published in *Proceedings of The Oxford Society of Historical Theology* 1959–60, reprinted in Austin Farrer, *Interpretation and Belief*, edited by Charles C. Conti (London: SPCK, 1976), 54–65. See also Farrer's response to Gardner in 'Inspiration: Poetical and Divine', originally published in F.F. Bruce (ed.), *Promise and Fulfilment* (Edinburgh: T&T Clark, 1963), reprinted in *Interpretation and Belief*, 39–53.

   [4]   Frank Kermode, *The Genesis of Secrecy: On the Interpretation of Narrative* (Cambridge, MA: Harvard University Press, 1979).

   [5]   Helen Gardner, *In Defence of the Imagination* (Cambridge, MA: Harvard University Press, 1982).

   [6]   David Jasper, *Coleridge as Poet and Religious Thinker: Inspiration and Revelation* (London: Macmillan, 1985), 149 / 124 in this volume [see also the note on structuralism].

   [7]   A point made by many observers, but explored in detail in R. Scholes, *Structuralism in Literature: An Introduction* (New Haven: Yale University Press, 1974), 168–70.

It was Gardner's initial contention, in 1956, that Austin Farrer had gone too far. He was accused of having trespassed against the proper business of criticism. He may even have sensed this himself, at least if we read literally and not ironically what he conceded in 1959: 'in my hotheaded youth, I unwisely wrote some studies in the typological interpretation of Scripture, and still more unwisely published them'.[8] He appeared to be somewhat puzzled (or did he, in fact, feel slightly honoured?) that Gardner had chosen, as he phrased it, 'such a butterfly as me to break upon her wheel', all the more so since he believed he had merely argued that there were parallels or analogies between the typological exegesis of Scripture and 'the sort of poetry-criticism which Mr Empson and in some places Charles Williams and some others had endeavoured'.[9] The juxtaposition of William Empson and Charles Williams is rather surprising, but, be that as it may, the point is that towards the end of his address Farrer vigorously defended himself and his 'method', as David Jasper notes. He was of the opinion that he had 'dissolved' those of Gardner's arguments that appeared to have undermined 'the charter of an exegesis' he believed in and wished to 'see practised'. So we may safely assume that he did not really believe it to have been unwise to publish his youthful attempts at a typological interpretation of Scripture.

And there *was* no reason for him to be defensive in the late 1950s. I do not know if Farrer was aware of the existence of Northrop Frye's *Anatomy of Criticism*, which came out in 1957 – that is to say, a year after Gardner's Riddell Memorial Lecturers – but Frye's *Anatomy* was nothing less than the final rehabilitation of a typological interpretation not only of the Bible, but of the whole of literature, since, according to Frye, secular literature is a displaced version of the Bible.[10] What Farrer had sensed in the early 1950s, and quite correctly I think, was that certain trends in contemporary literary criticism had made typological readings of the Bible possible again. By the end of the decade typological readings as such were taken for granted in certain progressive literary critical circles, but not, needless to say, in all.

Farrer, after all, wrote in the 1950s and in England, the time and place of the so-called Movement in poetry, of the neo-realism and anti-modernism of C.P. Snow and the Angry Young Men, and of analytical philosophy. It was a period when a poet was just like the man next door or, indeed, where he might in fact *be* the man next door.[11] Those high and idealistic hopes which Farrer had for poetry or poetic truth he certainly did not share with the poets of his time. All attempts to look below the surface of both life and literature appear to have been strictly censured at that time, if not by Helen Gardner then by the likes of Kingsley Amis,

---

[8]   Farrer, 'On Looking Below the Surface', 54.

[9]   Ibid.

[10]   Northrop Frye, *The Anatomy of Criticism: Four Essays* (Princeton: Princeton University Press, 1957).

[11]   The expression comes from A. Alverez, 'English Poetry Today', in R. Kostelanetz (ed.), *On Contemporary Literature* (New York: Discus Books, 1969), 86.

whose poem 'Against Romanticism' (1957) catches the spirit of the age quite successfully. The poem begins,

> A traveller who walks a temperate zone
> – Woods devoid of beasts, roads that please the foot –
> Finds that its decent surface grows too thin:
> Something unperceived fumbles at his nerves ...[12]

## II. Farrer's Theory of Mind

The Bible, says Helen Gardner, 'whatever else it may be, is certainly literature and presents to the human understanding literary problems, and demands that we exercise upon it the methods and skills appropriate to the discussion of such problems'.[13] The ending of Mark's Gospel presented Farrer a problem, and in order to solve the problem he used the methods and skills of literary criticism. But why were they not, according to Gardner, appropriate to the discussion? Did Farrer find that the Gospel's decent surface had grown too thin – St Mark used to be considered the least literary of the evangelists – and did he find patterns and allusions that could not be perceived? One of the fundamental principles of Gardner's literary criticism is that 'a poem is not whatever I choose to make of it. It is something which its author made with deliberation, choosing that it should say this and not that'.[14] At this point she appears to be echoing not only common sense but also the reconstructive hermeneutics of E.D. Hirsch's *Validity in Interpretation*.[15] What she calls the historical sense must be the arbiter in all interpretative controversies.

Since the Gospel of Mark is a kind of poem, St Mark must have made it with deliberation and must have chosen to say this, and not what Austin Farrer made him say. Farrer, as you may well know, set out to solve various puzzles, above all he wished solve the problem of the somewhat abrupt ending of the gospel text using literary methods or skills instead of traditional historical-critical ones. Now, who can deny that Farrer managed to make sense? The gospel ends with words that echo those of Joseph's brothers in the Old Testament – 'a glance at the Greek Old Testament will show the exactness of the verbal parallel'[16] – and Farrer continues, 'we have discussed the ending of St Mark, not to prove a thesis,

---

[12]   Amis's poem quoted from R. Ellmann and R. O'Clair (eds), *The Norton Anthology of Modern Poetry* (New York: Norton, 1973), 1012.

[13]   Gardner, 'The Poetry of St Mark', in *The Business of Criticism*, 79.

[14]   Ibid., 75.

[15]   E.D. Hirsch, Jr, *Validity in Interpretation* (New Haven: Yale University Press, 1967).

[16]   GV 145 / 116. [But see Robert Titley's comment, cited earlier on page 116 of this volume, that this verbal parallel, while suggestive, is not quite as 'exact' as Farrer perhaps wanted his readers to think. Nevertheless, Hauge's use of 'echo' above is certainly legitimate. While Hauge, following Farrer, writes 'quotation', 'quoted' and 'quoting' below, readers may wish to consider

but to show what sort of argument is appropriate'. But why was his argument not appropriate? Let us postpone Helen Gardner's answer to this question.

If the two last words of Mark's Gospel have an exact parallel in the Septuagint, then either the women at the grave were quoting, and St Mark was merely recording, or else St Mark quoted the words of Joseph's brethren in order to give finality and coherence to his gospel or poem. Farrer obviously believed that St Mark had chosen to end his poem in precisely this way and that the allusion to the Old Testament was deliberate. Furthermore Farrer was well aware of something else: namely, that his own essay belonged to a particular *genre*. His text belonged to the genre of literary criticism and, if someone wished to challenge him, he should be challenged as a literary critic not as a theologian. His only question to any future critic was: is this appropriate by way of literary criticism?

He was convinced, as he states it, that 'St Mark's words are shaped by a play of images and allusions of the subtle and elusive kind which belongs to imagination rather than to rational construction'.[17] Yet is this only a truth within the *genre* of literary criticism? Would it be equally true outside the genre – that is to say, inside another genre, such as scientific or historical criticism? Can one imagine Farrer drawing the same consequences as Northrop Frye, who distinguishes between historical truth, which is truth of correspondence, and poetic truth, which is 'contained within the verbal form and provides no external criterion for it'?[18] My point is that, if the final words in Mark's Gospel are a quotation, then that insight undermines the referential value of the same words, unless one is willing to say that the women were actually themselves quoting, and, if they were quoting, one would have to say that they weren't really afraid.

What does Farrer mean when he claims that what St Mark did belonged to the imagination and not to rational construction? On several occasions Farrer speculated upon the nature of language and of the imagination. Farrer takes his starting-point in the act of perception. When one sees a matchbox – and this is his example – one sees only a part of it. The imagination supplies the rest, aided by memory. In the case of language Farrer first holds that language consists of meaningless noises: 'a trail of sounds in the air'.[19] The meaning of these sounds is immediately supplied by the imagination. The meaning includes not only logical meaning but even the person who expresses the words – that is to say, the meaningless trail of sounds. Again memory offers assistance. The imagination, then, is a supplement, and it produces something which is not present but which once was present. Such past presences are stored in memory and reactivated by the imagination. Memory has priority over imagination. Blake, by the way, contended that imagination has

---

how the argument would go if 'allusion', 'alluded' and 'alluding' were used instead. Note also that Farrer eventually revised his earlier argument about the conclusion of Mark's Gospel.]

   [17]   GV 146 / 117.

   [18]   Northrop Frye, 'History and Myth in the Bible', in A. Fletcher (ed.), *The Literature of Fact* (New York: Columbia University Press, 1976), 12.

   [19]   Farrer, 'Inspiration: Poetical and Divine', 39.

nothing to do with memory. Farrer would then have to imagine a state of affairs, a perception or a use of language, where the imagination did *not* supply anything. Yet such a state, prior to the immediate use of imagination, cannot be remembered; it can only be imagined. The logical conclusion seems to be that the imagination supplies things that were never there at all.

In *The Glass of Vision* Farrer tries to spell out his, as we may call it, theory of mind. What is highest in the human mind, he argues, is the understanding. This faculty consists of wit and reason. 'Wit divines its object and begets a representation of it', he says. Reason, on the other hand, 'disciplines the product of wit and works out its inspirations to a systematic construction'.[20] The relation between wit and reason corresponds to the relation between imagination and rational construction – the words he used in connection with his reading of St Mark – or between imagination and memory. Wit, or imagination, is productive: it or they beget and divine objects and representations. The only thing that reason or memory can do is to discipline and systematise the products of the imagination. How the productive imagination works, and what its materials are, remains a mystery to Farrer. The only thing he can say is that they work upon signs or sense perceptions. When the imagination sees a sign it 'pictures another man's mind'. But is this picture really mimetic? Or is there not a great deal of arbitrariness in the workings of this power which Wordsworth called an 'unfather'd vapor' and which came athwart him so that he was 'lost in a cloud'?[21] What prevents a glass of vision from becoming a cloud of vision?

The interesting thing about Farrer's theory of imagination is that he moves from the act of perception of objects to the interpretation of texts. There seems to be no fundamental difference between perceiving a thing and a linguistic sign.

Let us proceed to how Farrer applies his theory to Mark's Gospel – that is to say, how he moves from the perception of a matchbox to the women by the empty grave. If a linguistic sign is merely a meaningless noise whose meaning has to be supplied by the imagination aided by memory, how can this idea be transferred to the textual problem we are debating? Are the women facing a meaningless sign which they supply with meaning, and in that case what memory can come to their aid? Or is it St Mark who uses his imagination-*cum*-memory; or, finally, is it the modern reader, *in casu* Farrer, who faces a trail of written, meaningless signs which he then supplies with meaning? First of all, Farrer contends that to understand a text is 'to understand the author'[22] and a text is simply the expression of the author's mind. To understand a text, or an author, is, as we have seen, to picture the author's mind in one's own mind. But a past memory always controls the present imagination.[23] It seems, in other words, as if Farrer has two theories of the imagination. On the one hand it begets and divines, as he says; on the

---

[20]   GV 147 / 117.

[21]   William Wordsworth, *The Prelude*, VI. 525–9.

[22]   Austin Farrer, 'The Mind of St Mark' (no date, published posthumously), *Interpretation and Belief*, 14.

[23]   Farrer, 'Inspiration: Poetical and Divine', 40.

other hand it is merely an instrument through which memory acts. It is thus his second theory of the imagination which is the basis of his reading of St Mark. If all understanding, whether of utterances or of sense perceptions, depends upon a past memory, then this explains why the only way in which St Mark could understand what he was writing was to let his past memory act through his present imagination. And his past memory was the Septuagint. Thus neither St Mark, nor Farrer in his reading of him, did anything unusual, nor did Farrer add anything to the original text; or, rather, he may have added something but what he added was based upon a past memory. Yet, if one can only understand something in terms of something which came before, does that not make it impossible to see anything new or to experience something unique? Is an event at all possible? As he says, 'apart from such a background of past memory acting through present imagination it is scarcely conceivable that any event or voice or thought could put itself upon any man as the act or utterance of God'.[24] Does he not say that the word of God can only be heard *as* the word of God if you have already heard the word before? How can one then account for the *kerygma*? The gospel as the *New* Testament or as good *news*? Is that not made inconceivable? Farrer says, for instance, that the news of the gospel did not consist in a 'Galilean Rabbi' who offered a 'new interpretation of Daniel chapter 7'.[25] Nor did Jesus do anything but give 'a new twist to the parables', since they were 'already alive in the faith of Israel'.[26]

However far removed from structuralism all this appears to be, it is nevertheless Farrer's notions of the relation between memory and imagination which made a structuralist appropriation of certain of his ideas possible. Structuralists, to be sure, have dispensed with such faculties as memory and imagination and have replaced them with linguistic categories. Instead of 'memory' they would say 'prior texts' or a 'code', and instead of the 'imagination' they would say 'variation' or 'transformation'. In a more modern vocabulary one could say that Farrer had hit upon the idea of *inter-textuality*. Any text, a dogmatic structuralist critic would say, is a transformation of a prior text. A present text is an acting out of a past text. A text is not an event, but a structure. Perhaps it was Gardner's intention to defend the text as event and not as structure. If that is so, we may legitimately characterise her literary criticism as hermeneutical.

## III. The Historical Sense

Helen Gardner's critical tool, her torch, is the historical sense. This sense she opposes to the concept of structure, as the following bears out: 'The discovery of a work's centre, the source of its life in all its parts, and response to its *total*

---

24   Ibid.
25   Austin Farrer, 'The Gospel as "Good News"' (BBC broadcast, 19 February 1963), in *Interpretation and Belief*, 34–5.
26   Farrer, 'Inspiration: Poetical and Divine', 41.

*movement* – a word I prefer to "structure", for *time is inseparable* from our apprehension of works of literature – is to me the purpose of critical activity' (emphasis added).[27] Gardner was well aware of the novelty and modernity of the concept of the historical sense, or the historical imagination as she sometimes calls it.[28] She was keenly aware, I think, of the incompatibility between structuralism and the hermeneutic concept of the historical sense.

In her essay 'The Historical Approach' she has very interesting things to say about Dryden's, Dr Johnson's and Coleridge's lack of historical sense. Dryden, she says, could deal lightly with the historical 'because he was writing before the development of the historical imagination'. In the case of Dr Johnson, 'the historical is something to be got out of the way'; and Coleridge 'when he approaches the work itself salves its imaginative integrity by ignoring the historical'. When one ignores the historical sense one does so, as she says Coleridge did, 'at the cost of remaking it [the text] in his own image'.[29] Twentieth-century critics fare no better than the three grand old men of English literary criticism. With Wilson Knight we have reached an extreme form of subjectivism because he spatialises the temporal, or, in Gardner's own words, 'Professor Wilson Knight shows clearly his attitude to the temporal by calling his method "spatial analysis"'.[30] Her essay, then, is an extended critique and diagnosis of a structuralism *before* French structuralism became fashionable. Structuralism spatialises the temporal and it is identified with subjectivism.

But what about the alternative: the historical study of literature and the use of the historical imagination or empathy? Is that alternative viable? No, Gardner contends. One cannot turn oneself into an Elizabethan reader, nor, one might add, into a contemporary of St Mark. For, as she shows, even the historical imagination is historically conditioned. Gardner knew that it is an illusion to suppose that we can think like men of another time. Here she is in perfect agreement with, for instance, Peter Winch, who in his *The Idea of a Social Science*, in connection with a discussion of Collingwood's notion of the historical imagination, says: 'though extinct ways of thinking may, in a sense, be recaptured by the historian, the way in which the historian thinks them will be coloured by the fact that he has had to employ historiographical methods to recapture them'.[31] I quote from Peter Winch in order to demonstrate how

---

[27]   Helen Gardner, 'The Sceptre and the Torch', in *The Business of Criticism*, 23–4.

[28]   She may have picked up the term from R.G. Collingwood's *The Idea of History* (Oxford: Clarendon Press, 1946).

[29]   Helen Gardner, 'The Historical Approach', in *The Business of Criticism*, 26, 28, 29, and 30. [Note that this lecture is from the first set of lectures complied in this book – *The Profession of a Critic* (1953) – and not the second set – *The Limits of Literary Criticism* (1959) – which includes 'The Poetry of St Mark', the lecture dealing with Farrer. The second set also contains a related lecture titled, 'The Historical Sense' (127–57), cited in note 40 below.]

[30]   Ibid., 30.

[31]   Peter Winch, *The Idea of a Social Science and its Relation to Philosophy* (London: Routledge and Kegan Paul, 1977), 182.

much Gardner, in her own way, had reached conclusions of the same kind as certain of the best English philosophers of the Wittgensteinian persuasion.

She does not deny, though, that there is some validity in trying to 'build up over the years a conception of a writer's life and times which has some consistency'. But she knows how the historical imagination works. It fabricates an 'imaginative construction'. The way she describes how such a construction is made corresponds largely to the way in which Farrer described how a present imagination 'pictures' something out of the materials furnished by past memory. Yet the most interesting thing about it is what she says about this construction. It is obvious that a construction is something like a structure and hence is a spatialisation. Therefore, she says, the imaginative construction 'must be kept *fluid* and not allowed to *harden* into a *fixed* background' (emphasis added).[32] What I have tried to argue by quoting from the essay 'The Historical Approach' is that Helen Gardner's approach to literature is radically hermeneutic, so radical indeed that structuralism seems conservative in comparison. She reached some of the same conclusions as Heidegger and Gadamer did almost certainly without any familiarity with their work (she was familiar with the work of Rudolf Bultmann, however, so one has to be very careful when making such assertions).[33] Is she, in her insistence on the historical sense, not being as radical as Nietzsche? In a section of his *Twilight of the Idols* he has this comment: 'You ask me about the idiosyncrasies of philosophers? … There is their lack of historical sense … they think they are doing a thing an honour when they dehistoricise it, *sub specie aeterni* – when they make a mummy of it'.[34]

Her critique of all attempts to spatialise, to construct, to fix and to harden in the name of a more basic and authentic temporality means that she had already superseded structuralism long before it came to Britain in the work of Frank Kermode and many others. It should be noted that she did not refute structuralism or deconstruction in the name of a native English common-sense empiricism. Her historical sense would make such a gesture impossible.

Something else characterises her version of a radical historical hermeneutics. In her case it was combined with a fundamental respect for the individuality of any text. A text is not a web of codes but a unique event, and so should a reading be. This respect for the imperatives of the text was furthermore the result of a *Christian* attitude towards literature, and it was directed against the worst danger of all, which she saw demonstrated in Coleridge and which she found several years later in Stanley Fish: the danger of *remaking the text in one's own image*. The iconoclastic overtones in this remark cannot be overlooked, nor should they.[35]

---

[32]   Gardner, 'The Historical Approach', 34.

[33]   Gardner, *In Defence of the Imagination*, 120: she takes Kermode to task for not discussing Bultmann in his *The Genesis of Secrecy*.

[34]   Friedrich Nietzsche, *Twilight of the Idols* [1889], trans. R.J. Hollingdale (Harmondsworth: Penguin, 1974), 35.

[35]   [See, for example, her comments about Fish on pages 3–4 of *In Defence of the Imagination*.]

We are now, I hope, well prepared for her criticism of Farrer. Farrer commits two errors: the Johnsonian and the Coleridgean. Both arise from and are a result of his lack of the historical sense. The Johnsonian error is found in the following quote from Farrer:

> We said that throughout the experiencing of one human person by another there works the activity of an immediate imagination untraceably complex in its ramifications. Nevertheless, through all this maze there runs one simple unchanging homespun thread of connection. All men are men; their instinctive passions are broadly identical; the relation of their will or purpose to their tongues and hands is essentially the same everywhere[.][36]

This is Johnsonian because, as Gardner says, 'the whole basis of Johnson's criticism is the belief that human nature is always essentially the same and that the poet's concern is with general truth'.[37] Coleridge, according to Gardner, ignores the accidents of history: 'he thereby preserves the integrity of the work, but he does so at the cost of remaking it in his own image'. Now, obviously Farrer committed the same error. He preserved the integrity of St Mark's text, but he remade it in his own image.

In her direct criticism of Farrer's reading of St Mark it should first of all be noticed that there is one critic whom she finds remarkable: Erich Auerbach. What Auerbach did in his *Mimesis, or the Representation of Reality in Western Literature* was to respect the historical reality of text and author, and he showed that St Mark's narrative was unique – an event, an individual style, not a rewriting.[38] Secondly, we should take note of what she means by historical reality so as not to come to the false conclusion that she was some sort of positivist historian. By the 'then' and the 'there' of memory, she relates, she did not mean 'detailed precision of testimony, but the deep sense of "happening"'.[39] Is she not here making the distinction between *historisch* and *geschichtlich*?

And what was wrong, basically, with Farrer's way of doing literary criticism, and with the New Criticism fashionable in the 1950s, was that it reduced the individual mind to 'schematic ways of thought'. And such ways of thought harden, 'mummify' (Nietzsche), fix and spatialise the text and thereby they conceal the authentic temporality of both text and man. Gardner advocates the view that the meaning of a text be kept fluid or open. She did not derive such ideas from Heidegger or Gadamer, but she found support and inspiration in such a critic as

---

[36]    Farrer, 'Inspiration: Poetical and Divine', 40.

[37]    Gardner, 'The Historical Approach', 28.

[38]    Gardner, 'The Poetry of St Mark', 118, referring to Erick Auerbach, *Mimesis, or the Representation of Reality in Western Literature* [1946], translated by Willard R. Trask (Princeton: Princeton University Press, 1953).

[39]    Ibid. [For the 'distinction between *historisch* and *geschichtlich*' below, see note 35 on page 129 of this volume]

Mary Lascelles. Mary Lascelles's study of *Measure for Measure* was exemplary because she left 'her reader with no theory, with no *scheme* of thought, but with a sense of the great *tides* of thought and feeling which *swirl* through the play' (emphasis added).[40]

## IV. Frank Kermode's Theory and Scheme of Thought

In *The Genesis of Secrecy* (1979) Frank Kermode tried to rehabilitate Austin Farrer. Kermode found Farrer's reading of St Mark 'exceptionally interesting'. Kermode also suggested that Farrer gave up his studies because of criticisms of them as 'farfetched'. Kermode here surely thought of Helen Gardner amongst others. Now, as I have tried to argue, Gardner did feel that Farrer had gone too far and that his reading, though imaginative, was far-fetched. Yet it was far-fetched because Farrer ignored his own historically conditioned position. In retrospect, we can see that what gave Farrer the idea of looking beneath the surface and finding hidden allusions came from the image-, paradox- and irony-hunting New Critics. The New Criticism was, among other things, a way of reading which derived from the New Critics' experience of reading modernist poetry such as T.S. Eliot's. Although the New Critical theory of poetic language derived from a particular kind of allusive and paradoxical poetry – modernist poetry and the Metaphysical Poets – the New Critics nevertheless universalised their theories to cover all poetry. This universalising tendency comes out most clearly in Cleanth Brooks's *The Well-Wrought Urn* – especially in his readings of Wordsworth.[41] In short, Farrer could be said to read St Mark as a modernist allusive poet, thereby converting the gospel into a coherent organic whole. In a similar way Frank Kermode makes sense out of the abrupt ending of Mark's Gospel – the enigmatic enclitic γάρ – by comparing it with the endings of Joyce's *Ulysses* and *Finnegans Wake* – that is to say, with the words *yes* and *the*. As he says: 'these ambiguities are not unlike those of Mark's problematical ending'.[42] Space does not permit me to describe Kermode's reading of St Mark. It is Gardner's criticism which is my concern. In a sense it is true that in her criticism of Kermode she repeats many of the points she made in her criticism of Farrer. From her perspective they commit exactly the same errors, although she admits that Kermode does so in a more sophisticated way.

---

[40]   Helen Gardner, 'The Historical Sense', 152 [referring to Mary Lascelles, *Shakespeare's* Measure for Measure (London: University of London/The Athlone Press, 1953]. It is difficult not to see some kind of parallel between Helen Gardner's sense of fluidity, the tide and the swirl, and the theories of certain contemporary French post-feminists. Luce Irigaray – I am fully aware of how monstrous the comparison is – has also written about 'the fluid' as a distinctive female value. See Toril Mos, *Sexual/Textual Politics* (London: Methuen, 1985), 141–2.

[41]   See Cleanth Brooks, *The Well-Wrought Urn: Studies in the Structure of Poetry* (New York: Harcourt Brace, 1947).

[42]   Kermode, *The Genesis of Secrecy*, 61, 67.

I am afraid that I disagree with David Jasper in his diagnosis of the debate between Gardner and Kermode. Jasper contends that Gardner wished to

> safeguard as normative the 'main' or 'literal' sense. A narrative, for her, is not a
> source of inexhaustible meanings, although she admits that great books may be
> almost inexhaustibly fertile. The debate can almost be defined in terms of the biblical
> fundamentalist who holds to the primacy of the literal sense of scripture against the
> structuralist, bred upon the structured typology of Farrer's analysis of St Mark.[43]

I shall return to the question of who is being almost a fundamentalist: Gardner or Kermode. A historically sensitive reader and scholar such as Gardner would know that the idea of the inexhaustible text is a Romantic one – Novalis's – which cannot be universalised to cover all texts. Perhaps she wished to safeguard the literal sense of St Mark's text. What she actually says is that the text is *naïve*.[44] She questions whether it is legitimate to compare St Mark's text with Joyce's. Are they comparable at all? If the gospel is fundamentally different from *Ulysses*, then the question is whether it is appropriate to use either New Critical or structuralist methods when reading the Gospel. To settle this issue is not easy and would involve us in a long discussion. Here one might mention that Northrop Frye argues that the Bible and *Ulysses* belong to the same genre, and hence are comparable. It cannot be denied that there is a tendency in structuralist readings to reduce differences between texts and to emphasise similarities, and it is, as we have seen, this tendency that Gardner castigates.

Frank Kermode raises another question in his discussion of St Mark: namely, the question of what makes an interpretation acceptable. In *The Genesis of Secrecy* he introduces the concept of an institution. He has developed this further in two articles, 'Can We Say Absolutely Anything We Like?' and 'Institutional Control of Interpretation'.[45] As soon as one introduces the idea of institutional control of interpretation, one has somehow moved out of a structuralist theory and into a pragmatic or hermeneutic one. Kermode is not a 'pure' structuralist, but has always seen himself as a mediator between British and Continental European literary criticism. He often tries to combine structuralist insights with hermeneutic ones. About Farrer's reading he says that, 'since he [Farrer] was not an adherent of the latest school of hermeneutics, he believed that Mark must have intended these [i.e. delicate, ironic] senses, and that he must have had an audience capable of perceiving them'.[46] The implication is that Mark did not necessarily intend them and that there was no audience capable of perceiving them. Poetic meaning, as both the New Critics and structuralists have it, depends neither upon intention

---

[43]   Jasper, *Coleridge as Poet and Religious Thinker*, 152 / 130 in this volume.

[44]   Gardner, *In Defence of the Imagination*, 123.

[45]   See Frank Kermode, *The Art of Telling: Essays on Fiction* (Cambridge, MA: Harvard University Press, 1983), chapters 7 and 8.

[46]   Kermode, *The Genesis of Secrecy*, 62.

nor upon effect upon the audience. This is familiar to us as the intentional and the affective fallacy. Farrer had the wrong theory but produced fine interpretations. But fine in terms of what criteria? Kermode's answer is: in terms of the institution.

The real reason, thinks Kermode, why Farrer's interpretations were unacceptable was that they were 'damaging to what remained of the idea that the gospel narratives were still, in some measure, transparent upon history'.[47] The idea that it is the institution, or as pragmatists such as Stanley Fish call it, 'the interpretative community', which decides which interpretations are valid or appropriate is, however, incompatible with any sort of structuralist theory. The structures found by structuralists inhere in texts. It is the text which makes a given reading valid. A pragmatist would deny this. Kermode seems to have moved in such a neo-pragmatist direction, since he claims that the text cannot prevent you from saying anything you like; only the interpretative community can. Kermode asks whether the constraints are in the semantic texture of the text or 'in the semantic texture of what we say about the text'.[48] I cannot tell if Kermode has made up his mind: are the constraints in the text or in the institution? In the case of Farrer, though, it seems to me that he says that Farrer was right, but that the institution was wrong. If that is the case it must have been St Mark's text that made Farrer's various readings possible.

In *The Genesis of Secrecy* there is no doubt that Kermode adhered to basic structuralist theories, as the following illustrates:

> To *restrict* or *halt* the free movement of senses within a text is ... thought [i.e. by certain French theorists] to be a kind of wickedness. It may be so; but it is our only means of reading until revolutionary new concepts of writing prevail; and meanwhile, remaining as aware as we can be of ideological and institutional constraints, we go about *our business of freezing* those senses into different patterns.[49]

This sums up Kermode's 'method'. The business of criticism accordingly is to freeze, to halt and to restrict. No alternative is given. Northrop Frye, whom Kermode has criticised so often, has the same idea. Those theorists who think that it is a kind of wickedness to halt, restrict and freeze the senses of a text may be such people as Roland Barthes and Derrida. But the whole hermeneutical movement also constitutes a viable alternative.

The German philosopher, Manfred Frank, has the following comments on this act of freezing the structure, so characteristic of structuralist activity:

> if meaning (*Sinn*) and significance (*Bedeutsamkeit*) arise in the being-related to each other of differing expressive substances, then the identity of a term could be guaranteed only by a state of closure ('*clôture*') and of the unchangeability

---

47    Ibid., 63.
48    Kermode, *The Art of Telling*, 157.
49    Kermode, *The Genesis of Secrecy*, 71 (emphasis added).

of the system. The model which underlies the classical structuralist theory of language ... is not by chance the crystal lattice, in which, if the temperature is low enough, all the molecules are *immobilized* in their places, both separated from all the others and bound to them as well. Now the world of symbolic interaction, as opposed to that of the elements, cannot be cooled down to absolute zero. It only flourishes in a certain *heat*, which permits the *flow*, the exchange and re-ordering, of the signs.[50]

I need hardly argue how similar, down to the very vocabulary, Manfred Frank's description of classical structuralism is to what we have heard Gardner say about how our reading-hypotheses have to be kept fluid and not allowed to harden. What was basically wrong with Farrer and Kermode was that they froze the text. They did not open texts; they closed them. That was their wickedness. Helen Gardner knew, just as Manfred Frank, that symbolic interaction only flourishes with that warmth which permits fluidity. To cool down the text is not only a kind of fundamentalism but it is, worst of all, to remake the text in one's own image. That is not only wickedness; it is perhaps *the sin of reading.*

---

[50]    Manfred Frank, 'Is Self-Consciousness a Case of *presence à soi*? Towards a Meta-Critique of the Recent French Critique of Metaphysics' (translated by Andrew Bowie), in David Wood (ed.), *Derrida: A Critical Reader* (Oxford, UK and Cambridge, MA: Blackwell, 1992), 218–34, citation from 227–8 (emphasis added). ['*Presence à soi*' is 'self-presence'.]

Chapter 6

# Austin Farrer's Shaping Spirit of Imagination [2006]†

## Douglas Hedley

Tell me where is fancy bred,
Or in the heart or in the head?
How begot, how nourished?
Reply, Reply.

Shakespeare, *Merchant of Venice* III ii 63

It requires little justification to discuss the thought of arguably the greatest English theologian of the twentieth century, Austin Farrer. Yet Farrer is in many respects an enigmatic and elusive writer. He belonged to no clearly defined school of theology and did not found one. His elegant and sometimes epigrammatic prose

† When Douglas Hedley wrote this chapter he was Senior Lecturer in Philosophy of Religion in the Divinity Faculty of the University of Cambridge. It was originally delivered at the Farrer centenary conference held in Oxford in 2004 and published in Douglas Hedley and Brian Hebblethwaite (eds), *The Human Person in God's World: Studies to Commemorate the Austin Farrer Centenary* (London: SCM Press, 2006). The gap of 14 years between this and the previous chapter does not indicate a cessation of scholarly interest in the interval, but rather a shift in focus towards other aspects of Farrer's thought than the themes explored in *The Glass of Vision*, particularly toward libertarian free will: see, for example, the relevant chapters in F. Michael McLain and W. Mark Richardson (eds), *Human and Divine Agency: Anglican, Catholic, and Lutheran Perspectives* (Lanham, MD: University Press of America, 1999). However, both this and David Brown's chapter in the centenary volume, 'The Role of Images in Theological Reflection', indicate a renewed desire to engage with *The Glass of Vision*. Mention has already been made of Brown's constructive use of Farrer's ideas in his own work. Likewise, soon after writing this chapter Hedley published a study that incorporated Farrer's arguments with his own original development of them: *Living Forms of the Imagination* (London and New York: T&T Clark International, 2008). This current chapter returns us both to the impact of Farrer on Basil Mitchell discussed in my introduction, and to the comparison between Farrer and Coleridge that was first encountered (positively) in Jasper's contribution and then again (negatively) in Hauge's. As most students of Farrer trace his intellectual genealogy to Thomism or analytic philosophy rather than the English Romantic tradition, this is a provocative proposal. Nevertheless, in joint review of Ann Loades and Robert MacSwain (eds), *The Truth-Seeking Heart: Austin Farrer and His Writings* and *The Human Person in God's World*, Lucy Beckett says of Hedley's chapter that 'the connections (or unconscious similarities) between Farrer and Coleridge become clearer and clearer': *Times Literary Supplement* (3 August 2007), 24. This link clearly requires further investigation.

does not flinch from real puzzles and apparent paradoxes. Farrer relentlessly fuses poetry, metaphysics and Scripture in his theology, brooding on images and ideas – often arguing in imaginary dialogues. A writer of great spiritual depth, his intellect is decisive and acute, fertile and suggestive. This chapter will consider Farrer from two perspectives. First, it considers the fertility of Farrer's intellectual legacy through the prism of Basil Mitchell's philosophy of religion, focusing on Mitchell's unjustly neglected *Faith and Criticism*.[1] Second, it explores the profundity of Farrer's thought in the light of the English Romantic inheritance.[2]

## Imaginative Belief

An important point of contact between Farrer and Mitchell lies in the centrality of human personality for understanding God. In Farrer, this is an explicit metaphysical principle: the 'union of will with the primal Will'. The only God who can mean anything to the human mind is the God about whom the human will has something to do. Furthermore, the analogy between finite and infinite creativity is central for Farrer. Again, 'we know the action of a man can be the action of God in him'.[3] This is the paradigmatic instance of 'double agency'. Brian Hebblethwaite insists that Farrer speaks of the *paradox* – not the contradiction – of double agency. It appears paradoxical because of our inadequacies: 'we lack access to the "causal joint" of supernatural and the natural'.[4] Double agency is a paradox which 'arises simply as a by-product of the analogical imagination'.[5] Farrer uses the literary analogy of the author who 'has the wit to get a satisfying story out of the natural behaviour of the characters he conceives'. But though the source of divine action remains hidden, the effects are obvious.

It seems to me that the kind of apologetic or justification which Basil Mitchell mounts in *Faith and Criticism* presupposes a vital connection between the soul's longing for God and the rationality of religious belief. Here is a sense of the 'vital connection' between religion and imagination: in that mysterious and inscrutable causal joint between human and divine activity:

> Our understanding of people, whose inexhaustibility entails that our knowledge
> of them is never final or complete, provides the closest analogy we have to our

---

[1]   Basil Mitchell, *Faith and Criticism* (Oxford: Clarendon Press, 1994). Page references to this volume will be given parenthetically in the main text.

[2]   [The first two sections of this chapter, which followed the introductory paragraph and dealt primarily with Basil Mitchell, have been cut for this current volume. See pages 107–13 of the original for this material.]

[3]   Austin Farrer, *Faith and Speculation: An Essay in Philosophical Theology* (London: A&C Black, 1967), 66.

[4]   Brian Hebblethwaite, *Philosophical Theology and Christian Doctrine* (Oxford: Blackwell, 2005), 140.

[5]   Farrer, *Faith and Speculation*, 66.

knowledge of God; and if it is true that it relies on a critical awareness of all sorts of signs and cues, as well as a defensible conception of what it is to be a human being, so must our awareness of God depend upon something comparable. (84)

On this model, the activity of the pupil does not exclude the initiative and the activity of the teacher. On the contrary, divine promising and forgiving are necessary to the model. Christian doctrine requires a concept of revelation and this depends upon the analogy of one person communicating to another truths about his character, purposes and intentions which that other person would not otherwise be in a position to know.[6] However, natural theology is insufficient to know God's purposes. God would have reason to communicate, and the Bible should be interpreted as God's self-revelation. The idea of communication presupposes some divine speech. For inspiration Mitchell uses the idea of a teacher inspiring a pupil.

One might pursue, by way of illustration, a passage in *Faith and Criticism* in which Mitchell discusses Jane Austen's *Emma*: 'In the novel, Emma learns through her mistakes, and the process of learning is one in which she comes to see more clearly and judge more wisely in proportion as she is freed from self-centred pride. Her education is watched over by Knightley' (85). Mitchell notes that, like the Romantics, Jane Austen was sensitive to the role of imagination and the will, and invoked Knightley's ability to 'imagine a range of different possible people that Emma might become and different choices she might make, and decide which one of them represents her real vocation' (86). He decides to trust her and by virtue of this he 'exerts his imagination to the full in order increasingly to understand her'. But Mitchell notes that if his judgment is to be well founded, his 'critical intellect' must also be really effective, if he wants to be sure that he understands her properly (86). Mitchell reasons further that despite starting with Christian revelation itself – and all that we are committed to by accepting it – there is no bar to the full exertion of our intellectual energies. Trust in a person, and even more so, trust in God, engages the emotions, the imagination, and the will, because it engages the whole person and, by that same token, engages the intellect as well. Faith is not so much opposed to knowledge as to vision.

One recalls that Farrer uses St Paul on seeing through a glass darkly as the motto of *The Glass of Vision*. In that theological masterpiece Farrer gave us a fascinating and intriguing piece of intellectual biography, from which Basil Mitchell quoted a passage in the first chapter of *Faith and Criticism*:

I had myself ... been raised in a personalism which might satisfy the most ardent of Dr Buber's disciples. I thought of myself as set over against deity as one man faces another across a table, except that God was invisible and indefinitely great. And I hoped that he would signify his presence to me by way of colloquy; but neither out of the scripture I read nor in the prayers I tried to make did any mental voice address me. I believe at that time anything would have satisfied me, but nothing came: no

---

[6]     See Basil Mitchell, *The Justification of Religious Belief* (London: Macmillan, 1973), 145.

'other' stood beside me, no shadow of presence fell upon me. I owe my liberation from this *impasse*, as far as I can remember, to reading Spinoza's *Ethics*. Those phrases which now strike me as so flat and sinister, so ultimately atheistic – *Deus sive Natura* (God, or call it Nature), *Deus, quatenus consideratur ut constituens essentiam humanae mentis* (God, in so far as he is considered the being of the human mind) – these phrases were to me light and liberation, not because I was or desired to be a pantheist, but because I could not find the wished-for colloquy with God.

Undoubtedly I misunderstood Spinoza, in somewhat the same fashion as (to quote a high example) St Augustine misunderstood Plotinus, turning him to Christian uses. Here, anyhow is what I took from Spinozism. I would no longer attempt, with the psalmist, 'to set God before my face'. I would see him as the underlying cause of my thinking, especially of those thoughts in which I tried to think of him. I would dare to hope that sometimes my thought would become diaphanous, so that there should be some perception of the divine cause shining through the created effect, as a deep pool, settling into clear tranquility, permits us to see the spring in the bottom of it from which its waters rise. I would dare to hope that through a second cause the First Cause might be felt, when the second cause in question was a spirit, made in the image of the divine Spirit, and perpetually welling up out of his creative act.[7]

This remarkable passage echoes Coleridge's words in his *Biographia Literaria* about Spinoza as helping him keep alive 'the *heart* in the *head*' and thus to 'skirt, without crossing the sandy deserts of utter unbelief'.[8] It also gives us an important insight into Farrer's theology. Though Farrer does not employ the traditional scholastic method of cosmological inference from world to God, he clearly wishes to avoid the other extreme of the personalism in philosophy and theology of Martin Buber and Karl Barth. He writes (NB in 1948): 'when the Germans set their eyeballs and pronounce the terrific words "He speaks to thee" (*Er redet Dich an*) ...they are not speaking to my condition'.[9] He is placing himself within the Platonic/Aristotelian tradition of which St Thomas is a good example. As such, he is allied to both the God of the philosophers and to the God of Abraham, Isaac and Jacob. This also explains why Farrer is at pains to insist upon the hierarchy of the mind: mankind is defined by the 'luminous apex of the mind' not the 'shadowy base'. *Pace* David Brown in his excellent article on Farrer, 'God and Symbolic Action', I do not think we can say that Farrer is hostile to the creative role of the un- or sub-conscious realm.[10] I

---

[7]    GV 7–8 / 19–20 [original pagination / this volume].

[8]    Samuel Taylor Coleridge, *Biographia Literaria* I [1817], edited by James Engell and W. Jackson Bate (London: Routledge, 1983), 152.

[9]    GV 8 / 20.

[10]    David Brown, 'God and Symbolic Action', in Brian Hebblethwaite and Edward Henderson (eds), *Divine Action: Studies Inspired by the Philosophical Theology of Austin Farrer* (Edinburgh: T&T Clark, 1990), 103–22; now reprinted in this volume (133–47).

think Farrer is making a point about anthropology. Man made in the image of God is primarily a rational creature.[11] This is the basic conviction lying behind the idea of 'a double personal agency in our one activity'.[12] God can act within and through finite human agents. Again, I think the target is the anthropological pessimism of Freud or Barth. Farrer is clearly standing in the tradition of natural theology and he wants a theory of inspiration as part of an account of divine action that coheres with his philosophical tenets, but the starting point for his natural theology is the experience of the believer – the fact of his own agency and the sense of his or her free and creative response to, and dependence upon God. He endeavours to use the principle of analogy based upon agency rather than a dialectical theology of the Word, but his metaphysics of analogy is based upon the necessarily inscrutable working of God. At one level God is necessarily hidden; at another he is evident to the imaginative eye of faith as it is *illuminated* by metaphysical reflection and *instructed* by revelation: 'Faith discerns not the images, but what the images signify: and yet we cannot discern it except through the images'.[13]

In this context, moreover, one might recall Farrer's employment of Gabriel Marcel's distinction between problems and mysteries. This is not to be confused with appeals to ignorance or the sacrifice of the intellect. Farrer accepts that we cannot articulate the facts of human personality; and yet we know these facts as realities. He thinks that metaphysics cannot be dispensed with. He argues that we have to distinguish the central problems of metaphysics, free will or the relation of the subject to the body, from scientific questions because natural science deals with specific *problems* relating to the specific questions and instruments of the inquiry. The results are real but 'highly abstract or selective'. On the other hand, philosophical puzzles depend upon the prior philosophical assumptions of any particular position. The relation of the active and the receptive intellect is a 'puzzle' for Aristotelians but not for behaviourists or Berkeleyans. God is a genuine mystery like free will or the nature of the self. Neither he nor they are open to scientific procedure, but they cannot be disposed of as factitious puzzles. Farrer sees the work of metaphysics as the 'sober criticism of images' that we can naturally employ to describe reality:

> The so-called problems of metaphysics are difficulties of description: that does not make them either unimportant, or easy to manage. On the contrary, they may be quite agonizing; nor are any questions of greater importance to a mind which desires to understand the nature of its real world. There is no finality about the description offered by metaphysics for the mysteries of existence, but there is advance in apprehension of the mysteries by the refining of the descriptions.[14]

---

[11]   Farrer, *Faith and Speculation*, 50.
[12]   GV 33 / 36.
[13]   GV 110 / 93.
[14]   GV 63 / 59.

The natural mystery which is the starting point of rational theology is the finite manifesting itself as the shadow of the infinite. Metaphysics is the description of natural mysteries by the criticism of analogies. And analogy is the name for 'sober and appropriate images'. Farrer's clear admiration for Aristotle should be allied to a certain scepticism towards the conceptual (for example *The Glass of Vision*, 45 / 44: 'the life of images, not of concepts').[15] The knowledge which literature and metaphysics can deliver is not to be confused with definitive articulation. This knowledge is, in a sense, experiential. I think it is clear from Farrer's excursion into the nature of metaphysical reasoning that he is concerned to do justice to the experiential component in metaphysics which eludes exhaustive definition: 'the soul does exist: there is nothing of which we are more aware, for it is we ourselves; only its uniqueness and singleness prevents our talking prose about it ...'[16] Farrer employs the Platonic language of participation:

> [I]n our degree we all participate in supernatural act, for we do not receive revealed truth as simply a tale told about God in the third person by others; we apprehend it as assured to us by God himself, or to put it otherwise, the description of divine mysteries ceases to be experienced by us as mere description: in the lines laid down by the description, the mysteries shine with their own light and presence; or rather with the light and presence of God.[17]

This is very close to the passage where he describes the liberating effect of Spinoza which helped him to think of the divine not as alien 'other', but rather as the 'underlying cause of my thinking'. So there might be a perception of the divine cause through the created effect.

But Farrer insists:

> If we surrender metaphysical enquiry, we shall vainly invoke supernatural revelation to make up for our metaphysical loss of nerve. For if our cravenheartedness surrenders the ground of metaphysics, it will have surrendered the bridgehead which the supernatural liberator might land upon. Get a man to see the mysterious depth and seriousness of the act by which he and his neighbour exist, and he will have his eyes turned upon the bush in which the supernatural fire appears, and presently he will be prostrating himself with Moses, before him who thus names himself 'I am that I am'.[18]

---

[15]   The same applies to Farrer's 'Thomism'. His debt to Aquinas is huge, his affinity to the textbook neo-Thomism of his contemporaries slender.

[16]   'Poetic Truth' (no date but circa 1943, posthumously published), in Austin Farrer, *Reflective Faith: Essays in Philosophical Theology*, edited by Charles C. Conti (London: SPCK, 1972), 34.

[17]   GV 32 / 35.

[18]   GV 78 / 68.

The move here to Exodus 3.14 is very important. It was this passage, partly as a result of a strange translation of the Hebrew, that came to be read as God's own identifying himself with ultimate being.

Here we come back to the 'Barthian captivity' of a theology that refuses to mediate between revealed and natural truth. The organic model of revelation through the medium of the imagination is linked, however paradoxical this may seem, to Farrer's passionate defence of metaphysics. Although God is 'absolutely unique' we expect, he claims, religious mysteries

> to bear some analogy with natural realities because they are revealed in the stuff of human existence. So it seems that God's encounter with us must be a sort of encounter, analogous to our encounters with men; and that the parables or symbols through which God teaches us to imagine his action must be some sort of symbols parallel, perhaps, to the symbols of valid poetry.[19]

The point is really about divine agency rather than religious language. Farrer is not trying to translate talk of divine action into the merely figurative expression of a sense of deity, but to give an account of the status of talk about divine action. I think Farrer's theory that the 'stuff of inspiration is living images' is indebted to a certain legacy of Christian Romanticism. Farrer's stress upon the *organic* and *imaginative* nature of inspiration rather than the mechanical is very 'Romantic':

> But what springs up through wit and inspiration is not the gratuitous gift of the imagination to the intelligence: the previous labour of the intelligence is thrown down into the imagination as into a cauldron, from which it emerges again fused into new figures and, it may be, enriched with materials from the subconscious sphere, which were never in distinct consciousness at all … Such inspiration (always using the word in the secular sense) belongs to what is most godlike in the natural man: but it also belongs to what is most centrally human in him.[20]

## Divine Uniqueness, Contemplation, Joy and the Mind's Eye

There is another sense of imagination linked to the soul's longing for God. Austin Farrer shares with his great North African namesake, St Augustine, a concentration upon the unique nature of the soul:

> The soul is unique when compared with that which is not a soul; for if we are classifying created things, we must put soul all by itself on one side of the division, and on the other the whole host of things which the soul knows, loves,

---

[19]   'Inspiration: Poetical and Divine' [1963], in Austin Farrer, *Interpretation and Belief*, edited by Charles C. Conti (London: SPCK, 1976), 45.

[20]   GV 24–6 / 30–1.

hates, feels, manages, copes with and exploits. But although the soul is unique by comparison with all that is not soul, it is in this respect not unique, that there are many souls, yours and mine and the next man's, and these have a common nature, and I can know something about several such. But God is uniquely unique.[21]

I think that Farrer would have regarded the contemporary prevailing functionalist orthodoxy in the philosophy of mind, where the mind is seen in terms of information processing in the process of which a Martian, a computer or a human being might share an equivalent functional economy, as just as pernicious, flat and sinister as its cruder forebears in behaviourism and verificationism. God is a reality, immanent and active in all creatures through his continual creative power. And it is the soul that is the fountain of the creative imagination. But we could not speak of God even if we attain the vision of God – not for the Gnostic reason that God is radically and incommensurably beyond our apprehension, but for the solid Platonic/Aristotelian reason of divine uniqueness: 'It is his uniqueness and not only his hiddenness, which prevents our saying anything perfectly exact about him, except that he is himself'.[22]

Coleridge's reflections upon poetry were driven by a metaphysical conviction that a merely mechanical view of the mind as primarily associative, a view derived from Hobbes and Hume, could not explain the distinctive creative genius of a true poet like Wordsworth. This is in part the impact of the presence of Wordsworth as a companion, collaborator and friend, but it is more deeply motivated by the conviction that the creative dimension of the mind points to a level untouched by mechanical explanation.

All statements about God are enigmatic, like those of the soul. Farrer then faces an objection: is he not just reducing theology to poetry? Farrer's reply is that the metaphors of the poet illuminate if there is a real analogy between the items compared. The poet, however, is not worried about the accuracy of the analogy. In theology 'we must get behind the poetry to the real analogies'.[23] Farrer states at this point that personal analogies are best: God can be compared with human will and intellect but not with human passions. Farrer takes the example of the phrase 'the eternal spirit' as an example of this work by analogy. It expresses the paradoxical coincidence of living personality and the immutability of mathematical verity.

Part of Farrer's argument must be about the capacity to see reality as a whole. The ability to do this is 'imaginative' – not in some pejorative and negative sense of 'phantasy'. The move from notional to imaginative assent to belief in God requires

---

[21]   Farrer, 'Poetic Truth', 34–5.

[22]   Ibid., 35. Compare Thomas Aquinas, *Summa Theologiae*, Ia. 3 on divine simplicity: God is not a member of a series, and this claim about God 'in himself' is decisive for questions 12 and 13 of the *Summa* about how we know or speak about God. I am grateful to Denys Turner for pointing this out to me.

[23]   Ibid., 36.

a disciplined imagination. In *Aids to Reflection*, Coleridge argued that: 'to believe and to understand are not diverse things, but the same thing in different periods of its growth. Belief is the seed, received into the will, of which the Understanding or Knowledge is the Flower, and the thing believed the fruit'.[24] Coleridge speaks of imagination as bringing the whole soul of man into activity. Farrer is quite explicit about the role of the imagination in a total response to God. The poet, the lover and the theologian are, in Farrer's thought, of imagination quite compact. However, 'The lover and the poet at least look at something and see it'.[25] The theologian should endeavour to. Farrer goes on to insist that the 'great impediment to religion in this age' is the loss of the capacity to contemplate:

> no one ever looks at anything at all: not so as to contemplate it, to apprehend what it is to be that thing, and plumb, if he can, the deep fact of its individual existence. The mind rises from the knowledge of creatures to the knowledge of their creator, but this does not happen through the sort of knowledge which can analyse things into factors or manipulate them with technical skill or classify them into groups. It comes from the appreciation of things which we have when we love them and fill our minds and senses with them and feel something of the silent force and great mystery of their existence. For it is in this that the creative power is displayed of an existence higher and richer and more intense than all.[26]

Is this not 'joy' in the Wordsworth/Coleridgean sense?[27] The contemplative mood of 'joy' in Coleridge's poem 'Dejection' is explicitly linked to his 'shaping spirit of imagination'.[28] Or Ruskin exclaims: 'to see clearly is poetry, prophecy, and religion, – all in one'.[29] It is such imaginative moods that 'lift', as Shelley puts it, 'the veil from the hidden beauty of the world'.[30] The joy described by some of our greatest poets can be seen as the pinnacle of an imaginative component in cognition which is evident in mundane experience and extends up to very elevated experiences of the world as a coherent and purposive theatre of divine

---

[24]    Samuel Taylor Coleridge, *Aids to Reflection* [1825, 1831], edited by John Beer (London: Routledge, 1993), 194.

[25]    Farrer, 'Poetic Truth', 37.

[26]    Ibid., 37–8.

[27]    One might compare Farrer with Coleridge: 'Hast thou ever raised thy mind to the consideration of EXISTENCE, in and by itself, as the mere act of Existing? Hast thou ever said to thyself thoughtfully, IT IS! Heedless in that moment, whether it were a man before thee, or a flower, or a grain of sand?' *The Friend* I, edited by Barbara E. Rooke (London: Routledge, 1969), 514.

[28]    Samuel Taylor Coleridge, *Poems*, edited by John Beer (London: Dent, 1986), 280–283.

[29]    John Ruskin, 'Modern Painters', in *The Works of John Ruskin*, edited by E.T. Cook and Alexander Wedderburn (London: George Allen, 1903–12), V, 177.

[30]    Percy Bysshe Shelley, 'A Defence of Poetry' [1821], cited in *Shelley's Poetry and Prose*, edited by Donald H. Reiman and Sharon B. Powers (New York: W. W. Norton, 1977), 487.

agency. One might think here of Coleridge's description of Wordsworth's poetry. Here 'objects observed', for which 'custom had bedimmed all the lustre' could be endowed with the 'depth and height of the ideal world'.[31] In such a way Coleridge muses that Wordsworth, in 'imaginative power', is closest to Shakespeare and Milton. Using Wordsworth's lines from 'Elegiac Stanzas, Suggested by a Picture of Peele Castle', Coleridge reflects upon Wordsworth. To employ his own words, which are at once an instance and an illustration, Wordsworth does indeed to all thoughts and to all objects,

> ... add the gleam,
> The light that never was on sea or land,
> The consecration and the poet's dream.[32]

Such a paean to 'joy' can be misleading for us, especially since purely secular writers, such as Proust with his *moments bienheureux* or Virginia Woolf, have accustomed us to imaginative epiphanies with no purely residual religious content. And many will associate Romantic epiphanies with pantheism. Yet I suspect that the concept of 'joy' is best understood as a name for the exalted mood of the contemplative liaison of the empirical eye and mind's eye by which the poet perceives items of sense experience as conveying, beyond themselves, the divine source.

To speak of the contemplative imagination is to reflect upon the relation of the empirical eye and what our great metaphysical bard William Shakespeare calls 'the mind's eye' (*Hamlet* I i 12). Wordsworth's power was primarily in this creative liaison of eye and mind's eye. And he was convinced that the poet's imaginative capacity is dependent upon the ability to penetrate truths obscured by the more narrow constraints of physical science and to envisage the hidden shape of reality. Here we are not so much talking of imagination in the sense of possession of mental images, the Kantian 'transcendental' power of the imagination, or of make-believe, but the imagination that enables the theist to see the world as real facts – discrete and apparently discordant and often grievously painful – and respect them as such, and at the same time to see these parts as belonging to a whole which one can affirm as grounded in a wholly good and transcendent God. This contemplative imagination is not the much-discussed capacity for 'seeing as' (whatever we see is seen *with the mind*) which is important, but the capacity to see *both x and y*. 'It is a capacity of the religious mind to see', as Coleridge observes, 'symbols: living *educts* of the imagination ... consubstantial with the truths, of which they are the *conductors*', as opposed to the 'unenlivened, generalising Understanding'.[33] It is not that the religious mind fails to see the same objects in the world as the purely secular observer, since to see them in *exclusively* religious terms would be what

---

[31]   Coleridge, *Biographia Literaria* I, 107.

[32]   Ibid., II, 151.

[33]   Samuel Taylor Coleridge, *Lay Sermons*, edited by R.J. White (London: Routledge, 1972), 28–9.

the eighteenth century called rampant 'enthusiasm' or what we might designate madness. It is rather the sober capacity to see the same objects as *both* themselves *and* as conductors or symbols of another dimension of reality.

Atheism for Coleridge or Wordsworth can be construed as a failure of imagination. Through imagination the reality of certain *facts* can be experienced, and hence to emancipate the mind from what Coleridge calls 'the despotism of the eye'[34] and to be open to the impact of certain objects upon the soul. A Caspar David Friedrich landscape is a good instance of an appeal to both the empirical and the inner eye. His depictions have a certain realism and yet are aimed at an effect upon the soul rather than any purely visual experience. Milton is even more extreme. He writes:

> Mine eyes he closed, but open left the cell of fancy
> Of fancy, my internal sight ...[35]

The blindness of the poet, whether Milton or Homer, is itself an image of the work of imagination. We are not mirrors of nature in any crude representational sense, and the Christian faith is a fidelity to the invisible causal joint of God and the soul, through the dark glass of our reason and imagination. The greatest poets explore and make articulate through images and analogies our often mute intimations of invisible reality, and I think Farrer's theological project is inextricably linked to this poetic and philosophical imagination.

## Poetic Truth

The exploration of the poetic within the canonical prophetic writings is largely a Romantic contribution to theology which goes back to another great Oxford divine, Robert Lowth [1710–87]. His *Sacred Poetry of the Hebrews* of 1753 discussed and analysed the poetic quality of the Hebrew prophetic writings. Farrer presents a fascinating account of how the lover, the theologian and the poet are all of an imagination compact in *The Glass of Vision*. But I wish to discuss in more detail Farrer's paper 'Poetic Truth' in the collection *Reflective Faith*. This is a discussion of the relation between poetry and theology and the use of metaphor in speaking of the soul and God: a great theme of the Romantics. Coleridge says that words are 'LIVING POWERS, by which the things of most importance to mankind are actuated, combined and humanized'.[36] Poets are transformers of the tongue. The poet diffuses a tone and spirit of unity that blends and (as it were) fuses. This fusing power of the poetic vision is in Farrer's mind when he draws analogies between poetical and prophetic inspiration: 'this strange

---

[34]   Coleridge, *Biographia Literaria* I, 107.

[35]   John Milton, *Paradise Lost*, Book VIII, line 461. [In the poem, the voice is Adam's, but the allusion to Milton's own lack of physical sight is most suggestive.]

[36]   Coleridge, *Aids to Reflection*, 10.

human passion for never saying what one means but always something else finds its most extreme and absolute development in the poets'.[37] What is the point of such bizarre convolution such as 'The curfew tolls the knell of parting day'? Why the use of metaphor? Is it mere drollery or relish of ingenuity? Sounding rather like John Ruskin, Farrer insists:

> the best figurative poetry speaks not to the frivolous intellect, but (if anything does) straight to the heart; and it does so better than plain prose. There seems then to be something which is better said with metaphor than without, which goes straighter to the mark by going crooked, and hits its aim exactly by flying at tangents. An odd fact, if true.[38]

Poetry, therefore, is not misrepresentation, as Bentham or Hume would insist, nor even ornament. It is descriptive. Farrer wants to attack two errors. One is that metaphor is the language of emotion. He makes the point that one can stir emotions often more effectively with literal language: 'A bull is charging you from behind' is more effective than talk of 'the playfellow of Europa'.[39] Farrer distinguishes between two senses given to the words 'subjective' and 'feeling'. Poetry does express 'something subjective' and 'what is felt about things'. However, Farrer thinks it quite illegitimate to infer that poetry *only* tells us about the poet's emotions. He uses an analogy from the provincial (poorly lit) aquarium and the murky phenomena behind the glass with two observers: the philosopher (I think he means what we would usually call a 'scientist') and the poet. The first tries to distinguish the genuine fish from the distorting impact of the factors of light, glass and so on. The poet tries to describe the whole effect of the phenomenon of the fish in the tank in figurative language as a sea monster. The work of the poet is *descriptive*; but his domain of description is broader than that of the philosopher. 'The poet describes things just as he feels them, he does not describe what he feels *about* the things'.[40]

Coleridge proposes, in the famous chapter 13 'On the Imagination' of his *Biographia Literaria*, that the imagination is a *tertium aliquid* or 'an inter-penetration of the counteracting powers, partaking of both' – that is, a middle point between subjective and objective.[41] Ultimately, Coleridge is trying to capture, I think, a similar insight about the nature of a poem as descriptive. Farrer distinguishes between the task of analysis and description. The scientist wishes to analyse the constituent elements of reality. The poet wishes to describe, '*to know what it is like*'. If a lover wants to describe his beloved, no scientific analysis of her skin will do. 'You will have to compare her skin to flowers'. Does the emotion blind or open the

---

[37]   Farrer, 'Poetic Truth', 24.

[38]   Ibid., 25.

[39]   Ibid., 25–6.

[40]   Ibid., 27–9, citation from 29.

[41]   Coleridge, *Biographia Literaria* I, 300. Coleridge is rather elliptical in this passage, but this is how I interpret him.

eyes of the lover? Farrer argues that it is reasonable to assume the latter. Perhaps the violence of passion can 'break down the dull custom of incomprehension, the blindness of the eyes and the hardness of heart'. 'It would be a strange fact if being passionately interested in something were always a bar to appreciating it truly.'[42] This is a point that Burke and the Romantics (including Newman) made against the quasi-objectivity of 'sophisters, economists and calculators'. Knowledge is much more likely to be obtained if the mind is really committed and passionate about truth.[43] But this must mean a greater role for the emotions and imagination in the formation of belief than classical empiricism can concede.

Farrer writes:

> In poetic vision, then, and amatory passion, we are convinced that the object of our contemplation has a vividness of being, a distinctness of incommunicable individuality which scientific analysis would in vain hope to express – we are driven into metaphor. Science considers things in so far as they are the same; poetry, in so far as each is irreducibly itself. But what can we say about that which is truly unique?[44]

What is it like means, 'What other thing does it resemble?' This is a question of analogies:

> All the unique creatures God has made resemble one another, at a greater or less distance; for all reflect in diverse manner or degree their one creator, and imitate his existence, as far as their lowliness allows, by being each themselves. But if they have family resemblance, they have an unlikeness too.[45]

Furthermore, Farrer insists, 'it is only by comparison and contrast with other things that we become aware of their individualities, and find out, as the saying is, what they are like'. Basil Mitchell has a telling argument against any exhaustive and exclusive dichotomy between the literal and the metaphorical. Drawing on Berkeley's distinction between metaphorical and proper analogy he argues that it is perfectly reasonable to apply concepts such as knowledge, faithfulness or love as attributes of the deity. This can be done in a manner which vastly exceeds our experience of these properties, while avoiding relegating these terms to mere metaphor. Stretched these concepts may be, but they express *literal* truths about God. Through a 'controlled exercise of imagination' by the use of proper analogy we can develop a 'framework of theistic theory'.[46] Within such a context Farrer's

---

[42]   Farrer, 'Poetic Truth', 30–31.

[43]   Edmund Burke, *Reflections on the French Revolution* [1790] (London: Dent, 1910), 73.

[44]   Farrer, 'Poetic Truth', 31.

[45]   Ibid., 32.

[46]   'The Place of Symbols in Christianity', in Basil Mitchell, *How to Play Theological Ping-Pong: Collected Essays on Faith and Reason*, edited by William J. Abraham and

claim that 'divine truth is supernaturally communicated to men in an act of inspired thinking which falls into the shape of certain images' does not itself have to be regarded as a metaphor that we are at a loss to interpret; for the language of 'speaking' or 'communicating' in this context is an instance of 'proper' rather than 'metaphorical analogy'. There is good metaphysical precedence for this in one of the greatest poets. When Dante speaks of the love moving the sun and the stars, it would make a nonsense of his *Commedia* if that were just a metaphor.

In *The Glass of Vision*, Farrer compares the post-Renaissance poet with Jeremiah. Jeremiah, like Shakespeare, is a poet who 'sets images moving by musical incantation' and allows them to arrange and express themselves as they 'ought'. But what is the 'ought' that constrains Jeremiah? The 'ought' that constrains Shakespeare is not a metaphor. Farrer observes that there are certain facts about human nature to which great poetry is responsive. But Jeremiah is constrained by the impact of the will of God upon his mind. 'He is not [like Shakespeare] responding to the quality of human life, he is responding to the demands of eternal will on Israel as they make themselves heard in the determinate situation where he stands.'[47]

The difference between the two controlling pressures is enormous. The scope of prophecy is much narrower than poetry because of the 'elastic possibilities of human nature', and the determinate nature of the divine will. The poet is a maker, the prophet is a mouthpiece. But there is control in both cases. Poetry is a technique of divination, Farrer insists: it is in the poetic process that the prophet receives his message.

> Whatever signs or omens set the incantation of shapely words moving in the prophet's mind, it went on moving and forming itself with a felt inevitability, like that of a rhapsodical poetry which allows for no second thoughts: it formed itself under a pressure or control which the prophet experienced as no self-chosen direction of his own thinking, but as the constraint of the divine will.[48]

Here we can see a clear instance of Farrer's theory of *double agency*. The emphasis is upon the organic and vital nature of the process. The great images are 'alive and moving', 'vital images'. Farrer writes:

> When I think of God as addressing man in revelation, I naturally fall into the same posture and become the victim of my parable. If you address me you are outside me; so, then, I suppose, is God. But then, on serious reflection, none of us can really maintain this. God is no more outside me than within; I am his creation just as much as you are, or as the physical world is. He has the secret key of entry into all his creatures; he can conjoin the action of any of them with his will in such fashion as to reveal himself specially through them. God speaks without and within; he reveals himself both through the situation with which he

---

Robert W. Prevost (London: Hodder and Stoughton, 1990), 193.

[47]   GV 126–7 / 104.

[48]   GV 128–9 / 105.

presents the recipients of revelation, and through the imagination, in terms of which he leads them to see and hear the voices and the sights surrounding them. How should it – how could it – be otherwise? The process is gradual; God has employed, he has not forced, the action of his creatures; he teaches us also to discern revelation from revelation and see where the flower and fruit borne by the branching plant of sacred truth are to be found.[49]

Furthermore, Farrer notes that 'from the fact that the craftsman is preparing materials you may guess that he is about some work, but it may be impossible for men or angels to infer what the work is to be without communication with the craftsman's mind'.[50] And it is the whole point of Farrer's typological analysis of St Mark's Gospel that the 'act of God always overthrows human expectation: the Cross defeats our hope: the Resurrection terrifies our despair'.[51] Yet Farrer's emphasis is upon continuity between inspiration poetic and divine rather than the gulf. It is by means of the images which are 'implanted' that revelation 'grows', images that 'in growing, are transformed, they throw out fresh branches, they fertilize neighbouring and as yet purely natural imaginations'.[52] Farrer presents us with a metaphysics of the imagination.[53]

## Conclusion

In his illuminating essay, 'The Place of Symbols in Christianity', Basil Mitchell describes the oscillation within the Christian tradition between an insistence upon the inadequacy of images or symbols (the negative or mystical way) and an excessive credulity in images (idolatry). Yet he observes:

> Philosophically speaking, I believe that we are in a better position now than for a very long time to maintain a proper balance between these two tendencies, the apophatic and the anthropomorphic. We are now much more aware of the essential part played by the imagination in all creative thought, not excluding natural science, and also of the mysteriousness of personal life.[54]

Farrer, too, emphasises that 'the excellence of mind consists of conscious intelligence, but of a conscious intelligence based always on acute senses and riding upon a vigorous imagination. For although the excellence of mind is an act

---

Farrer, 'Inspiration: Poetical and Divine', 44.

GV 30 / 34.

GV 139 / 112.

GV 136 / 109.

See Ingolf Dalferth's critical but illuminating essay '"Esse Est Operari": The Anti-Scholastic Theologies of Farrer and Luther', *Modern Theology* 1 (1985), 183–211

Mitchell, 'The Place of Symbols in Christianity', *How to Play Theological Ping-Pong*, 189.

of thinking, the act of thinking is not self-sufficient, but has constant recourse to the imagination; and out of such recourse wit and (in the secular sense) inspiration arise'.[55] Farrer is explicitly repudiating any crass opposition between reason and imagination. He uses the image of the cauldron to describe the fusing activity of imagination as distinct from mechanical patterns of association. And he is also pointing to the importance of imagination in touching those levels of mind that lie beneath consciousness. The imagination is 'a sort of focus into which is drawn together much that seems to us most important in the common essence of our human existence. The phrase which is just right has infinite overtones: or it awakens echoes in all the hidden caves of our minds'.[56]

Farrer's suggestion can be put like this: do we follow the path of so much twentieth-century philosophy and give up metaphysics and philosophical theology as the product of the bewitching capacity of language to hypostatize practices and dispositions as substances and entities, and proceed, like the wily Ulysses, to withstand these sirens and purge our concepts of folk and theological leaven? Or, is it conceivable that our language can reasonably strain to express facts and phenomena that are real but genuinely puzzling and which resist exhaustive conceptual articulation? Perhaps, ultimately, only images suffice to express some of these mysterious realities. Such is Farrer's claim: 'the stuff of inspiration is living images'.

It is the great virtue, I believe, of both Austin Farrer and Basil Mitchell to have defended a vision of theology in which the continuum of human creativity and divine action is so ably asserted. Why does this emphasis upon the continuum of human and divine freedom and creativity matter? A century ago the great German sociologist Max Weber gave an oration to young scholars, *Wissenschaft als Beruf*.[57] He observed that the modern world is one of re-emergent polytheism. The beautiful, the true – to say nothing of the good – have no overarching unity in contemporary culture. The legacy of this is a science stripped of values, art devoid of beauty, ethics divorced from truth, a milieu in which the very idea of the human person in God's world seems at best quaint and anachronistic, at worst simply incoherent and erroneous. This was for the Romantics a debilitating legacy of the Enlightenment, and was eloquently excoriated by Coleridge, who was particularly fond of the biblical adage: 'WHERE NO VISION IS, THE PEOPLE PERISHETH'. But theological positivism as a reaction merely reinforces the malaise and becomes itself a variant of Gnosticism. The thinking of Austin Farrer and Basil Mitchell constitutes a rich, subtle and imaginative articulation of the relation of faith and criticism, religious belief and rational justification. We can be particularly grateful for the shaping spirit of Farrer's vision.[58]

---

[55]    GV 24 / 30.

[56]    GV 119 / 99.

[57]    Max Weber, 'Wissenschaft als Beruf', in W.J. Mommsen and W. Schluchter with B. Morgenbrod (eds), *Max Weber, Gesamtausgbe* (München: Mohr/Siebeck, 1992), 99–101.

[58]    I wish to thank Mark Wynn, Dave Leal, Tim Mawson, Chris Insole and Denys Turner for helpful comments. I have a special debt to Brian Hebblethwaite for detailed comments and to both Basil Mitchell and Ann Loades for their help and encouragement.

# Selected Bibliography

**Primary Sources: Books Published in Farrer's Lifetime**

*Finite and Infinite: A Philosophical Essay* (Westminster: Dacre Press, 1943; Second Edition with a revised preface, 1959).

*The Glass of Vision: Bampton Lectures for 1948* (Westminster: Dacre Press, 1948).

*A Rebirth of Images: The Making of St John's Apocalypse* (Westminster: Dacre Press, 1949).

*A Study in St Mark* (Westminster: Dacre Press, 1951).

*The Crown of the Year: Weekly Paragraphs for the Holy Sacrament* (Westminster: Dacre Press, 1952).

*St Matthew and St Mark* (Westminster: Dacre Press, 1954; Second Edition, 1966).

*The Freedom of the Will: The Gifford Lectures delivered in the University of Edinburgh, 1957* (London: Adam and Charles Black, 1958; Second Edition, including a 'Summary of the Argument', 1960).

*Lord I Believe: Suggestions for turning the Creed into Prayer*, Beacon Books Number 10 (London: The Church Union, 1955); Second Edition, Revised and Enlarged (London: SPCK, 1962).

*Said or Sung: An Arrangement of Homily and Verse* (London: The Faith Press, 1960). Published in the United States as *A Faith of Our Own*, with a preface by C.S. Lewis (Cleveland, OH and New York: World Publishing Company).

*Love Almighty and Ills Unlimited: An Essay on Providence and Evil, Containing the Nathaniel Taylor Lectures for 1961* (New York: Doubleday, 1961/London: Collins, 1962).

*The Revelation of St John the Divine: A Commentary on the English Text* (Oxford: Oxford University Press, 1964).

*Saving Belief: A Discussion of Essentials* (London: Hodder and Stoughton, 1964).

*The Triple Victory: Christ's Temptations According to St Matthew* (London: The Faith Press, 1965).

*A Science of God?* (London: Geoffrey Bles, 1966). Published in the United States as *God is Not Dead* (New York: Morehouse-Barlow).

*Faith and Speculation: An Essay in Philosophical Theology, containing the Deems Lectures for 1964* (New York: New York University Press/London: Adam and Charles Black, 1967).


**Primary Sources: Posthumous Collections of Sermons and Essays**

*A Celebration of Faith*, edited by Leslie Houlden (London: Hodder and Stoughton, 1970).

*Reflective Faith: Essays in Philosophical Theology*, edited by Charles C. Conti, foreword by John Hick (London: SPCK, 1972). Contains 'Poetic Truth' (24–38).

*The End of Man*, edited by Charles C. Conti, introduction by John Austin Baker (London: SPCK, 1973).

*The Brink of Mystery*, edited by Charles C. Conti, foreword by J.L. Houlden (London: SPCK, 1976).

*Interpretation and Belief*, edited by Charles C. Conti, foreword by E.L. Mascall (London: SPCK, 1976). Includes 'Inspiration: Poetical and Divine' (39–53) and 'On Looking Below the Surface' (54–65).

*The Essential Sermons*, edited and introduced by Leslie Houlden (London: SPCK, 1991).

*Words for Life: Forty Meditations Previously Unpublished*, edited by Charles Conti and Leslie Houlden, preface by Charles Conti, introduction by Leslie Houlden (London: SPCK, 1993).

*The Truth-Seeking Heart: Austin Farrer and His Writings*, edited and introduced by Ann Loades and Robert MacSwain (Norwich: Canterbury Press, 2006).

## Secondary Sources: Selected Monographs

Conti, Charles, *Metaphysical Personalism: An Analysis of Austin Farrer's Theistic Metaphysics* (Oxford: Clarendon Press, 1995).

Curtis, Philip, *A Hawk Among Sparrows: A Biography of Austin Farrer* (London: SPCK, 1985).

Eaton, Jeffrey C., *The Logic of Theism: An Analysis of the Thought of Austin Farrer* (Lanham, MD: University Press of America, 1980).

Hefling, Jr, Charles C., *Jacob's Ladder: Theology and Spirituality in the Thought of Austin Farrer* (Cambridge, MA: Cowley Publications, 1979).

MacSwain, Robert, *Solved by Sacrifice: Austin Farrer, Fideism, and the Evidence of Faith* (Leuven: Peeters, 2013).

Titley, Robert, *A Poetic Discontent: Austin Farrer and the Gospel of Mark* (London and New York: T&T Clark International, 2010).

## Secondary Sources: Essay Collections

Eaton, Jeffrey C. and Ann Loades (eds), *For God and Clarity: New Essays in Honor of Austin Farrer* (Allison Park, PA: Pickwick Publications, 1983).

Hedley, Douglas and Brian Hebblethwaite (eds), *The Human Person in God's World: Studies to Commemorate the Austin Farrer Centenary* (London: SCM Press, 2006).

Hebblethwaite, Brian and Edward Henderson (eds), *Divine Action: Studies Inspired by the Philosophical Theology of Austin Farrer* (Edinburgh: T&T Clark, 1990).

Hein, David and Edward Hugh Henderson (eds), *Captured by the Crucified: The Practical Theology of Austin Farrer* (New York and London: T&T Clark International, 2004).

Loades, Ann and Michael McLain (eds), *Hermeneutics, the Bible and Literary Criticism* (London: Macmillan/New York: St Martin's Press, 1992).

McLain, F. Michael and W. Mark Richardson (eds), *Human and Divine Agency: Anglican, Catholic, and Lutheran Perspectives* (Lanham, MD: University Press of America, 1999).


**Secondary Sources: Additional Books and Essays Relevant to this Volume (excluding the chapters in Part II)**

Allen, Diogenes, 'Farrer's Spirituality', in David Hein and Edward Hugh Henderson (eds), *Captured by the Crucified: The Practical Theology of Austin Farrer* (New York and London: T&T Clark International, 2004), 47–65.

Blakesley, John, 'Pictures in the Fire? Austin Farrer's Biblical Criticism and John's Gospel – a Comment', *Journal of Literature and Theology* 1 (1987), 184–90.

Brown, David, *Tradition and Imagination: Revelation and Change* (Oxford: Oxford University Press, 1999).

——. *Discipleship and Imagination: Christian Tradition and Truth* (Oxford: Oxford University Press, 2000).

——. 'The Role of Images in Theological Reflection', in Douglas Hedley and Brian Hebblethwaite (eds), *The Human Person in God's World: Studies to Commemorate the Austin Farrer Centenary* (London: SCM Press, 2006), 85–105.

Crombie, I.M. (revised), 'Farrer, Austin Marsden (1904–1968),' in H.C.G. Matthew and Brian Harrison (eds), *Oxford Dictionary of National Biography: Volume 19* (Oxford: Oxford University Press, 2004), 121–3.

Forsman, Roger, 'Revelation and Understanding: A Defence of Tradition', in Ann Loades and Michael McLain (eds), *Hermeneutics, the Bible and Literary Criticism* (London: Macmillan/New York: St Martin's Press, 1992), 46–68.

Gardner, Helen, *The Business of Criticism* (Oxford: Clarendon Press, 1959).

——. *In Defence of the Imagination* (Cambridge, MA: Harvard University Press, 1982).

Gill, Jerry H., 'Divine Action as Mediated', *Harvard Theological Review* 80 (1987), 369–78.

Goulder, Michael, 'Farrer the Biblical Scholar', in Philip Curtis, *A Hawk Among Sparrows: A Biography of Austin Farrer* (London: SPCK, 1985), 192–212.

Harries, Richard, '"We Know On Our Knees": Intellectual, Imaginative, and Spiritual Unity in the Theology of Austin Farrer', in Brian Hebblethwaite and Edward Henderson (eds), *Divine Action: Studies Inspired by the Philosophical Theology of Austin Farrer* (Edinburgh: T&T Clark, 1990), 21–33.

Hebblethwaite, Brian, 'The Communication of Divine Revelation', in Alan G. Padgett (ed.), *Reason and the Christian Religion: Essays in Honour of Richard Swinburne* (Oxford: Clarendon Press, 1994), 143–59.

Hedley, Douglas, *Living Forms of the Imagination* (London and New York: T&T Clark International, 2008).

Hefling, Jr, Charles C., 'Origen *Redivivus*: Farrer's Scriptural Divinity', in Jeffrey C. Eaton and Ann Loades (eds), *For God and Clarity: New Essays in Honor of Austin Farrer* (Allison Park, PA: Pickwick Publications, 1983), 35–50.

—— 'Farrer's Scriptural Divinity', in David Hein and Edward Hugh Henderson (eds), *Captured by the Crucified: The Practical Theology of Austin Farrer* (New York and London: T&T Clark International, 2004), 149–72.

Kermode, Frank, *The Genesis of Secrecy: On the Interpretation of Narrative* (Cambridge, MA: Harvard University Press, 1979).

Lewis, H.D., *Our Experience of God* (London: George Allen and Unwin Ltd/New York: The Macmillan Company, 1959).

Loades, Ann, 'Farrer, Austin Marsden,' in Alister E. McGrath (ed.), *The SPCK Handbook of Anglican Theologians* (London: SPCK, 1998), 120–3.

Loughlin, Gerard, *Telling God's Story: Bible, Church and Narrative Theology* (Cambridge: Cambridge University Press, 1996; corrected paperback edition, 1999).

MacSwain, Robert, 'Above, Beside, Within: The Anglican Theology of Austin Farrer', *Journal of Anglican Studies* 4 (2006), 33–57.

—— 'Centenary Perspectives on Austin Farrer: A Review Article', *Philosophy Compass* 5 (2010), 820–9: available at http://onlinelibrary.wiley.com/doi/10.1111/j.1747-9991.2010.00322.x/abstract.

—— 'Documentation and Correspondence Related to Austin Farrer's Baptism in the Church of England on 14 May 1924', *Anglican and Episcopal History* 81 (2012), 241–76.

Mitchell, Basil, 'War and Friendship', in Kelly James Clark (ed.), *Philosophers Who Believe: The Spiritual Journeys of 11 Leading Thinkers* (Downers Grove, IL: InterVarsity Press, 1993), 23–44.

Peterson, Jeffrey, 'A Pioneer Narrative Critic and His Synoptic Hypothesis: Austin Farrer and Gospel Interpretation', in *Society of Biblical Literature Seminar Papers 2000*, Society of Biblical Literature Seminar Paper Series 39 (Atlanta: Society of Biblical Literature, 2000), 651–72.

Smart, Ninian, 'Revelation and Reasons', *Scottish Journal of Theology* 11 (1958), 352–61.

Wright, T.R., 'Regenerating Narrative: The Gospels as Fiction', *Religious Studies* 20 (1984), 389–400.

# Index

As the main title of this volume indicates, it has three primary topics: 'Scripture', 'metaphysics', and 'poetry'. However, in addition to these primary topics, Farrer also states that the overarching theme of *The Glass of Vision* is 'the form of divine truth in the human mind'. By this Farrer means supernatural revelation conveyed through inspired images to human intellects and imaginations—inspired images which are then written down in Holy Scripture and made accessible to inspired readers. Thus, in addition to the three primary topics there are also several major themes such as 'God', 'Jesus Christ', 'truth', 'nature', 'supernature', 'revelation', 'inspiration', 'images', 'imagination', and the '(human) mind'. These primary topics and major themes are pervasive throughout both Parts I and II, and in this index they are often cited only selectively or by entire lecture from *The Glass of Vision* and/or entire chapter in Part II.

Printed in Great Britain
by Amazon